# Physical Development with Expressive Art and Design

Mavis Brown
and Maureen Warner

# Publisher's information

**Brilliant Publications**
Unit 10
Sparrow Hall Farm
Edlesborough
Dunstable, Bedfordshire
LU6 2ES

Tel: **01525 222292**
Fax: **01525 222720**
e-mail: **info@brilliantpublications.co.uk**
Website: **www.brilliantpublications.co.uk**



Revised and updated by Debbie Chalmers
Illustrated by Claire Boyce and Kirsty Brown

Printed ISBN 978 0 85747 674 6
e-book ISBN 978 0 85747 677 7

First published in the UK in 2013.
10 9 8 7 6 5 4 3 2 1

Printed in the UK.



There are three books in the Foundation Blocks series, each covering one of the prime areas and one or two of the specific areas of the *Early Years Foundation Stage*. Each book contains a wealth of activities, ideas and suggestions, clearly described and illustrated. Further details on how these books are structured and how they can make it easy to implement the Department of Education's new, revised *Statutory Framework for the EYFS* (September 2012) are given in the Introduction.

The other books in the Foundation Blocks series are:
*Communication and Language with Literacy by Irene Yates*
Encourages children to speak and listen, express themselves clearly, use language confidently, use and enjoy books, link sounds and letters, develop phonic knowledge and begin to read and write.

*Personal, Social and Emotional Development with Understanding the World and Mathematics by Mavis Brown and Rebecca Taylor*
Encourages children to develop self-confidence and positive attitudes and relationships, manage feelings and behaviour, explore the environment and community, investigate, experiment, begin to use technology and develop skills in counting, addition and subtraction, understanding and using numbers, problem solving; and describing shape, space and measures.

# Contents

## Contents continued

## Contents continued

# Introduction

This book has over 150 differentiated activities set in real-life contexts relevant to children in the Early Years Foundation Stage (EYFS). The activities aim to develop children's skills and to meet the Department of Education's learning and development requirements in the areas of *Physical Development* and *Expressive Arts and Design*. They offer opportunities for practitioners to follow the guidance document *Development Matters* and to encourage and support children as they work towards the Early Learning Goals (ELGs) of the new, revised Statutory Framework for the Early Years Foundation Stage (September 2012).

There are two ELGs for the prime area Physical Development:

- Moving and Handling
- Health and Self-care

A table showing specific learning opportunities addressed by each activity can be found on pages 195–204.

Physical development in the foundation stage involves providing opportunities for children to be active and encouraging and supporting them as they improve their skills in coordination, control, manipulation and movement. They are developing both gross and fine motor control and need time, space and an enabling environment to practise large and small movements, both indoors and outside. Practitioners must maintain a postive attitude to movement, offering children enough challenges and allowing them to take acceptable risks and to gradually learn to decide for themselves which risks may be taken.

Children need to learn how to move with confidence and imagination, as well as with control and coordination. They need to be aware of space, for themselves and others, and able to sit or stand in their own place, allowing room for others around them, or to negotiate a safe pathway when moving around or interacting within a group, avoiding collisions while following their chosen directions. Children must also learn to handle toys, equipment and tools effectively. They may lift, carry, transport and build on a large scale with blocks, cartons, crates, boxes and outdoor equipment and toys, move around on wheeled toys, or bouncing toys and with balls or skipping ropes, challenge themselves on climbing frames, trampolines and balancing and jumping equipment, explore natural materials like sand, water, sticks, stones and mud, and practise skills such as running, jumping, hopping, skipping, crawling, rolling, kicking, throwing and catching.

Equally important are the smaller movements, from striking, rolling, throwing, waving and balancing equipment such as bats and balls, skittles, beanbags and ribbons, to digging, sieving, moulding and pouring malleable materials like sand and water, exploring paint, clay, playdough and cookery ingredients, using glue and scissors, and holding pencils, pens and crayons effectively for mark making. Children should be encouraged to make marks outside, painting with water and drawing with large chalks on the ground, and to scribble, draw, colour and write on paper, both indoors and outdoors, when they are ready. These skills will develop if adults support children's efforts, provide ideas and materials to enhance their ideas and celebrate their achievements.

Practitioners must provide a safe, well-planned and well-resourced learning environment and give children plenty of time to explore, experiment and refine movements and actions. They should enable children to learn through using all their senses and aim to support all other areas of learning through physical activity.

Physical activities help children to feel more confident about using their bodies and enable them to feel the positive benefits of being healthy and active. Adults should talk with children about ways to keep healthy and safe and about the importance for good health of physical exercise and a healthy diet. Children need to learn which foods and drinks are healthy and what their bodies need for growth and effective physical development, in order to develop a positive sense of well-being.

Adults must also support children as they learn to manage their own basic hygiene and personal needs successfully. Opportunities and encouragement must be provided for them to learn to manage their own dressing and undressing, including manipulating fastenings, understanding when they might need a coat or a sunhat, going to the toilet independently, choosing when to drink water or eat a snack and asking for help when it is needed, in order to promote a healthy degree of self-confidence and independence within a secure and supportive atmosphere.

There are two ELGs for the specific area Expressive Arts and Design:

- Exploring and using media and materials
- Being imaginative

Expressive arts and design activities provide multi-sensory creative opportunities through which practitioners can encourage and support children in the foundation stage to extend their play, develop their own ideas and communicate them through art, music, dance, role-play, drama and imaginative play. If children begin to acquire knowledge and learn and practise creative skills and techniques, they will be able to develop them more effectively in the future when exploring visual and performing arts.

Paintings and sculptures cannot be appreciated through pictures and photographs, so it is recommended that children are taken to an art gallery or exhibition if possible, to see and experience actual works of art and their sizes, textures and materials. Within the setting, children need to explore art and craft media and materials, both indoors and outside, as a part of their continuous provision every day.

Music, dance and drama can be explored through singing and making up songs, playing with rhyming, rhythm and pitch, using percussion instruments and listening to recorded music, watching performed music and dance, live or on television or DVD, dancing and moving to music, leading and following, presenting and performing.

Children should be encouraged to listen to stories and poems, play with small world toys and puppets, dress up and create role play situations. Adults can enhance and sustain imaginative play by joining in with the children and encouraging their ideas, rather than over-planning a play activity or trying to steer it in a particular direction. Developing children's abilities to experience with all their senses and to verbalize their ideas will allow them to respond imaginatively to stimulii and to imitate and create stories.

It is important to allow children to use and build upon their knowledge, skills, techniques and processes to choose their own creative methods of communicating and expressing their responses to experiences. They may then develop the abilities to think in non-verbal and visual images and to express their ideas and emotions symbolically, translating them from one creative area to another. Along with these, they will be building skills to assist in reading and writing, self-discovery and exploration of the world, appreciating similarities and differences between past and present and between cultures and identities, co-operative working strategies and respect for the contributions of others.

Practitioners need to provide a large quantity and variety of good quality materials, objects and experiences and encourage children to concentrate on creative processes rather than outcomes or finished results. This will allow children to practise making connections, choices and comparisons and solving problems, so that they feel that their work is all their own. It will also help them to develop the qualities of motivation, self-confidence, curiosity, independence and persistence.

The *EYFS Statutory Framework* states that children learn most effectively by investigating, experiencing and 'having a go', concentrating, trying again and enjoying their own achievements, creating, linking ideas, thinking critically and developing their own strategies for doing things.

Most of the activities in this book can be adapted to fit any topic or project that is being explored by a group of children. The tasks are designed to allow practitioners to choose their own directions and to include opportunities for exploration and new challenges as children's skills are being developed.

The activities are divided into four sections to indicate which prime or specific area and which of the ELGs each one will particularly contribute to. Practitioners may use this information when planning, to ensure that they are not concentrating too much on one area at the expense of another. They should be providing enough encouragement and experiences for all children to move confidently, negotiate space, handle equipment and tools, understand good health, manage personal needs and hygiene, use, explore and experiment with materials and techniques and represent original and imaginative ideas, thoughts and feelings through design and technology, art, music, dance, role-play and stories.

Some activities contribute to more than one ELG and many are also strongly linked to other learning and development areas and their ELGs, as shown in the chart on pages 195–204.

To avoid the clumsy 'he/she', the child is referred to throughout the book as 'she'.

# Planning

Where relevant, the activities have been linked to sixteen popular topics that are frequently used in early years and primary settings. These are:

- Animals
- Families
- Health
- People who help us
- Toys
- Weather
- Celebrations
- Food and shopping
- Homes
- Seasons
- Travel and transport
- Colours
- Gardening
- Myself
- Shapes
- Water

The topic appears in a shaded box at the top of each page. The other books in this series use the same topics. However, these are only suggestions and all of the activities can easily be modified to fit with any topic that a practitioner needs material for. The majority of activities in this book can be used with any topic.

All activities are designed with the *Statutory Framework for the EYFS* in mind and, therefore, link with other learning and development areas, offering opportunities to explore them all with the children. Practitioners will be aware of needing to provide a balanced curriculum and to explore, along with Physical Development and Expressive Arts and Design: Communication and Language, Personal, Social and Emotional Development, Literacy, Mathematics and Understanding the World.

Prior knowledge is not expected for any of the activities, but practitioners should use their own judgement to choose activities to suit children's developmental stages.

Although plenary sessions have not been included, practitioners will recognize the importance of reviewing activities and encouraging children to verbalize what they did, how they felt about it and what they think they achieved. It is also important, of course, to discuss with parents and carers how they might build upon the children's experiences, so that they can learn consistently in the setting and at home.

## Display

It is important to display children's work as it adds value and worth to their endeavours. If the setting has a multiple use or limited wall space, use double sided display boards or wheeled panels which can be stored between sessions and keep collections of models for table displays in labelled, accessible boxes.

Work can also be hung from a washing line across the room (high enough not to be a hazard) or from the ceiling, from wire coat hangers, as mobiles, or attached to draped fabric. Mount individual pieces of artwork on paper or card before adding them to a display. Encourage children to work together and use different techniques, such as collage, painting or printing, to create group murals.

## Logos used on the activity sheets

### Box 1 – group size

This box indicates the number of children recommended for the activity, keeping safety and level of difficulty in mind. Less able children can achieve more difficult tasks with a smaller child to adult ratio. The group size indicates the size of group for the activity itself, rather than for any introductory or plenary sessions.

### Box 2 – level of difficulty

This box uses a scale between 1 and 5 to depict the level of difficulty or challenge the task might present to the children. Children still developing skills described in the 22-36 months age band of the Development Matters guidance document will find 1 most suitable, whilst 2 and 3 will apply to children as they move through the 30-50 months age band. Children just entering the 40-60+ months age band will appreciate 4, while 5 will be suitable for older and more able children who are already meeting the Early Learning Goals. As most settings have mixed age groups, the majority of the activities have been classified as easy, so that the whole group can be involved. Higher levels can be achieved for particular children, as appropriate, by encouraging them to develop their own ideas and to participate in the suggested extension activities.

### Box 3 – time needed to complete the activity

The suggested time slots are only a guideline. Children need time to practise their skills, test their ideas and reflect upon their findings. Some children will wish to extend the original activity to pursue their own enquiries or improve upon their experiment.

### Safety

Where relevant, additional safety notes are included on the sheets. You are advised to read these before commencing the activity.

## Links to home

- The word 'parent' is used to refer to all those persons responsible for the child, and include mothers, fathers, legal guardians and primary carers of children in public care. The 'Links to home' suggest ways in which parents can continue and reinforce the learning that is experienced at the setting.

- Parents can share important information about their children and their experiences, upon which practitioners can build. It is essential that practitioners find out from parents details of any special or additional needs, allergies, intolerances or medical conditions.

- Parents can be a valuable resource, giving support when extra help is needed during visits out of the setting, and with more complex activities during designing and making. They can become the knowledgeable visitor, bringing their own language, culture and experiences to the setting.

- Parents are also a useful source of recycled materials, which are required for many of the tasks.

## Safety

- Children are active learners, and investigative, exploratory and construction activities invariably involve the use of potentially dangerous equipment. Part of the learning process involves offering the child the opportunity to learn to use this equipment safely. As young children cannot anticipate danger, practitioners have to be vigilant and take part in a regular risk assessment exercise relevant to their own setting.

- Any rules issued by your employer or Local Authority should be adhered to in priority to the recommendations in this book; therefore check your employer's and LEA's Health and Safety guidelines and their policies on the use of equipment.

## Templates and other resources

On pages 188–192 there are photocopiable templates to be used in conjunction with relevant activities. The pieces will last longer if they are laminated.

A glossary of creative terms appears on pages 193–194.
Characteristics of effective learning can be found on pages 195–196
A table of learning opportunities appears on pages 197–206.
An index of topics appears on pages 207–209.

# Assessment

- Each activity has learning objectives which are linked to the prime area of Physical Development and/or the specific area of Expressive Arts and Design.

- To assist practitioners in planning a balanced educational programme of experiences, the charts on pages 195–204, shows which activities address which of the Department of Education's EYFS Early Learning Goals.

- Comments on these activities and other evidence of children's achievements, such as dated examples of early writing, dictations, drawings, paintings and photographs of 3D models and 'work in progress', can be kept in a file or portfolio and given to parents as a celebration and record for the future.

- These records should be retained for inspection.

# Physical Development

# Moving and Handling

- Children instinctively know and understand the importance of physical activity. Movement is their first form of communication and it provides the stimulation and responses that they need for healthy development. Research has found that the exploration and use of a wide range of movement patterns and abilities during the early years contributes to the healthy growth of the brain and development in all other areas.

- Working effectively through each of the valuable and important stages of movement is vital for children's health and well-being and also contributes to their physical, cognitive and emotional development. These stages, from the first arm and leg movements in the air and in water, through rolling, creeping and slithering, crawling on hands and knees, standing up and balancing on two feet while holding on, to eventually walking and running, all have a crucial impact on future learning skills. Children must be offered lots of opportunities for physical and movement play at each stage and not hurried through them to reach the 'goal' of walking unaided too quickly.

- Balance skills and the strong and healthy development of vision and hearing are developed through play activities involving swinging, rocking, climbing, sliding, spinning and hanging from hands or feet. These are also important later for reading and copying from charts, posters, displays, boards or screens. Crawling develops muscle strength and flexibility in the arms, wrists and hands, which will be used in drawing and writing in the future.

- Children also need to have a good sense of where their bodies are, in order to develop control and coordination and to learn to safely negotiate space for themselves and others. Movements in muscles, joints and limbs send messages to the brain to develop this sense.

- Primitive reflexes that babies need from birth are gradually replaced by more complex ones if they have enough opportunities for independent movement. This is essential, as, if these reflexes continue to exist as a child grows up, they can cause difficulties with motor control, hand/eye coordination and perception.

Sensory stimulation is also vital and children need to learn to handle many senses at the same time. An environment will contain sights, sounds and smells and the feelings of things to touch and sometimes to taste, and, if children's brains cannot process all of the information, they may suffer emotional or behavioural difficulties.

- The development of fine motor control should be encouraged, alongside the larger 'whole body' movements, through activities that develop hand strength, different grasps and grips and manipulative skills. Picking up small items or pieces of food with the finger and thumb, using a pincer grip, sorting, threading, making puzzles, moulding malleable materials, messy play, craft activities, cookery, cutting out, mark making and eventually drawing and writing are skills that may be learned and refined through play, with supportive adults in an enabling environment.

Moving and Handling

# Five Currant Buns

## Topic
Food and shopping

## Resources
- Pictures of buns and cakes
- Card
- Glue
- 'Five Currant Buns' from *This Little Puffin*, compiled by Elizabeth Matterson (Puffin)
- Small coins
- Paper
- Soft pencils
- Paint
- Paintbrushes
- Cardboard
- Scissors

## Learning objectives
- To experiment with different ways of moving
- To show good control and coordination and safely negotiate space within a group of children
- To listen attentively and respond to what is heard with relevant actions

## Preparation
- Arrange pictures of buns and cakes, or play food, or even real food, on a table. Make sure that there is at least one for each child. Collect enough real coins or play money for the group to use, or make pretend coins from paper.

## What to do
### Movement activity
- Gather the children on the floor or carpet and begin the song 'Five Currant Buns'. When it comes to the line 'Along came a boy with a penny one day', substitute the name of a child in the group and a price value, for example 'Along came Lucy with 2p one day'.
- Encourage all children to listen carefully for their names and get up to take their turns when they hear them. The named child should travel to the table using any movement of her choice, such as hopping, skipping, tiptoeing or walking backwards. She should then choose a bun, leave her money on the table and return to the group to sit down. Repeat this until the verse with no buns and then begin the whole activity again until all the class have had a turn at the activity.

## Extensions/variations
- Make pretend money by sticking small coins under a piece of thin white paper and rubbing the surface gently with soft pencils. Cut out and stick onto card discs.
- Make a shop window. Draw a large square or rectangle on white card or paper. Fill in the window with painted bread, cakes and tarts.

# Can you grow like a bean?

**Moving and Handling**

## Learning objectives

- To show good control and coordination in whole body movements
- To be aware of others, moving confidently and safely negotiating space
- To express thoughts and ideas and create simple and imaginative representations of an event

## What to do

**Circle activity**

- Show a packet of seeds, a bulb and a bean to the children. Ask them if they know what happens to them once they have been planted.
- Read the story *Jody's Beans*.

**Movement activity**

- Invite the children grow like a bean. Ask them to pretend to be seeds. Curl up as small as possible on the floor.
- Either use music or read the story. As the shoots begin to push through the soil, ask the children to uncurl and crouch on the floor like small shoots then to gradually rise up from the floor and stand up straight. Ask them to stretch up high on their legs and to stretch out their arms as far as possible until they are as high and as wide as they can possible be, like a fully grown bean.

## Extension/variation

- Use the following rhyme while they stretch upwards on their toes and extend their arms and fingers outwards.

  *Grow ever so high*
  *Up into the sky*
  *Birds passing me by*
  *Wish I could fly*

## Topic

Gardening

## Resources

- Packet of seeds, bulb and a bean
- *Jody's Beans* by Malachy Doyle (Walker Books)
- Large space
- Music if wished

Be aware of others in the movement session.

# Holiday homes

## Topic
Homes

## Resources
- 'Here's a House Built up High' from *This Little Puffin,* compiled by Elizabeth Matterson (Puffin)
- 'The Caravan' by Madeline Nightingale, from *The Book of a Thousand Poems* (Evans)
- Matchboxes
- Glue
- Paper
- Card
- Straw
- Twigs
- Scissors
- Junk boxes

## Learning objectives
- To perform actions and movements confidently, safely negotiating space within a group of children
- To sing a song, make up movements and experiment with ways of changing them

## What to do
**Circle time**
- Talk to the children about holidays. A holiday home is still a home, however temporary. Discuss the types of homes they may occupy while on holiday, for example apartment, caravan, log cabin, houseboat, hotel. Perhaps the children can share their experiences.

**Movement activity**
- Read and act out the action rhyme 'Here's a House Built up High'. The children will need to be standing, giving each other plenty of space. Encourage the children to exaggerate the actions with their arms and hands.

- Read 'The Caravan'. Ask the children whether they have ever taken a holiday in a caravan, and whether they know anyone who lives in a caravan.
- Some gypsies live in caravans pulled by horses. Encourage the children to engage in role-play, trotting around as horses, holding the reins and guiding the horses, or pretending to cook outdoors and sleep in a caravan.

## Extension/variation
- Make a holiday village. Stick matchboxes together to form houses. Fold a piece of card to make a pointed roof. Stick pieces of straw on the roof to resemble thatch. Collect twigs and cut into small lengths. Stick on matchboxes or other junk boxes to make log cabins.

## Links to home
- Ask parents if they could lend any photographs of the family on holiday in a caravan or holiday village, for their child to show to the group.

# The Queen's palace

**Moving and Handling**

## Learning objectives

- To develop control and coordination in large and small movements
- To negotiate space successfully when playing games with other children
- To show increasing control over a ball and develop throwing and catching skills

## What to do

### Movement activity

- Talk to the children about the grand palace where the Queen lives. Tell them that she will not always be the Queen and one day we will have a King instead.
- Ask a volunteer to be the Queen. Ask her to stand with her back to the other members of the group. They stand about six steps behind her. She throws her golden orb (usually a tennis or soft ball) backwards over her shoulder, or upwards between her legs.
- Before the ball hits the ground, the others try to catch it so that they can become the Queen. Whoever catches it, hides it behind his/her back. The other players put their hands behind their backs too so that they appear to have the ball. Someone then shouts, 'Queenie ball. Queenie ball.'
- The Queen turns around and tries to guess who has the ball. When she decides who it is, she calls the child's name and says, '(Lucy) has the ball.' If she is correct, Lucy returns the ball to her and the game begins again. If she is incorrect, the person with the ball says, 'Queenie, Queenie, I have the ball,' and becomes the Queen.
- The game can be as long or as short as necessary, but, where possible, try to continue until each child has had a turn at being the Queen.

## Topic

Homes

## Resources

- Tennis or other soft ball
- Large box or lots of shoe boxes
- Thin card
- Paint
- Paintbrushes
- Scissors
- Beads
- Glitter
- Glue
- Stapler or sticky tape

Provide a safe space so that ball-playing is not too near a window. Be alert to the safety of the group.

## Extensions/variations

- Build a palace from a large box, or individually from shoe boxes. Decorate it with paint and glitter.
- Make royal crowns. Cut strips of thin gold card, or white card painted yellow, long enough to fit around the children's heads. Stick beads and glitter around the crowns. Staple or stick the sides together.

## Links to home

- Ask the parents if they have any photographs of Buckingham Palace or any other royal palace visited in another country.
- Ask permission to borrow the photographs for a short time and make a display to share and discuss with the children.

**Moving and Handling**

# Catch the robber

## Topic
People who help us

## Resources
- Apparatus
- Paper cups
- Scissors
- String
- Pencil

Ensure the safety of each child when on the apparatus.

Ensure clothing is safe and will not hamper activity.

## Learning objectives
- To jump between objects and land appropriately
- To travel with confidence and skill around, over, under and through balancing and climbing equipment
- To move in a range of ways, negotiating space and stopping safely
- To understand and talk about ways to keep safe

## Preparation
- Set out the apparatus, putting some pieces close enough to each other that the children can jump from one object to another. Arrange other pieces so that the children have to land on the floor in order to climb up on to a new piece of apparatus.

## What to do
### Movement activity
- Play 'Catch the robber' by using the game 'Off ground touch'. Choose two robbers and one police person. Ask the robbers to start moving across the room across the apparatus. Tell them they have big bags of gold and are running away from the police person, but as long as they stay on the apparatus they cannot be caught. However, they must keep moving. As soon as they touch the floor, the chasing police person can catch them. Repeat this game until everyone has had a turn.

## Extensions/variations
- Arrange for a police person to visit and talk to the class about safety.
- Make walkie-talkie radios. Find two empty paper cups. Using the point of a pencil, make a hole though the centre of the cup base. Thread string through and help the children to knot it tightly so that it will not pull through. Ask one child to put one cup over her ear. Ask another child to speak into the cup so that the sound waves travel across the string. They will need to hold the string tightly.

## Related activity
- Fire! Fire! (see page 78)

# Let's play trains



## Learning objectives

- To move confidently, showing good control and coordination
- To move with others, starting and stopping safely
- To negotiate space safely when running with other children

### Topic

Transport and travel

### Resources

- Large space

## What to do

**Movement activity**

- Choose a driver and a guard. The driver stands ready to drive his/her train.
- The driver and the guard shout to the remaining children, 'Ride on the train!' While the driver remains at the front the guard at the end allows others to join in front of him.
- Twisting and swaying they run around like a fast train.
- When the driver decides it's time to stop the train he takes his followers round and round in an effort to touch the guard at the end. Once caught, the guard is 'out' and the last child becomes the new guard. The game continues until only the driver is left and a new game can begin.
- Initiate language such as *before*, *after*, *take turns*, *wait*.

## Related activity

- Let's ride the train (see page 48)

Moving and Handling

# Sing a limb

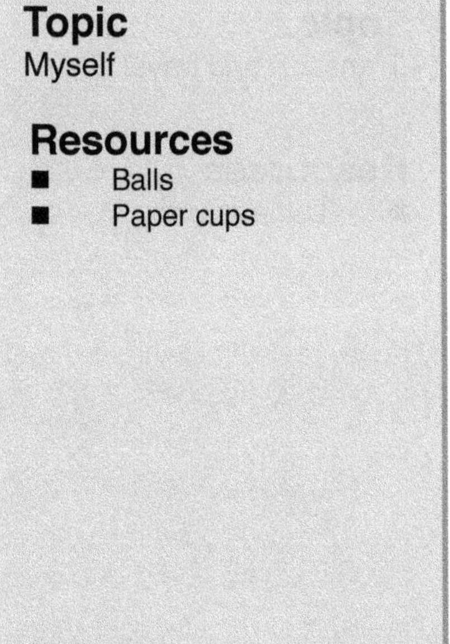

## Topic
Myself

## Resources
- Balls
- Paper cups

## Learning objectives
- To experiment with different ways of moving, using all parts of the body
- To move, freeze and balance with good control and co-ordination
- To develop increasing control over an object, such as a ball
- To initiate new combinations of movement and gesture to express ideas
- To play alongside other children who are engaged in the same theme

## What to do
### Music activity
- Sing to the tune of 'Three Blind Mice'. Ask children to sing the following words, while moving the relevant part of the body:

  *Here's my hand, here's my hand*
  *Here's my hand, here's my hand*
  *I wiggle my fingers upon my hand*
  *I wiggle my fingers upon my hand*
  *It would be all right if I played in a band*
  *Here's my hand.*

  *Here's my eye, etc*
  *I see everything that I want with my eye*
  *The sun and the rain and the moon in the sky*
  *Here's my eye.*
- Perhaps you can think of other words to fit with other parts.

## Extensions/variations
- Provide a range of balls and encourage children to explore and find out what they can do with them.
- Throw a ball up into the air and catch it. Throw it up in the air, clap hands and catch it.
- Bounce a ball and catch it. Bounce a ball, turn around and catch it.
- Hold the ball between the knees and try to walk.
- Roll the ball across the floor to a friend.
- Make skittles with upside-down paper cups. Invite children to roll balls to knock them down.

## Related activity
- The Queen's palace (see page 21)

# Use your senses

Moving and Handling

## Learning objectives

- To handle and manipulate objects and materials safely and with good control
- To explore a variety of materials and their textures
- To use different senses to explore and identify objects and textures
- To match senses to facial features

## Preparation

- Set up a corner or table with as many different things you can from the **Resources** list.
- Stick various pieces of fabric (velvet, cotton, woollen, nylon) and different papers (tissue, sugar, crumpled cellophane, film) on to a piece of cardboard.

## What to do

**Table activity**

- Invite the children to come to the prepared area and investigate the items on display.
- Practitioners need to be available to the children and involved in the activity throughout, suggesting and modelling ways of exploring and demonstrating which items are for touching, listening to, smelling or tasting.
- Have a feely bag, filled with familiar objects. Ask them to guess the objects inside by feeling the outside of the bag.

## Extensions/variations

- Discuss the different shapes, sizes and colours of the children's eyes.
- Explain that blind people use a system called Braille to read. Pushing a pin through some stuff paper can imitate Braille, allowing children to feel raised dots with their fingers. It may be possible to borrow a Braille book from a library for the group to explore, very carefully.
- Talk about the way deaf people can communicate through sign language and teach the children some simple signs to use when speaking or singing.
- Make faces using paper plates. Ask the children to include all the features. Point to the various features and ask what they do. Attach cut-out card for ears. A good short verse to remember these senses is:

## Topic

Health

## Resources

- Salt and sugar
- Perfume
- Items – soft, hard, prickly, sticky, smooth, rough
- Pieces of fabric
- Different types of paper
- Different types of card
- Small radio
- Hard-boiled eggs
- Table tennis balls
- Paints
- Paintbrushes
- Felt-tipped pens
- Pin
- Paper plates
- Glue
- Hand bells and shakers

Supervise children in the sensory area, especially when they are tasting things.

*Eyes to see*
*Nose to smell*
*Ears to hear*
*Mouths to tell*

## Links to home

- Explain the activity to parents in advance and take careful note of any children with allergies, intolerances or preferences who may not taste a particular substance or should not be exposed to strong perfumes etc.

Moving and Handling

# Horsey, Horsey, Don't You Stop

**Topic**
Animals

**Resources**

- Cardboard boxes
- Glue
- Paint
- Paintbrushes
- String or wool
- Felt
- Bits of wool, fur, straw
- Wooden skewers
- Corks
- Cardboard
- Broom handle
- Kitchen roll inner

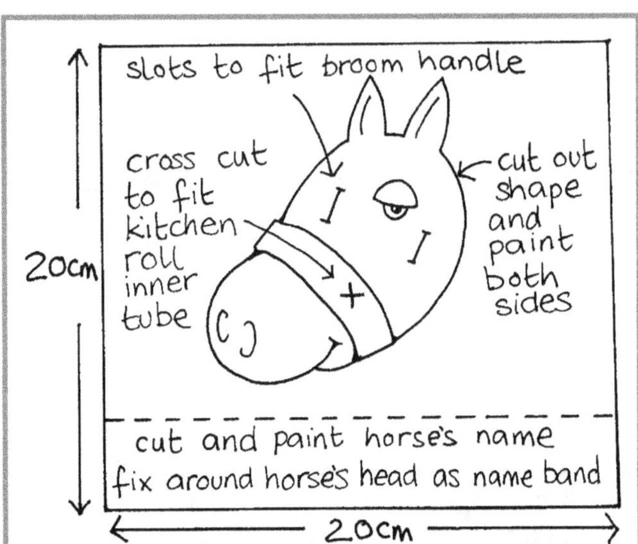


## Learning objectives

- To move confidently in a range of ways, safely negotiating space
- To handle tools, objects, construction and malleable materials safely and with increasing control
- To construct with a purpose in mind, using a variety of resources
- To sing a familiar song and move rhythmically

## What to do

**Movement activity**

- Teach the children the rhyme:

  *Horsey, horsey, don't you stop*
  *Just let your feet go clippetty, clop*
  *Your tail goes swish and your wheels*
  *go round –*
  *Giddy-up, you're homeward bound!*

- Encourage the children to pretend to be horses, galloping around the room as they say or sing the rhyme.

**Art activity**

- Make a small horse from cardboard boxes. Let the children cover or paint in any colour they prefer. Stick on string or wool for a tail. Cut out cardboard ears and paste to head.
- Paint eyes or stick on felt shapes. Make the mane from bits of fur, wool, or straw. If you wish to add reins, push a wooden skewer through the head and cover each end with a cork. Attach string for the reins.

## Extensions/variations

- Make a hobby horse. Draw, paint and cut out a horse head shape. Decorate with features. Cut two slits as in the diagram to accommodate the broom handle. Push the kitchen roll inner through the head as illustrated, to aid stability and as a handle for the children to hold on to. A name could be printed on a strip of cardboard and attached across the horse's nose. Invite the children to take turns to climb across the broom handle and gallop around the room.
- All the children could make miniature hobby horses using pencils and small horse heads.

# Spring plants and animals

Moving and Handling

## Learning objectives

- To use one-handed tools and equipment
- To handle a variety of objects, resources and craft materials effectively
- To develop awareness of features and changes within the natural environment during spring

## Preparation

- Photocopy the Tree template on page 188 onto thin card.
- Cut out circles of thin card.
- Prepare a safe floor space.

## What to do

**Circle time**

- Discuss the arrival of spring with the children, mentioning the new green leaves on the trees that were bare in winter and explaining how trees provide shelter for many small animals and birds. Talk about whether seeds have been planted in the garden and if new daffodils are growing.

**Art and craft activity**

- Ask the children to look out of the window and describe what they see. Give each child an outline of a bare tree. Invite them to draw or paint birds or leaves in their tree. Older children may prefer to draw and cut out birds and leaves. If they cannot see anything, ask them what might live in the tree. Cut some scraps of brown felt or fur and apply to the tree as squirrels.
- Using the circles of card, weave some drinking straws in and out, glue them to the circles and make some nests. Stick some table tennis balls inside for eggs.

## Extensions/variations

- Take the children to the floor space. Invite them to pretend to be different spring animals, such as: a baby lamb frisking, a baby bunny hopping, a baby bird standing uncertainly on the edge of the nest before fluttering away, a squirrel holding a nut and nibbling it, a caterpillar or a worm crawling on the floor.
- Stick a twig on to a piece of sugar paper. Ask the children to finger print blossoms.

## Topic

Seasons

## Resources

- Tree template on page 188
- Thin card
- Felt-tipped pens
- Paints
- Paintbrushes
- Glue
- Unwanted felt
- Scraps of fur
- Scissors
- Drinking straws
- Table tennis balls
- Twigs
- Pastel sugar paper
- Sticky tape
- Damp cloth (for finger wiping)

 Supervise the use of scissors carefully.

The practitioner can cut out the blossom and twig shapes and fix them to the wall as an attractive spring border.

## Related activity

- Can you be a tree? (see page 141)

Moving and Handling

# What's the time, Mr Wolf?

## Topic
Animals

## Resources
- Large safe space
- String, hoop or chalk

Children excite easily. Watch for pushing and jostling.

## Learning objectives
- To negotiate space successfully when playing chasing games with other children, adjusting speed or changing direction to avoid obstacles
- To develop their running skills and be able to stop safely
- To work as part of a group, understanding and following the rules of a game and behavioural expectations and boundaries

## Preparation
- Provide a safe space in a playground or hall. Use a circle of string, a hoop or a chalked area to indicate zones for the wolf's den and the safe den.

## What to do
**Movement activity**
- Explain to the children how to play the game. Introduce language such as *run, chase, catch,* and *wait.*
- Choose a player to be Mr Wolf. He/she stays in the wolf's den. The other players stay in the safe den.
- Slowly Mr Wolf creeps out from his den. He pretends not to notice the other children and walks away with his back towards them. The other players follow behind, shouting, 'What's the time, Mr Wolf?'
- For a while Mr Wolf shouts any time he can think of, for example 'Nine o'clock' or 'Ten o'clock!' When the Wolf decides that the other players are far enough away from their safe den, he shouts 'Dinner time!'
- Whirling around, the wolf tries to catch them. The players scream in pretend fright. They race back to their safe den. The first player that is caught becomes Mr Wolf and the game begins again.
- Allow sufficient time for each child to become the wolf.

## Extension/variation
- Talk about the environment of a wolf and ask if the children have ever seen a wolf at a wildlife park or zoo, or on television.

## Related activity
- Peter and the Wolf (see page 184)

# Acting out colours

Moving and Handling

## Learning objectives

- To move freely and with pleasure and confidence in a range of ways, negotiating space successfully within a group of other children
- To improve control and coordination in large and small movements
- To represent and express ideas, thoughts and feelings through movements and actions
- To engage in imaginative role-play based on first-hand experiences

## Topic

Colours

## Resources

- Different shaped foil dishes
- Paint
- Paintbrushes
- Leaves of different shapes and sizes
- Paper
- Different coloured wax crayons
- Toys and other objects
- Large cardboard box

## What to do

### Circle time

- Talk about the colours blue, green, red and yellow. Ask children to think of things that are blue (the sky, the sea because it reflects the sky), green (leaves, grass, apples), red (the setting sun, strawberries, raspberries) or yellow (sand, bananas, lemons).

### Movement activities

- Invite the children to mime actions and create imaginative movements and role-plays for each of the colours.
- For blue, they could pretend to play in a paddling pool, walk through puddles, splash in the bath, fish in the river, row a boat or roll over and over like a wave.
- For green, they could run around and hide behind the trees, climb a tree, flutter like leaves falling down or pretend to eat green fruits and vegetables.
- For red, they could shade their eyes from the sun or pretend to pick berries.
- For yellow, they could pretend to dig and build sand castles on the beach, peel a banana or squeeze a lemon.

## Extensions/variations

- Draw pictures of fish or boats inside foil dishes and hold them up to the light to make the drawings show up as blue lines.
- Collect different leaves and stick them onto card to make collages or lay them under paper and make rubbings with wax crayons.

In spring or summer, they will be green, but, in autumn, they will also be red and yellow.

- Place various toys and objects around the room or outdoor area and invite children to take part in a treasure hunt for red things, blue things, etc.
- Make a large cardboard box into a stall selling drinks, ice creams and beach toys.

Moving and Handling

# Shape necklaces

## Topic
Shapes

## Resources
- Ingredients for salt dough: 100g salt, 340g plain flour, 300ml tepid water
- Kebab skewers
- Paint
- Varnishes
- Paintbrushes
- Beads
- Coloured dough

 Take care with skewers.

## Learning objectives
- To handle equipment, tools and malleable materials safely and with increasing control
- To develop hand/eye coordination, fine motor control and threading skills
- To develop skills in planning and design, experimenting with colour, shape and form

## What to do
**Craft activity**
- Ensure that everyone has washed their hands before beginning the activity. Stir the flour and salt together. Carefully add the tepid water. Mix to a soft dough. Make sure that the children wash their hands again to remove any stickiness before moving onto the next task.
- Invite each child to take small pieces of dough and roll them into whatever shapes they would like their beads to be (cubes, spheres, sausages etc). Help them to push the dough beads on to the kebab skewers. Bake on these skewers at 160°C/325°F/Gas Mark 3.
- Allow the beads to cool and remove them from the skewers. Invite the children to paint them in bright colours and patterns. Varnish them after the children have left and leave them overnight to dry.
- Support the children as they slide the beads onto strong thread and fasten with a knot.

## Extensions/variations
- Make coloured beads using coloured dough. Bake as per the manufacturer's instructions.
- Thread beads collected from home.

## Links to home
- Ask the children's families to donate any unwanted beads to the setting for children to use in threading and design activities. Make sure that they are safe to use (not too tiny or made of glass).

# Fishes in the sea

## Learning objectives

- To negotiate a safe pathway between obstacles as a member of a group
- To travel with confidence and skill around, under, over and through balancing and climbing equipment
- To introduce a storyline or narrative into play

## Preparation

- Find a safe space in or out of doors. Arrange simple apparatus to form barriers and obstructions. This will represent undersea rocks, caves (cardboard boxes) and seaweed (a curtain of strips of paper). Drape clothes from some of the apparatus to portray nets. Make a marked zone at the end of the apparatus.

## What to do

**Movement activity**

- Play the game 'Follow that fish!' Choose an adult to be leader fish first and to lead the group of children safely under the sea, over rocks and seaweed, through caves and avoiding fishing nets. Their safe spot (a shallow pool) will be the marked zone at the end of the apparatus. Once the children are confident, allow them to take turns to lead each other as they wish.

## Extension/variation

- Make a collage of what lies and swims beneath the surface of the sea. Paint and cut out fish shapes. Decorate the shapes with milk-bottle tops, foil, bubble wrap, beads, sequins and stick some of them to a blue background. Attach a piece of netting to the background so that it forms a pocket. Place some fish shapes inside the net. Cut out foil fish shapes and suspend them from a wire coat hanger. If the collage is placed on the wall above a table, shells and pebbles can be displayed on the table for greater effect.

## Related activities

- Cross the forest canopy (see page 45)
- Pets help to keep us healthy (see page 60)

## Topic
Animals

## Resources

- Simple apparatus
- Large cardboard boxes
- Pieces of paper, cut into strips
- Scarves and clothes made from light fabrics
- Paint
- Paintbrushes
- Paper
- Milk-bottle tops
- Foil
- Bubble wrap
- Beads, sequins
- Blue paper for background
- Netting
- Wire coat hangers
- Shells and pebbles

Moving and Handling

# Build a house

## Topic
Homes

## Resources
- Huge box (appliance or furniture)
- Scissors
- Felt-tipped pens
- Paints
- Glue
- Fabric scraps, cut into squares
- Blanket or rug
- Cushion
- Books and toys
- Flat lolly sticks
- Small cardboard boxes
- Wood shavings
- Tissue paper
- Foil
- Buttons
- Interlocking plastic bricks (eg Lego®) or other construction sets

⚠ Make sure the children are standing well away from the box before you start cutting

## Learning objectives
- To handle construction materials safely with increasing confidence
- To demonstrate increasing skill and control when using construction sets
- To use simple tools to make changes to materials

## What to do
**Craft activity**
- Place the big box on the floor using the open side at the back for the children to crawl inside.
- Invite the children to draw the windows and door. The practitioner should ensure that the children are well away from the box and proceed to cut out the windows and door. These may be cut out entirely or left as flaps to open and shut.

- Allow the children to paint their own designs on the house, or to draw flowers trailing or growing up the wall.
- Glue curtains on each side of the windows.
- Place a blanket on the floor of the house and a cushion. Arrange books and toys inside.

## Extensions/variations
- Make a log cabin. Use a small box. Cut out the windows and door. Glue flat lolly sticks over the rest of the house.
- Make a highway of houses. On a long wall panel make a collage of houses in different materials: wood shavings, crumpled tissue paper, foil, buttons.
- Allow the children plenty of opportunities to build houses and other structures using interlocking plastic bricks and other construction sets.
- Provide a range of construction kits of different sizes. Ensure that they are made of different materials, such as plastic, wood, rubber, metal and foam. Look for bricks and pieces that fit together in a variety of ways, such as interlocking, balancing, twisting, pushing, slotting and magnetism.

## Links to home
- Perhaps a parent can provide the large box.

# Reflections

## Learning objectives

- To show good control and coordination in large and small movements
- To move confidently in a range of ways, safely negotiating space
- To imitate movements
- To move in response to music

## Topic

Homes

## Resources

- Book: *Rosie's Room* by Mandy and Ness (Milet Publishing Ltd)
- Small plastic mirrors
- Large plastic mirror
- Music: 'Andante Second Movement', from *Violin Concerto No. 1 in A Minor* by Johann Sebastian Bach
- CD player

## What to do

### Circle time

- Read *Rosie's Room.*
- Invite the children to experiment with making faces and actions while looking into mirrors.
- Explain how their movements are opposite (when they move their right arm, their reflection shows the left arm moving).

### Dance activity

- Remind them of their reflections.
- Sit the children opposite each other in pairs. (It helps if one of the pair is more able. Ask one of them to be leader and make some movements.) Their partner should match the movements as though they are the first child's reflection.
- Swap roles and repeat.
- Repeat the exercise but moving around in the space.
- Suggest holding one hand.
- Suggest facing each other and putting the palm of their hands together.

## Extension/variation

- Play slow music (see Resources), and encourage the children to listen first, then modify their sequence of movements to fit to the music.

**Moving and Handling**

# A bear hunt

## Topic
Toys

## Resources
- Book: *We're Going on a Bear Hunt* by Michael Rosen and Helen Oxenbury (Walker Books)
- Teddy bear

## Learning objectives
- To move freely and with pleasure and confidence in a range of ways
- To safely negotiate space within a group of moving children
- To create a sequence of movements to express and respond to feelings, ideas and experiences
- To play cooperatively to develop and act out a storyline or narrative

## Preparation
- Hide a teddy in a cupboard or other dark place in the setting.

## What to do
**Circle time**
- Read *We're Going on a Bear Hunt* and perform appropriate actions.

**Imaginative play activity**
- Tell the children that they are going on a bear hunt to find Teddy.
- Act out the poem with the children, pretending to travel through the obstacles.

## Extension/variation
- Other stuffed animals/toys could be substituted.

## Related activities
- How will Teddy get there? (see page 174)
- Goldilocks and the Three Bears (see pages 168–169)

# Can you squirm like a worm?

Moving and Handling

## Learning objectives

- To move freely with confidence and pleasure
- To move in a range of ways
- To initiate new combinations of movement and gesture to respond to an idea

## Topic

Animals

## Resources

- 'Slithery' music, such as *Carnival of Animals* (Fish or Swan) by Saint-Saens. (CD Children's Classics LSO)
- Paper
- Paints
- Paintbrushes
- Scissors
- Large cardboard box, big enough to crawl through

## What to do

### Movement activity

- Talk about earthworms that live in the garden. Ask the children if they have seen them slithering and burrowing in the soil.
- Invite the children to pretend to be worms. Ask them to lie face-down on their tummies on the floor and try to squirm, then to kneel on the floor and make undulating movements. Ask them to rise up and fall down again and swivel from side to side.
- Then ask the group to kneel on the floor, keeping close to each other. Perhaps you can think of some 'slithery' music. Ask them to weave in and out as they cross the 'soil'.

Ensure that floor space is free from splinters.

## Extensions/variations

- Make a tunnel out of a large cardboard box by removing two opposite ends. Ask the children to cut out and paint some coloured paper leaves (or use sugar paper). Strew these across the floor near the cardboard box tunnel. Ask the 'worms' to crawl through the tunnel to aerate the soil. Ask them if they can drag the leaves through their tunnel. Explain to them the good they are doing to the soil.
- Cut and paint some paper worms, or twist a long piece of black or dark-coloured sugar paper into a spiral shape. Discuss with the children which worm is the heaviest and whether it feels like a worm.

**Moving and Handling**

# British bulldog

## Topic
Animals

## Resources
- Large safe space such as playground, field or large hall
- Paper
- Pencil

⚠ Watch the children carefully when they are running. Remind the children to take care not to touch or run into each other.

## Learning objectives
- To move freely with confidence and pleasure in a range of ways, such as running, skipping, swerving and dodging
- To show good control and coordination in large movements and negotiate space safely, adjusting speed or direction to avoid collisions with other runners
- To follow instructions involving several ideas and actions
- To play cooperatively within a group, taking turns with others

## Preparation
- Provide a safe area where the players can move safely without collision.

## What to do
### Movement activity
- Explain the game to the children. Decide who is to be the bulldog. This player stands alone. The others gather on the other side of the playground, field or large hall. The bulldog shouts, 'British bulldog!' This is the cue for the others to run across the ground without being caught by the bulldog. The bulldog can stop the runners by shouting a ridiculous dog's name like 'Silly spaniels' or 'Terrible terrier'.
- At the sound of her voice, everyone must then remain where they are. The bulldog must tap another player on the shoulder three times to catch him/her. The player who has then been caught becomes a catcher together with the existing bulldog. Future players caught in this way also become catchers.
- The last player left can be awarded a title such as "champion bulldog" and allowed to take the first turn next time the game is played.

## Extension/variation
- Play animal charades. Draw familiar animals, such as a cat, dog, horse, rabbit, mouse, frog or elephant on separate pieces of paper. Pass one of the drawings to one of the players. The children will enjoy acting out the characteristics and movements of the animal, while the others try to guess which animal it is. The first child to guess takes the next turn.

## Links to home
- Ask parents if they have any photographs of pet animals that the children can bring to school to show to the group and talk about.

# Battle ball

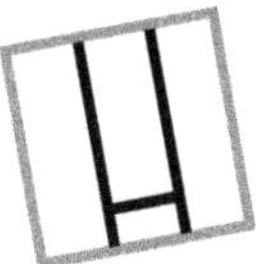

## Learning objectives

- To develop increasing control over objects by rolling and throwing balls and placing skittles
- To handle tools and craft materials safely and effectively
- To play cooperatively, taking turns with others
- To understand the game's link to Hanukkah and that families and communities may celebrate different festivals and traditions

## Preparation

- Use a large, safe space, either outdoors or indoors.
- Encourage children to learn and think about similarities and differences between cultures. If there are Jewish children within the group, invite them to talk about Hanukkah, if they would like to, as the activity is linked here to the Jewish holiday of Hanukkah. It could be linked to another theme, or simply played as a skittle game.

## What to do

### Craft activity

- Ask the children to use either coloured sugar paper or gummed shapes to make a face on the white paper.
- Stick the white paper around the bottles or packets. Apply the features as chosen. These are now the enemies. Help the group to stand the enemies up like skittles.
- Ask the children (who represent the Macabees) to stand approximately 8–10 paces away, depending on their size. Tell them that they have to recapture the Holy Temple. The only way they can do this is to knock down the enemies. Ask them to roll or throw the ball to see how many they can knock down.
- Ask the children to take it in turns to have one throw or roll at a time and knock down as many of the objects as they can.

## Extensions/variations

- Make a rebus card. Use pictures, letters and words and support the children in composing a very simple message, for example Happy Day:

## Topic

Celebrations

## Resources

- 8–10 junk boxes or plastic bottles (eg cereal packets or lemonade or squeezy bottles)
- A4 white paper
- Coloured sugar paper or gummed shapes
- Glue
- Soft ball
- Thin card
- Foil
- Glitter
- Thread
- Scissors

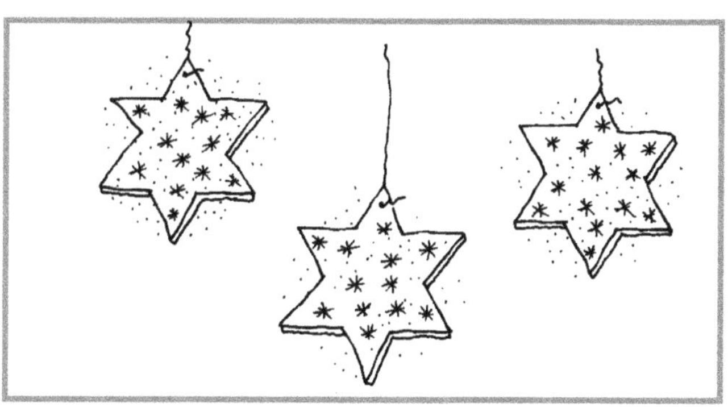

- Make a star of David (6 points). Use thin card. Help the children to draw the star shape and cut it out. If they find cutting the points very difficult, an adult could help by holding the shape for them or making some snips for them to continue. Either wrap foil around the star or paste it with glue and add glitter. Suspend with thread.

# Packing groceries

## Topic

Food and shopping

## Resources

- Large furniture boxes or zones
- Smaller boxes
- Packets in a variety of shapes and sizes
- Grocery wrappers
- Glue
- Paper

Be alert to the safety of each child.

## Learning objectives

- To demonstrate good control and coordination
- To negotiate space safely and carefully around others
- To listen attentively and respond to what is heard with relevant actions
- To count children and boxes, with support

## What to do

**Movement activity**

- Give each child the name of a grocery item. Ask them to remember it carefully because, when you call it out, that child will need to climb into a big box (if you have no boxes, ask them to pretend the marked zones are empty boxes).
- Begin by saying, 'Today I went to the grocer's shop and I bought some sugar.' The child who is sugar will climb into the box or zone and stand up straight. Carry on with the shopping until the first box or zone is full to the brim and tightly packed. Then begin on the next box or zone. When everyone has managed to fit themselves into boxes, examine the outcome. Encourage them to count along with you and to discuss how many items you bought and how many boxes they filled.

**Individual activity**

- Now use some boxes for the children to pack their own shopping. Give them each a box and ask them to pick out some different shaped packets. Ask them to try and fit all of them into their boxes. If they can't, encourage them to take them all out and pack them in a different order, to squeeze in more than before.

## Extensions/variations

- Ask the children to remember which item of grocery they were. Begin a game of 'Shopping'. For example, one child says, 'I went shopping and I bought some sugar.' The next child continues. 'I went shopping and I bought some sugar and some butter.' The game continues by adding another item and remembering the ones that came before. As the list becomes longer the game grows more complicated, so it may be best to begin with younger and less confident children and allow those who are older and more able to take their turns later. The practitioner can help them to remember the items.
- Collect clean food wrappers and make a large wall collage of as many grocery items as possible.

## Links to home

- Ask parents to collect clean wrappers for the second extension activity.

# Body shapes

Moving and Handling

## Learning objectives

- To experiment with different ways of moving
- To balance while holding a body shape and freeze in position
- To safely negotiate space within a group of other children

## Preparation

- Use a large safe space with a bare wall. Chalk or mark a starting line approximately 10–20 paces back from the wall.

## What to do

**Movement activity**

- Ask an adult to be the first leader, then allow children to take turns to lead and play the game for themselves, with and without adults, once they are confident.
- Ask the leader to stand facing the wall. The others stand on the starting line. The children on the starting line have to creep forwards slowly and stealthily and try to touch the wall without the leader seeing them. The leader meanwhile counts to 5 or 10 (depending on the age and ability of the group). He/she suddenly twirls around and tries to catch out anyone who moves even the slightest muscle or limb. The other children have to stand in whichever position they happen to be in when the leader turns around. If anyone moves, they return to the starting line and begin again. The first child to touch the wall without being seen is the new leader.

## Extensions/variations

- Make a shaped printing wedge. Use some self-hardening clay (or salt dough) and make a square. Now make your shape and fix on top of the square (in relief). When the printing wedge has hardened, dip it into the paint and print your shapes.
- Make a building using shapes from square or rectangular boxes, cones, circular and semi-circular boxes, and triangular cartons. An interesting block of buildings can be made this way.

## Topic

Shapes

## Resources

- Paper
- Paint in shallow dish
- Paintbrushes or sponges
- Self-hardening clay or salt dough
- Shaped boxes (variety of shapes and sizes)
- Glue
- Chalk

Moving and Handling

# Treasure trail

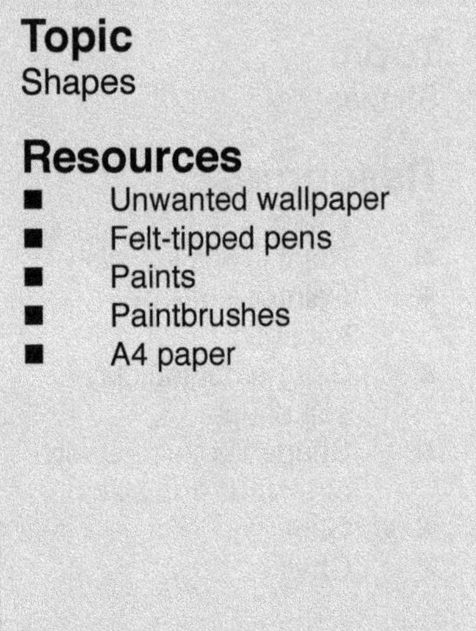

## Topic
Shapes

## Resources
- Unwanted wallpaper
- Felt-tipped pens
- Paints
- Paintbrushes
- A4 paper

## Learning objectives
- To handle equipment and tools effectively
- To draw lines, patterns, circles and other shapes, holding and using a pencil with good control.
- To explore characteristics of shapes and to use both everyday and mathematical language to describe them
- To extend vocabulary, including rhyme and alliteration, to link statements and connect ideas

## Preparation
- Invent a story about Peter, the pirate who has landed on a beach to find the hidden treasure left by another pirate a few days before.

## What to do
### Art activity
- Give the children a roll of unwanted wallpaper. Place it face downwards. Invite them to make a map so that Peter can find the treasure. Ask them to use as many different shapes as possible. Suggest triangles for rocks, cylinder shapes for caves, rectangles and circles for the trees. The tops of the trees could be large daisy shapes; use small circles and oval shapes for boulders, pebbles and stones. Suggest long wriggly shapes for pathways and wavy shapes for the sea. Mark the treasure site with a big **X**.

## Extensions/variations
- Invite children to take turns to describe a shape and ask the group to try to guess which one it is.
- Make some shape books. Make a booklet from A4 paper folded to A5 and ask the children to fill it with as many shapes as they can think of.
- Work with the children to think up alliterative names for shapes, such as: Tommy Triangle, Sally Circle, Sammy Square, Cyril Cylinder, Rex Rectangle, Connie Cone, Oliver Oblong etc. Then together, try to make up a story involving them all.
- Encourage children to notice shapes at home or when they are out with their families and to share their findings with the group.

# Journey to the stars

Moving and Handling

## Learning objectives

- To jump on and off an object and land appropriately
- To move freely in a range of ways and directions, including sideways, backwards and forwards
- To adjust speed and direction to avoid obstacles and collisions
- To travel around, under, over and through balancing and climbing equipment
- To introduce a storyline or narrative into play

## Preparation

- Invite a few of the more confident and more able children to work with an adult to plan a route through various obstacles and apparatus. Either call the session simply 'Follow the leader' or name it more adventurously with 'Journey to the stars'. Advise the leader (captain) to be cautious and not too speedy when leading younger children through and around obstacles.

## What to do

**Movement activity**

- Pretend they are venturing out in a spaceship. Start by sitting on a large box or a wall. When it's time for blast off, ask them to sit safely and still while the rocket leaves the Earth. Now imagine they have left Earth's orbit and are travelling through dark space through the stars. Find the way though the apparatus (call them comets or asteroids) and arrive at the nearest planet. (This should be at a lower level.) Make sure they jump off the piece of apparatus and land safely on the planet.
- Once on the planet they may see weird people and rock formations. Ask them to step sideways to avoid bumping into these rocks. Ask them to step backwards if they see an alien advancing towards them. Perhaps you can involve a couple of children who are not on the planned route to appear from the opposite direction. The children may wish to jump back on to their rocket ship to avoid confrontation.

## Topic

Myself

## Resources

- Various outdoor apparatus and obstacles
- Paint
- Paintbrushes
- Foil
- Glitter
- Glue
- Wire coat hanger
- Scissors

Watch the session carefully to avoid any unfortunate collisions.

## Extension/variation

- Make a mobile of the stars, planets and the moon. Cut the shapes from cardboard and either paint and cover with glitter, or use foil to cover the objects. Suspend them from a wire coat hanger.

# Look what I can do

## Topic
Myself

## Resources
- Space
- Chalk or tape or a long piece of string/ribbon

⚠ Observe carefully when balancing on lines and touching each other's feet.

## Learning objectives
- To move with good control and coordination in various directions
- To follow a line, demonstrating good balance skills, standing momentarily on either foot and stopping safely

## Preparation
- Draw a chalk line on the ground outside or inside, or lay down a long piece of string, ribbon or tape.

## What to do
### Movement activity
- Divide the class into two teams. Invite two children to stand back to back on the line, in the centre. They then take approximately eight steps walking apart on the line. One of them (either) shouts, 'Ticky tacky'. They turn around on the line so that they face each other. They walk towards each other in a straight line, with their heels hard against their toes in each step.

- When there is no longer space for them to put down their feet without touching each other, they should jump off the line and allow the next two children to take their places. Continue until everyone has had a turn.

## Extensions/variations
- Play the same game, this time a slightly more complicated version. Instead of heels touching toes, try twisting one leg so that the toe touches the other toe and try to balance on the line.
- Jumpy jumpy. Play the same game again but but this time jump towards each other. When the players cannot jump any more without landing on each other's feet, they could try turning around and jumping back again to the ends of the line.
- Children could try walking or jumping forwards, towards each other, until they meet in the middle and then try to walk or jump backwards, away from each other, back to the ends of the line.

# Find the smugglers' cave

## Learning objectives

- To experiment with different ways of moving
- To move confidently in a range of ways and directions, safely negotiating space within a group of children
- To jump on and off apparatus and land safely
- To travel around, under, over and through balancing and climbing equipment
- To use one-handed tools and equipment safely and with increasing control
- To introduce a storyline or a narrative into play and work alongside other children to develop it and act it out

## Topic

Water

## Resources

- Apparatus
- Large cardboard boxes
- Long pieces of cardboard
- Table
- Sheet
- Big box of gifts
- Thin card
- Scissors
- Coloured tissue paper
- Coloured cellophane
- Glue
- Foil tray
- Paint
- Paintbrushes

## Preparation

- Prepare a large area. Arrange small pieces of climbing apparatus to be the rocks. Form some caves by making tunnels with large open-ended cardboard boxes. Place long pieces of cardboard on the ground to form crocodiles. Drape a large sheet over a table. Hide the treasure chest underneath it in the smugglers' cave. Have the chest filled with small gifts, such as pencils, apples, and pictures.

## What to do

**Movement activity**

- Tell the children that there is a treasure chest in the smugglers' cave. Ask them who can be the first to find it. Tell them that they can 'swim' around the crocodiles, jump on and off the rocks and crawl through the tunnels. The first child to find the treasure chest is allowed a gift from it. Continue the game until everyone has had a gift.

## Extension/variation

- Suggest to the children that they make some fish and some ships/boats and support them as they draw them and cut them out. Invite them to cut 'scales' from the tissue paper and cellophane and use them to decorate the fish, and to paint the ships in colours of their choice. Explain the 'fish and ships' joke to those who do not understand.

## Related activity

- Shipwreck (see page 51)

**Moving and Handling**

# Cross the sea

## Topic
Water

## Resources
- Ice cubes
- Water
- Bowl
- Paper
- Glue
- Sand
- Paint
- Paintbrushes
- Bubble wrap
- Scissors

Be watchful when the children are using scissors. The younger ones will need help from the practitioner. Carefully observe water play.

## Learning objectives
- To move confidently in a range of ways, safely negotiating space
- To move with control and coordination
- To explore materials and textures and experiment with colour and design
- To follow instructions involving several ideas or actions
- To observe changes and how things happen

## Preparation
- Provide a safe floor space.

## What to do
### Circle time
- Discuss the many different kinds of water – fresh, sea, river.

### Movement activity
- An adult should take on the role of 'boatman' to begin the game. Once the children know how to play and are confident, they can take turns to be the boatman too. The boatman stands alone, pretending to be on 'an island across the sea'. The other children shout, 'Boatman, boatman, can we cross the sea?'

- The boatman chooses a colour and replies by naming the colour for example, 'Not unless you wear yellow.' The children who are wearing *any* yellow clothes attempt to cross the sea. Suddenly the boatman shouts, 'The waves are too big. You will drown!' The children in the 'sea' have to hurry to try to get across it without being swamped by a big wave.
- Show the children how to walk across big waves. Tell them that the water will feel heavy and they must push it out of the way with their legs. When the boatman has chosen enough colours for all the children, the last child to cross the sea becomes the new boatman.

## Extensions/variations
- Provide a bowl of warm water and some ice cubes. Show them how ice cubes melt in warm water. Children will love this gentle way of playing safely with water but they should be carefully supervised. A practitioner playing alongside the children will be able to encourage them to discuss what is happening and introduce new ideas and vocabulary.
- Make a frieze of the sea. Brush glue on to the bottom edge of the paper and sprinkle on some sand. Paint the rest of the paper blue to resemble the sea. Stick on bubbles from bubble wrap packaging material. Suggest that the children paint pictures of fish and cut them out to stick by the bubbles.

# Cross the forest canopy

**Moving and Handling**

## Learning objectives

- To experiment with different ways of moving
- To negotiate space successfully when playing games with other children, adjusting speed or direction to avoid collisions
- To travel with confidence and skill around, under, over and through balancing and climbing equipment
- To communicate through expressive movements linked to imaginative ideas

## Topic

Animals

## Resources

- Climbing frame
- Climbing ropes
- Sturdy safe boxes
- Paints
- Paintbrushes
- Plain cardboard
- Die
- Chalk
- Cotton reels, beads, buttons or matchboxes
- Strong thread

## Preparation

- Set out the apparatus, either indoors or outside, so that the children can find an easy pathway across the floor or ground.

## What to do

**Movement activity**

- Ask the children to pretend to be animals in the jungle or forest. They could pretend that other animals are chasing them and they must climb up the tree or rock to be safe.
- Designate zones to represent the beginning and the end of forest.

## Extensions/variations

- Make a snakes and ladders game. Choose a piece of plain cardboard and divide it into as many squares as you think fit. Number them. Talk to the children about the squares and numbers. Perhaps they would like to paint wriggly snakes and long or short ladders to and from the numbered squares. Obtain a die and teach them the game.
- If there is enough space outside (and you are allowed to draw on the ground with chalk), draw out the game on a hard ground surface. The children can use varied movements, for example hopping, skipping, walking, and running up the ladders or down the snakes.
- Make wibbly, wobbly snakes using cotton reels, beads, buttons or matchboxes and strong thread.

## Related activity

- Fishes in the sea (see page 31)

Moving and Handling

# Archway touch

## Topic
Celebrations

## Resources
- 'Oranges and Lemons' (traditional) from *Rub a Dub Dub Favourite Nursery Rhymes* complied by Val Biro (Happy Cats)

⚠ Supervise the children closely and remind them frequently not to run too fast or pull each other, especially when holding hands.

## Learning objectives
- To move confidently in a range of ways
- To negotiate space successfully when playing chasing games with other children, adjusting speed or changing directions to avoid obstacles and collisions
- To play cooperatively, taking turns and following the rules of the game

## Preparation
- It is preferable to use a playground or garden containing a wall.

## What to do
- This is a fun activity suitable for summer parties and celebrations.

**Movement activity**
- Choose two players to be 'chasers' and two to be 'lookouts'.
- The chasers begin by chasing the other children in the group. The first child caught has to stand near a wall with one arm stretched out against the wall to make an archway. The other players have to run through the arch. The next child caught stands making an arch beside the first child. As soon as several players have been caught, their arms against the wall form a long archway. While the children are running through the archway, the lookouts try to prevent them from escaping from the arch.
- The game ends when all the children are standing against the wall.

## Extensions/variations
**String touch**
- The chaser chases the other players. Once caught, he holds hands with the captured player and continues to chase. This is repeated until a string of children are chasing and holding hands, with the end players touching and catching the remaining children. The last player caught is the winner.

**Oranges and lemons**
- Two children form an archway by lifting their arms high in the air and joining hands. As the song 'Oranges and Lemons' is sung, the others run through the arch as quickly as possible to prevent being caught in the last line: 'Here is a chopper to chop off your head!' When the last pair are caught, they take their turn to form the archway.

*'Oranges and lemons'*
*Say the bells of St Clement's.*

*'You owe me five farthings,'*
*Say the bells of St Martin's.*

*'When will you pay me?'*
*Say the bells of Old Bailey.*

*'When I grow rich'*
*Say the bells of Shoreditch.*

*'When will that be?'*
*Say the bells of Stepney.*

*'I do not know'*
*Says the great bell of Bow.*

*Here comes a candle to light you to bed*
*And here comes a chopper to chop off your head!*

# I can balance

Moving and Handling

## Learning objective

- To practise balancing skills
- To move confidently in a range of ways
- To develop good control and coordination in large and small movements

## Topic

Myself

## Resources

- Long plank of wood
- Books
- Kitchen towel roll inner
- Thick cardboard

## Preparation

- Prepare the area with one long narrow piece of wood, for example a plank, resting on piles of books at each end.

 Supervise carefully to ensure no falls.

## What to do

**Movement activity**

- Ask the children to take turns in walking across the 'bridge'. Suggest that they hold out their arms to the sides to achieve balance. Have a number of balancing movements in mind, such as: lifting one leg and balancing on the other, jumping gently on the bridge, crawling along the bridge, sitting down and getting up again without touching the floor.
- Move the books to underneath the middle of the piece of wood so that it resembles a seesaw. Invite children to walk up it and make it go down again on the other side of the books or to make it straight and balanced by standing with feet apart.
- Ask the children to come off the bridge, and repeat the movements on the floor. Ask which is easier and which they enjoy more. Encourage them to try standing on one leg, to find out how long they can balance and whether they can balance for longer on one leg than the other.

## Extensions/variations

- Ask children to try walking sideways and backwards and to say whether they find it difficult.
- Make a seesaw. Cut a kitchen towel roll inner into three or four pieces. Place a strip of thick cardboard across one piece with the kitchen towel roll inner acting as a pivot underneath. Push the seesaw up and down.

Moving and Handling

# Let's ride the train

## Topic
Transport and travel

## Resources
- Very large boxes (one per child)
- Paint
- Paintbrushes
- Scissors
- String
- Travel brochures
- Paper
- Glue

Take care with scissors and big boxes.

## Learning objectives
- To handle tools, objects and construction materials safely and with increasing control
- To use one-handed tools and equipment with confidence
- To construct with a purpose in mind, using a variety of resources
- To experiment with colour, design and function
- To to play cooperatively as part of a group, introducing a narrative into role-play

## What to do
**Art activity**
- Help the children to remove the ends of the large boxes. Make two holes in two opposite sides of the box near the top ready for the string handles. Paint in bright colours and allow to dry. When dry, ask the children to thread a long piece of string through the holes to form a handle. The practitioner should knot the strings in place.

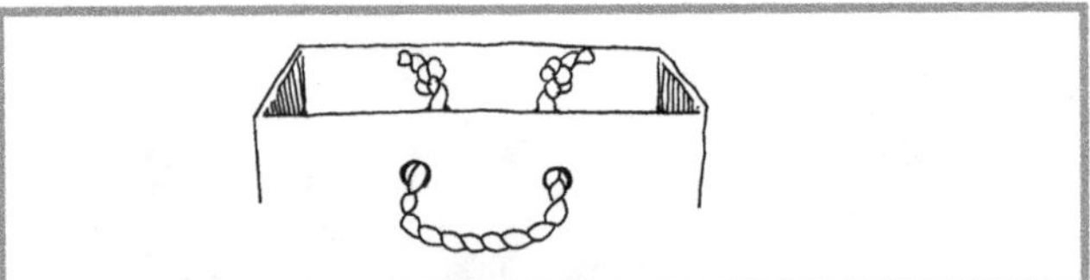

**Movement activity**
- Now it's time to ride the train. Ask the group to line up with their boxes. They should stand inside the boxes and pull them up around their waists. Hang the string handles on their shoulders. Ask them to trot around the floor, keeping close together like carriages.
- To attain the correct rhythm, the following rhyme (using whichever town or city you prefer), assists:

  *Over the track,*
  *Bristol and back,*
  *Riding the train,*
  *And home again.*
- Encourage children to make up their own stories about train journeys and enjoy imaginative role-play together.

## Extensions/variations
- Collect some travel brochures. Cut out favourite pictures and make an interesting collage of all the places the children would like to visit.
- Make railway posters, perhaps of places they have been to on holiday. Paint a seaside or country scene. Help them print the words, for example 'Come to lovely Devon' (or wherever they wish).

# Bony business

## Learning objectives

- To explore the bones and joints of the body and the movements they can make
- To experiment with different ways of moving
- To use and explore a variety of materials and techniques
- To manipulate materials to achieve a planned effect

## Topic

Health

## Resources

- Skeleton template on page 189 (photocopy onto card)
- Card
- Paper fasteners
- Tubes and boxes from the junk box
- Cheese boxes
- String
- Wool
- Paper
- Paints
- Paintbrushes
- Glue
- Ruler or tape measure

## What to do

**Circle time**

- Talk to the children about our bones and joints. Show them the skeleton template on page 189.
- Ask the children to guess how many bones they have. They will be surprised to know that children have approximately 300. Some of these bones fuse together in later life.
- Encourage the children to count the bones in their arms and legs. Explain what a joint is and tell them that joints are protected by cartilage and lubricated to allow them to move. Invite them to find all the joints in their bodies, supporting them as they discover their elbows, knees, ankles, wrists, and hips.
- Make cardboard joints. Cut out arm or leg shapes from thin card. Join together with paper fasteners. Watch the joints at work.

**Make jointed people**

- Use both big and small tubes from the junk box. Paint skin colour. Paint or cover a cheese box lid for the head. Make small cardboard discs to hold the joints in place. Help the children to thread string through the tubes. The body is now jointed. Ask them to paint eyes, nose and mouth on the head. Glue strands of wool for hair.

## Extensions/variations

- Measure legs and arms and discuss who has longer arms and who has shorter arms.
- Using a long rule, or a measuring tape, help the children to measure each other's heights.
- Make a simple block graph of their different heights.

**Moving and Handling**

# Winter

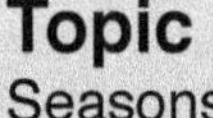

## Topic
Seasons

## Resources
- Thin card, cut into pieces approximately 7.5 x 5cm
- Paints
- Paintbrushes
- Scissors
- White socks
- Felt-tipped pens
- Scraps of material and wool
- Glue

## Learning objectives
- To use and manipulate materials, equipment and one-handed tools safely and with increasing control
- To construct with a purpose in mind, competently using a variety of resources, tools and techniques

## What to do
### Games
- Give each child two cards. Discuss the things they might see or do in winter and invite them to choose one of the ideas and paint two pictures of it, one on each card. (Examples might be: a robin, snow and ice, a polar bear, a Christmas tree, a snowman, a tree with no leaves and a woolly scarf.) If the children are not able to paint two pictures that are similar enough, ask them to each paint one and photocopy them once they are dry. Collect up the cards when they are dry. Continue until all the cards are used up.
- Now play 'Remember winter'. Place all the cards face upwards on the floor and invite the children to sit around them and look at them. Then turn the cards over to hide the pictures. Ask one child to choose a card and turn it over, then to try to remember where the matching card is and turn it over too.
If they guess correctly, they keep the two cards. Older children will enjoy a competitive element and try to find the largest number of pairs. Encourage younger children to take turns to guess, but to work together and help each other when someone is stuck and try to match all the pairs as a group.

## Extension/variation
- Make a snowman sock puppet out of unwanted white socks. Ask the children to put on the sock with their thumb in the heel, therefore making a mouth shape. Mark the positions for eyes and nose with a felt-tipped pen. Stick on small scraps of material for features and wool for hair. Tie a piece of material around the 'neck' for the snowman's scarf.

# Shipwreck

## Learning objectives

- To move with confidence and imagination and experiment with different ways of moving
- To negotiate space successfully when playing racing and chasing games with other children
- To jump off an object and land appropriately
- To travel around, under, over and through balancing and climbing equipment
- To follow instructions involving several ideas or actions

## Topic

Water

## Resources

- Apparatus
- Sturdy junk boxes
- Small chairs
- Climbing frame
- Squares of coloured cardboard
- Scissors
- Stiff paper
- Craft matchsticks
- Matchboxes
- Glue

 Be observant when scissors and glue are in use.

## Preparation

- Provide a safe area and, depending on the age of the children, arrange boxes or apparatus to resemble islands, rocks, or trees. If the children are very young, make off-ground zones from cardboard circles or squares for rocks, islands and trees.

## What to do

**Movement activity**

- Challenge the children to cross the 'water' without falling in. Invite some children to volunteer to be 'chasers'. While a player stands on a piece of apparatus, off the ground, they cannot be caught, but they must attempt to keep moving and running between places. When a player is caught, he/she becomes another chaser.

## Extension/variation

- Make sailing boats out of matchboxes. Cut a square or triangle sail from stiff paper. Pierce a craft matchstick through the sail and down through the middle of the matchbox. Put some glue on the matchbox-end of the stick to ensure it stays put.

## Related activities

- Find the smugglers' cave (see page 43)
- Cross the sea (see page 44)

Moving and Handling

# Family coach

## Topic
Families

## Resources
- Safe floor space
- Unwanted wallpaper
- Crayons
- Scissors
- Coloured wool
- Glue
- Scraps of fabric

## Learning objectives
- To move confidently, with control and coordination, safely negotiating space within a group of children
- To listen attentively to a story and respond to what is heard with relevant actions
- To maintain attention, concentrate and sit quietly when appropriate
- To understand and adjust behaviour to fit expectations, boundaries and rules

## Preparation
- Sit in a group with the children in a large, safe space, either indoors or outdoors
- Prepare a story, containing names of people animals or objects. Try to repeat each name several times.

## What to do
### Movement activity
- Give everyone a name of a person, an animal or an object mentioned in the story.
- Read or tell the story. As soon as the children hear their name, they should get up, turn around and sit down again. It can be done in ones, twos or several people at once (if there is enough room).
- As soon as the words 'family coach' are said, the whole group gets up, turns around, and sits down. You can imagine the jostling and laughter that will accompany this. Encourage the children to enjoy the game, while reminding them not to push or fall on each other deliberately.

## Extension/variation
- Make life-sized self-portraits by drawing round the children, one at a time, on sheets of unwanted wallpaper. (Other children can help with the drawing.) The children can add features using crayons. Coloured wool can be added for hair and pieces of fabric for clothes. When all the figures are finished, stick them all on a large wall frieze.

# Toy ball

## Learning objectives

- To move confidently, safely negotiating space for self and others
- To develop and improve control over an object such as a ball
- To practise coordination skills, such as throwing and catching
- To accept challenges, persevere when learning new skills and independently recognize and enjoy achievement and success

## Topic

Toys

## Resources

- Balls
- Balloons
- Newspaper
- Wallpaper paste without fungicide (alternatively make your own paste by mixing plain flour with tepid water)
- Paints
- Paintbrushes

## Preparation

- Find a safe space with a blank wall.
- Inflate some balloons.

## What to do

**Movement activity**

- Ask the children to queue up behind each other facing the wall. The first child in the queue throws the ball against the wall and allows it to bounce on the floor once. He then jumps over it and at the same time shouts the name of a toy. The second child tries to catch it, running after it to bring it back if they miss. That child then throws the ball against the wall and shouts the name of another toy, while jumping over the ball.
- The next child continues the game in the same way.

## Extensions/variations

- Have some inflated balloons and cover with papier-mâché. Tear up the newspaper into small pieces. Dip into the glue, then place on the balloon. Cover the balloon with two or three layers. When dry, paint the balloon balls.
- Demonstrate for the children how to keep the ball (or balloon) in the air by patting it upwards.

## Related activity

- I prefer this hand (see page 55)

Moving and Handling

# Careful not to bump!

## Topic

Health

## Resources

- Large space
- Small cartons (one for each child)

Watch out for collisions!

## Learning objectives

- To use good control and coordination
- To judge and negotiate space successfully when playing with other children, avoiding obstacles and collisions
- To work as part of a group, adjusting behaviour to different situations and understanding that actions affect other people.

## Preparation

- Find a large safe space inside or outdoors. Be sensitive to those who are unable to take part. Find enough small cartons for each child to have one each. Deposit these at each side of the space.

## What to do

### Circle time

- Talk about the space around us and how we might feel if the world was so crowded there was no space around ourselves. Ask the children if they think they would bump into each other all the time and how they would cope if others were so close to them all the time that they were unable to move where they wished.

### Movement activity

- Play 'Here We Go Gathering Strawberries in June'. (Sing to tune of 'Nuts in May'.)

  *Here we go gathering strawberries in June,*<br>*strawberries in June, strawberries in June*<br>*Here we go gathering strawberries in June,*<br>*on a warm and sunny morning.*

  *Here we go gathering gooseberries in June,*<br>*gooseberries in June, gooseberries in June*<br>*Here we go gathering gooseberries in June,*<br>*on a warm and sunny morning.*

  *We're all coming over to pick your berries,*<br>*pick your berries, pick your berries*<br>*We're all coming over to pick your berries,*<br>*on a warm and sunny morning.*

- Divide the group into two halves. Ask one half to join hands and form a line at one side of the room. Ask the other half to do the same at the opposite side. During the first verse one line skips as far as the other line and then moves backwards to their side. In the second verse the other line does the same. Before the third verse starts, they each pick up a small carton to carry to the other side. In the third verse they all skip up to each other. When they meet they let go of each other's hands and try to pass through each other's line to the opposite side.
- As they cross over the space and intermingle with each other, there will probably be much hilarity!

# I prefer this hand

## Learning objectives

- To begin to show a clear preference for a dominant hand
- To move confidently in a range of ways
- To show increasing control over a ball when throwing, catching or kicking it
- To use one-handed tools and equipment

## Topic

Myself

## Resources

- Balls of varying sizes
- Cardboard boxes
- Scissors, for both left- and right-handers
- Paper

 Supervise the use of scissors carefully.

## What to do

**Movement activity**

- Work with two children at a time and ask them to throw a ball to each other and try to catch it with both hands. Then ask them to try again, catching first with one hand and then the other, and to decide which hand they prefer to catch with.
- Ask them to sit facing each other on the floor. Roll the ball and repeat the above.
- Suggest that they bounce the ball on the floor so that a partner can catch it after it has bounced, then bounce the ball, lift a leg over the ball and bounce it in the direction of a partner, deciding which leg they prefer to use and whether they can use one more easily than the other.
- Invite them to kick the ball to each other and decide which leg is more comfortable and effective for kicking.

## Extensions/variations

- Try kicking the ball so that it rolls into a cardboard goal to find out which is the best foot for kicking.
- Try table-top ball. Roll balls with hands into a cardboard goal.
- Cut out paper people. Assess which hand is more comfortable.

## Links to home

- Ask parents if they have noticed their children's preferences for a dominant hand and check that their observations match practitioners observations. If there are left-handers in the group, make their parents aware that most shops and all educational suppliers sell equipment for left-handers and for right-handers, as well as items that can be used equally in either hand. Tell them where you obtain supplies or suggest that they search online for left-handed children's scissors, etc. If a family is unable to do this, consider lending small items of equipment when a child needs them to work on a skill at home.

Moving and Handling

# Obstacle course

## Topic
Transport and travel

## Resources
- Lots of cardboard boxes of a similar size
- Paper
- Fabric scraps
- Glue

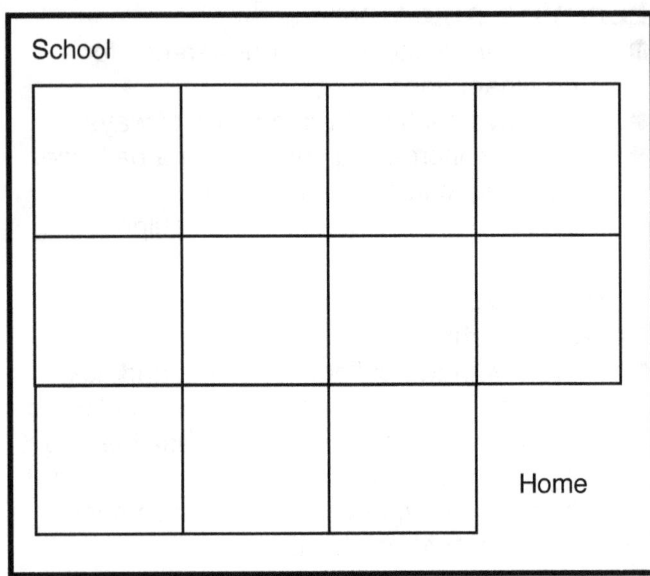


## Learning objectives
- To show good control and coordination in large movements
- To confidently and safely negotiate space
- To manipulate materials to achieve a planned outcome

## Preparation
- Set up the room as in the diagram with plenty of cardboard boxes, leaving one space only. Mark a start zone as home and a far end zone with the name of your setting.

## What to do
### Movement activity
- Invite the children one at a time to attempt to find their way to the setting, by moving the boxes one at a time to negotiate their way through the other boxes.
- They must not climb over and can only move forward by moving one box at a time.

## Extension/variation
- Invite children to make collage pictures of the routes they take from home to the setting, using scraps of fabric. These could include the houses, trees, buses, cars, and roads, etc that they see on the way.

## Links to home
Ask if any parents can supply the boxes. (They may be able to get them from work.)

# Scare the crows

Moving and Handling

## Learning objectives

- To handle tools, objects and materials safely and with increasing control and coordination
- To construct with a purpose in mind, using a variety of resources
- To manipulate materials effectively to achieve a planned effect
- To work cooperatively with others

## Preparation

- Find a suitable place for a scarecrow in the outdoor area.

## What to do

**Circle time**

- Discuss scarecrows with the children and ask whether they have ever seen any standing in farmers' fields, preventing the birds from eating seeds.

**Design and technology activity**

- Children will probably find this activity an immense pleasure and may adopt the idea at home for their own gardens.
- Tie the two sticks together in a cross shape. One stick forms the outstretched arms. Use either the turnip for the head or a piece of fabric stuffed with foam, tights or rags and tied into a head shape. Stuff a hat with straw or rags and stick or tie on to the head. Dress the scarecrow in an old coat or shirt and stuff the body and arms with straw. Glue on felt eyes. Add some flowers or leaves to the hat.
- Stick the scarecrow firmly in the earth.

## Extensions/variations

- Make paper flowers from sugar paper. Here's one method you could use: Fold a piece of sugar paper in half lengthways and cut into a fringe. Twist round and stick to form the flower. Cut out green paper for leaves. Stick to the end of a straw.
- Decorate empty containers with painted flowers. Use as vases for gifts.
- Make a wall frieze of a long garden. Fill it with every conceivable flower, tree or plant. Use collage materials: flowers and leaves, glitter, pasta shells and pebbles.

## Topic

Gardening

## Resources

- 2 sticks
- Large turnip or piece of fabric stuffed with foam, tights or rags
- Old hat
- Straw
- Old clothing
- Old scarf
- Bits of felt
- Glue
- String
- Scissors
- Sugar paper
- Empty containers
- Unwanted wallpaper for frieze
- Collage materials: flowers and leaves, glitter, pasta shells, pebbles

Be careful with scissors and sticks. Ensure the children wash hands after working in the garden.

# Water wheel

## Topic
Water

## Resources
- Circular cheese box
- Scissors
- Pencil
- Pictures of water wheels or other machines driven by water
- Cardboard
- Water
- Sink with tap
- Plastic bottle

Watch out for slippery floors after the water activity. Supervise the use of scissors carefully.

## Learning objectives
- To handle tools, equipment, objects and construction materials safely and with increasing control
- To observe and talk about why things happen and how things work

## Preparation
- Cut 6–8 slits around the edge of a circular cheese box. Make a hole in the middle and insert a pencil.

## What to do
- Discuss the power of water, and explain that it can be used to make enough power to drive machines. Share some pictures of water wheels, water mills and other water-driven machines with the children.

**Make a water wheel**
- Show the circular cheese box to the children. Cut small pieces of cardboard and fit them into the slots that you previously cut.
- Hold the wheel under a running tap (using the pencil) so that the water falls on the cardboard flaps. Encourage the children to watch closely as the weight of the water begins to turn the wheel around.

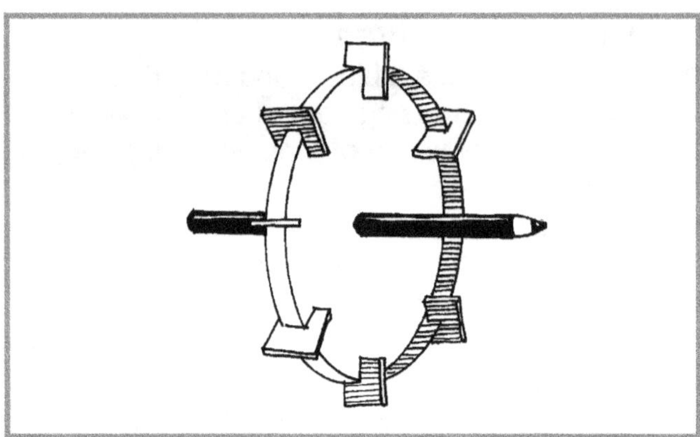

**Movement activity**
- Invite a group of children to form a circle with some adults, and to become a water wheel. Dance round and round singing the following song to the tune 'Here We Go Round the Mulberry Bush':

  *See how the wheel goes round and round*
  *Round and round*
  *Round and round*
  *See how the water splashes down*
  *Splashing on the ground*
- When they reach the words 'splashes down', bend down from the waist, and fall gently to the floor as the water forces the wheel to move around. Encourage the children to imitate the actions and to join in.

## Extensions/variations
- The practitioner should pierce some holes in a plastic bottle. Invite the children to fill the bottle quickly. Hold it over the sink and see what happens to the water.
- Talk about swimming. Ask the children whether they need to wear armbands to keep them afloat. Lead a movement activity involving various swimming strokes.

## Links to home
- Ask parents if they share swimming sessions with their children and remind them that it is a healthy family activity that they might enjoy.

# Physical Development

# Health and self-care

- Practitioners need to ensure that children know how important physical exercise is for achieving and maintaining good health. They must also encourage talking and learning about a healthy diet and ways to keep safe. This involves supporting children as they become aware of risks and learn to assess and choose levels of risk for themselves, rather than removing all risks, and therefore challenges and development opportunities, in the interests of 'health and safety'.

- Developing skills in self-care and attending to personal needs and hygiene are important as children move through the early years. They need to learn to manage their own dressing and undressing, handwashing and using the toilet by themselves in order to gain valuable independence and self-control. They should come to identify and understand their own feelings of hunger, thirst or tiredness, or being too hot or too cold, and know how to satisfy their needs or relieve their discomfort, or how to ask an adult for help.

- Putting on clothes and shoes develops coordination and manipulative skills, while washing before eating or after messy activities or using the toilet, offers opportunities for children to learn and talk about germs and hygiene. Taking responsibilty for their own personal needs allows children to feel more confident, more mature and more in control of their emotions and behaviour.

- It is, however, important to allow children to work through the developmental stages at their own pace, without rushing them towards achieving learning goals too quickly. Dependence during the early years does not lead to children expecting to be helped throughout their lives. Withdrawing from care routines with special adults too soon can mean that children miss out on some important sensory stimulation.

- The sensitivity, affection and intimacy that children share with their families and other carers during nurturing routines form and strengthen secure attachments and are vital for the development of emotional confidence and well-being, which supports academic and creative abilities and brain function in later years.

Health and Self-care

# Pets help to keep us healthy

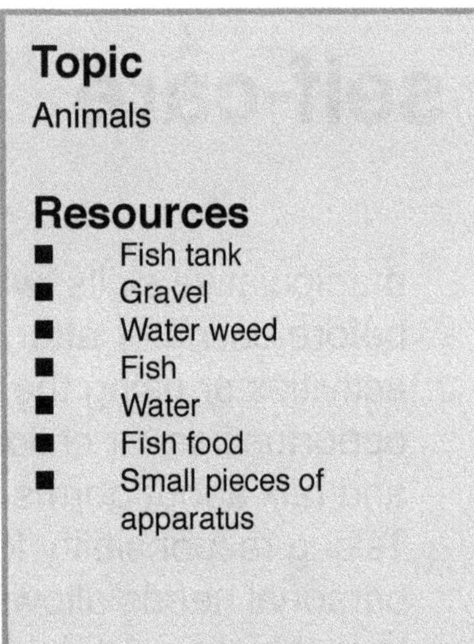

## Topic
Animals

## Resources
- Fish tank
- Gravel
- Water weed
- Fish
- Water
- Fish food
- Small pieces of apparatus

Ensure hands are washed after touching any animals.

## Learning objectives
- To recognize that exercise, eating, sleeping and good hygiene practices contribute to good health
- To behave safely and responsibly both with and without direct supervision
- To ask for help from adults when it is needed

## Preparation
- Set up a fish tank in the classroom. Watching fish is a very relaxing activity. Scatter gravel and stones in the bottom of the tank. Add water weed, perhaps a decorative archway and the water. Add the fish.
- Place a few small pieces of apparatus in a large floor space.

## What to do
- Support children in taking turns to feed the fish and help to clean out the tank regularly, making sure they understand the responsibility of keeping pets and the importance of caring for them properly. Discuss the need to wash hands thoroughly after touching any animals or their equipment, as they could have germs that make people ill, and ensure that all children remember to do this. Ask all the children to watch the way the fish move.

**Movement activity**
- Invite the children to show how their pets move. They could lie on the floor and wriggle their bodies like a fish
- Discuss other pets. Ask children if they have pets at home and if they could show the group how the animals move. Here are a few ideas:
  - Dogs – run around the room, jump over small obstacles (apparatus).
  - Rabbits – hop across the room, twitch noses and crunch carrots.
  - Cats – spring and pounce, walk sedately around the room, lick paws and then use them to clean ears.
  - Birds – flap wings and hop on perches or glide around the room.

## Extensions/variations
- Talk about specially trained dogs who work as guide dogs for the blind or hearing dogs for the deaf. Find out whether a working dog could visit the setting, with its owner or trainer, to demonstrate its job to the children.
- Ask the children if they can think of other working dogs. They may know dogs who work on farms, but may not have heard of dogs who search for dangerous substances in luggage or for people lost on mountains or in snow.

## Links to home
- Ask parents if they would be willing to take turns to care for class pets during weekends and holiday periods. Make up a rota including the names of those who are willing, so that the children know when it is their turn to take the fish or other pets home. Provide a suitable tank or cage and clear instructions for care and feeding.

# Healthy eating



## Learning objectives

- To understand which foods are considered healthy and how a varied diet of these contributes to good health
- To learn the importance of good health and how to stay safe by eating a healthy diet and observing good hygiene practices
- To be sensitive to the fact that different people's food choices are influenced by medical conditions, cultures and religions, preferences, likes and dislikes

## Topics

Food and shopping/Health

## Resources

- Empty washed margarine containers
- Paper
- Glue
- Paint
- Paintbrushes
- Plasticine or modelling clay
- Variety of fruit (eg orange, apple or tomato)
- Knife (for use by practitioner)

## What to do

**Circle activity**

- Talk to the children about healthy food. Tell them it keeps us well and provides energy and growth. Ask whether they know or can guess which foods are healthy and which are not.
- Ensure that they are aware of the importance of cleanliness and good hygiene. Be aware of any children or adults who have food allergies or intolerances and talk about them with the group. Explain that many people cannot safely eat nuts, or dairy products, or gluten or citrus fruits etc.

**Art activity**

- Explain to the children that they are going to make 'a bowl of goodness'.
- Give each child an empty washed margarine container. Support children as they cover them with paper and paint them with colourful patterns. Then encourage them to think of healthy foods, such as fruits and vegetables and use plasticine or modelling clay to make them. For example, make: bananas, oranges, apples, tomatoes, carrots and celery.

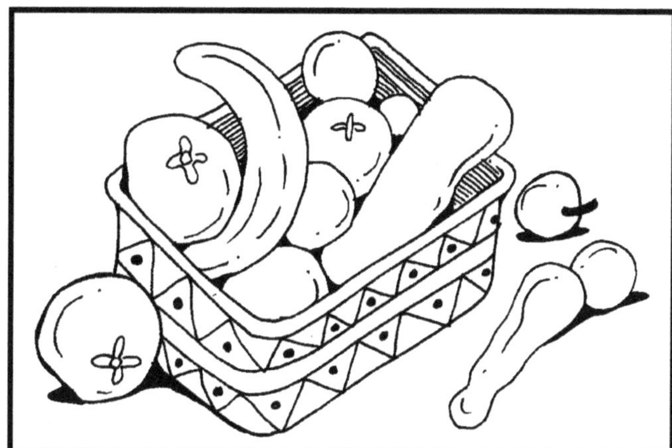

## Extensions/variations

- Make a daily menu chart. Ask the children to draw pictures of the meals they have eaten or will eat in a day. For example, for breakfast, draw a boiled egg or a bowl of cereal; for lunch, draw sandwiches or meat and potatoes. Don't forget to include drinks.
- Cut in half various fruits such as oranges, apples and tomatoes. Ask the children to dip them into paint and print the shapes, then ask their friends if they can recognize the fruits used.

## Related activity

- Vegetable and fruit faces (see page 62)

# Vegetable and fruit faces

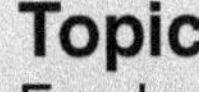

## Topic
Food and shopping

## Resources
- Tomatoes
- Cucumbers
- Cress
- Cottage cheese
- Apples
- Oranges
- Cherries
- Paper plates
- Wooden skewers
- Margarine cartons
- Paper
- Paint or felt-tipped pens
- Paintbrushes
- Glue
- Scissors
- Stapler

## Learning objectives
- To eat a range of foods and to understand the need for a varied and healthy diet
- To represent original ideas using fruits and vegetables as creative media

## Preparation
- Provide a variety of chopped vegetables and fruit.

## What to do
**Cooking activity**
- Give everyone a paper plate and ask them to design their own picnic. Put a variety of chopped vegetables and fruit in the centre of the table. Let them design their own faces. If they don't know how to get started you could prompt them. For example, suggest they use slices of cucumber for eyes. Cress or cottage cheese are good for hair. They could use a cherry for the nose and a slice of tomato for the mouth. Apple slices or orange segments make excellent ears.
- Now invite them to eat their designs and enjoy!

## Extensions/variations
- Cold kebab fruit: use any kind of fruit and vegetables and place chunks and slices on a wooden skewer. Eat the kebabs straight away.
- Berry baskets: cover margarine cartons with paper and paint patterns. Staple handles from paper strips. Fill with fruit.

## Related activity
- Healthy eating (see page 61)

# We need to eat and sleep



## Learning objectives

- To understand that good health relies upon a healthy diet, exercise, sleep and good hygiene practices
- To recognize the ways in which adults must support children and to know how and when to ask for help
- To show an interest in different occupations and ways of life and to appreciate the people who work in the caring professions or provide services

## Topic
Health

## Resources
- Role-play area with dolls, baths, beds, highchairs

## What to do

**Circle time**

- Discuss 'people who help us' with the children. Ask them who we need and what would happen if those people were not there.
- Talk about doctors, fire fighters, and police officers etc. Think of other essential trades and professions, such as mending and sweeping the roads, repairing gas and electric mains, driving buses and trains, delivering post and working in banks and shops.
- Talk about the things that parents do to help their children every day, such as bathing, washing clothes, providing food and working to earn money.

**Movement activity**

- Use some nursery rhymes to support some of the ways parents help.
- Sleep is most important. Tell the group that unless they rest when they are tired they will not keep well or active. Find a big space and have some children running around, others asleep on the floor. Ask your chosen Wee Willie Winkie to stride through the 'town' calling, 'Are the children in their bed? It's past eight o'clock!'
- Tell them how important it is to dry themselves if they get wet. Use the rhyme 'Dr Foster went to Gloucester'. Role-play his character, stamping through puddles. Talk about where he might have been going; possibly to the hospital to see his patients or to a house to visit sick children?

- Discuss the food that their parents cook and what the family would do without their meals at home. Role-play Jack Horner sitting in the corner eating his Christmas pie.

## Extension/variation

- Set up the role-play area with dolls, cooking and feeding equipment, baths, and beds. Provide on-going time for all children to role-play being parents and children.

Health and Self-care

# Effects of activities on the body

## Topic
Myself

## Resources
- Floor space
- *Did You Ever See a Lassie?* from Oki-tokki-unga (A&C Black)

## Learning objectives
- To become aware that physical activity and exercise can contribute to good health.
- To experiment with different ways of moving
- To move with increasing control and coordination
- To negotiate space successfully while moving around other children, avoiding collisions
- To observe the affects of activity on the body

## Preparation
- Prepare an empty space suitable for many exercising activities and encourage children to move around freely and to assume a variety of positions. Allow the children to rest when they are tired.

## What to do
- Discuss exercise with the children. Ask if they noticed any difference in their body after exercise. Use a playground or a hall to practise some of the following activities.
- To the tune of 'Frère Jacques', complete these actions:

  *Lift your right arm, lift your right arm.*
  *Your right arm, your right arm.*
  *Can you lift it higher, can you lift it higher?*
  *Up, up, up.*
- Repeat with left arm, right leg, left leg, feet, fingers, head, back, etc. Sing and practise types of movement instead of parts of the body, such as 'run around', skip, hop, etc.

## Extensions/variations
- Sing 'Did You Ever See a Lassie/Laddie?' Have the lassie or laddie stand in the centre of a circle of children and perform as many ungainly and awkward actions as possible. When the verse has finished, invite all the other children in the ring to perform the same actions. Let the children take turns in being the one in the middle.
- In a floor space, ask the children to think of many different postures. Ask them to run, jump or skip, and to balance on one leg as long as they can.
- Once again to the tune of 'Frère Jacques':

  *I am walking, I am walking,*
  *Walk walk walk, walk walk walk,*
  *I am walking, I am walking ,*
  *Walk walk walk, walk walk walk.*
- Try jumping, skipping, hopping, dancing, etc, singing along to the movements to maintain a steady beat and rhythm.

## Related activity
- Can you be a doctor? (see page 75)

# Hygiene in role-play

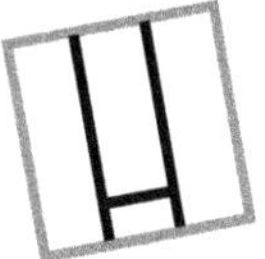

## Learning objectives

- To understand that observing good hygiene practices contributes to good health
- To practise managing basic hygiene and personal needs independently
- To know when and how to ask for adult support

## Preparation

- Provide equipment and resources for pretend washing and brushing in the role-play area. Have empty bowls ready for pretend hand and face washing.

## What to do

**Role-play activity**

- Discuss the importance of hygienic habits. Reinforce the importance of washing hands before handling food and before eating.
- Maintain the role-play as a part of your continuous provision while the children's interest lasts. Play alongside them to model how to pretend to wash their face and hands, how to shower and use a towel to dry their backs and legs. Pretend to wash hair, towel it dry, use a pretend hair dryer, and pretend to brush hair.
- Play 'Here We Go Round the Mulberry Bush' as a ring game, using these verses:

  *This is the way we wash our hands, hair, etc*
  *This is the way we brush our teeth, etc*
  *This is the way we take a bath, shower, etc*
  *This is the way we brush our hair, etc*

## Extensions/variations

- Make as many signs as you can to remind children of hygienic practices. For example: 'Now wash your hands' on toilet doors, and 'Is your hair tidy?' beside a mirror.
- Help the children write or copy these words on to large pieces of cardboard. Illustrate as necessary and suspend/display in prominent positions.
- Make a hygiene collage. Collect some soap wrappers, toothpaste cartons, shampoo sachets and a flannel, sponge or old towel cut into small pieces, and paste them on to a large piece of paper.

## Topic

Homes

## Resources

- Towels
- Soap
- Bowls
- Empty shower bottles
- Empty shampoo bottles
- Cardboard
- Glue
- Felt-tipped pens
- Empty shampoo sachets
- Toothbrush cartons
- Soap wrappers
- Old towel, flannel or sponge

It would not be wise for children to share brushes or combs.

## Related activity

- Hairdressing salon (see page 140)

Health and Self-care

# Teddy bears celebrate!

## Topics

Food and shopping

## Resources

- Teddy bears
- 'The Teddy Bears' Picnic' by John W Bratton (Past Times CD)
- Slices of bread
- Margarine
- Marmite
- Lemonade ingredients: 60ml fresh lemon juice, 250ml orange juice, 175ml water
- Blender
- Half banana per child
- Paper cups and plates
- Plastic spoons
- Cardboard
- Scissors
- Paper fasteners
- Glue
- Fabric scraps in assorted colours
- Felt-tipped pens

 Check with parents regarding food allergies.

## Learning objectives

- To understand the need for variety in food, to eat a healthy range of foods and be willing to try new foods
- To follow good hygiene practices and to understand that they contribute to good health
- To handle malleable materials, modelling tools and cookery equipment safely and effectively
- To engage in group imaginative role-play based on first hand experiences

## Preparation

- In advance, ask the children to each bring a teddy bear (or another soft toy) to the setting for a picnic party. (If anyone can't bring one, or forgets, they can choose a soft toy from the setting.)
- Prepare a clean surface for the children to use to prepare food for themselves.

## What to do

### Cooking activity

- Ensure the group wash their hands. Tell them that all their teddies are going to a picnic and they have been invited too, but first they need to get the food ready.
- Make whirly sandwiches. Show them how to spread the margarine (not too thickly) on a slice of bread. Help them to spread (even more thinly) some marmite on top of the margarine. Show them how to roll up the bread like a Swiss roll. The practitioner can cut the roll into slices. Store in the fridge.
- Make lemonade. Blend all the ingredients together in a blender and store in the fridge until ready.
- Slice the bananas and put aside with some plastic spoons.
- Ask the children to make small sandwiches, cakes and other foods (such as fruit and vegetables) from play dough, for the toys to have at the picnic party. Provide unlit candles to be pushed into some of the cakes.
- Ask the children to form a circle (with their teddies holding hands too) and sing 'The Teddy Bears' Picnic'.
- When it is a reasonable time for the picnic, for example break time or lunchtime, arrange for the children to sit at the table, around a tablecloth on the floor, or al fresco outside depending on the weather and insect seasons. Play suitable music while they are picnicking.
- Suggest that it might be one or more of the teddies' birthdays. Offer them the playdough cakes with candles and sing 'Happy Birthday' together.

## Extensions/variations

- Make cardboard teddies with jointed limbs by cutting out heads, bodies, arms and legs and fixing them together with paper fasteners. Children could decorate them with coloured pens or scraps of fabric and draw on features with black pens.
- Make birthday cards for the teddies, using art and craft materials or a computer program.
- Discuss the teddies' names and think up names for any toys that don't yet have them.

## Links to home

- Explain the activity to parents in advance and ask them to remind their children to bring a teddy bear or soft toy on the right day.
- Check and discuss any allergies and intolerances with parents before offering picnic food to all of the children.

# Healthy food for celebrations

**Health and Self-care**

## Learning objectives
- To recognize that some foods contribute to good health, while some should only be eaten occasionally.
- To eat a range of healthy foods and to understand the need for variety in food
- To understand the need for good hygiene practices when handling food
- To manage basic hygiene and personal needs, such as handwashing, independently
- To use tools and equipment, such as knives, competently and safely, with support
- To extend the theme with other art and craft activities

## Topic
Celebrations

## Resources
- Celery sticks
- Cottage cheese
- Variety fresh fruit
- Knives
- Carrots
- Lettuce
- Watercress
- Brown bread
- Hard-boiled eggs
- Chives
- Margarine
- Cinnamon
- Lemon juice
- Baking dish
- Felt-tipped pens or paints
- Paper plates
- Pastry cutters
- Sultanas
- Flag template on page 190

## Preparation
- Prepare a space for the children to work at the food activity. Ensure hands are washed before and after the activity. Promote tidiness and cleanliness in the food area.
- Wash all fresh fruits and vegetables.

## What to do
### Cooking activity
- Discuss healthy food with the group. Advise them that most party food should not be eaten too often as it doesn't contribute to good health and is sometimes called junk food. Explain that the following food ideas are still very tasty, just right for parties and beneficial to their health.
- Make some Celery tubes. The practitioner should slice (or help the children slice) the celery lengthwise. Stuff the middles with cottage cheese or fresh fruit.
- Carrot sticks. The practitioner should cut (or help the children cut) the carrots into small sticks. Use these to dip into cottage cheese or mashed banana. Or add to a salad with lettuce and watercress.
- Fruit-topped cheese. Ask the children to chop strawberries or raspberries into small pieces and add them to a bowl of cottage cheese.
- Brown wedges. Use sliced bread and ask the children to spread margarine lightly over the slices. Chop the eggs and mix with chives. Place a lettuce leaf on the bread and add the egg mixture. Help them cut the wedges into dainty triangles.
- Golden pears. Grease a shallow baking dish with margarine. Mix up 1 teaspoon cinnamon with 30g margarine and a little lemon juice. Add fresh sliced pears and coat with the mixture. Bake for approximately 20 minutes at 185°C/375°F/Gas Mark 5.

Be aware of food allergies. Supervise the use of knives carefully.

## Extensions/variations
- Decorate the shells of hard-boiled eggs using paints or felt tip pens. Children could try designs, faces or pictures.
- On paper plates make designs with healthy food to tempt even the smallest appetite. For example, cut sandwiches into circle shapes. Arrange carrot sticks and celery to form a face. Add sultanas for eyes. Use slices of apple for ears.
- Suggest to the children that they make flags (on sticks or as bunting) to add to their celebrations. Talk about different flags for different countries and choose which countries you wish to represent. Templates for the English, United Kingdom and Scottish flags are on page 190. Look up others in books and atlases.

## Links to home
- Ask parents if they can supply their child with a hard-boiled egg for decorating.

Health and Self-care

# Water is great to drink!

## Topic
Water

## Resources
- Yoghurt pot with water
- Small cardboard box
- Pencil
- String
- Chopped carrots, celery and potatoes
- Knives
- Water
- Saucepan
- Stock cube
- Salt
- Either saucepan and cooker, or microwave dish and microwave

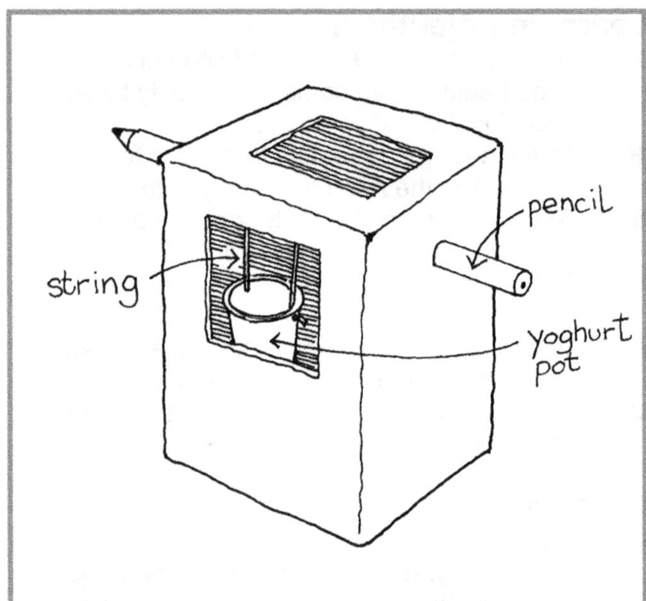


⚠ Keep children well away from the hot cooker. Supervise the use of knives carefully.

## Learning objectives
- To understand that drinking water is essential for good health
- To be aware of how it feels to be thirsty
- To learn that people in some other parts of the world do not have easy access to fresh drinking water

## Preparation
- Cut a hole in the front of the cardboard box and a hole in the top of the box (see diagram). Cut a slit each side for the pencil.

## What to do
**Movement activity**
- Explain that some people in other countries cannot turn on a tap to have water as we do. They have to fetch their water from a well, which may be a long way away. Explain that the water is drawn from underground and people have to walk miles to fetch water. Invite the children to role-play this situation by dragging their feet across the room, as if they are very tired, hot and thirsty

**Make a well**
- Thread the pencil through the slits in the sides of the box. Attach the yoghurt pot of water to the pencil with string. Ask the children to twirl the pencil around until the pot rises with the water. Watch the 'bucket' of water rise through the viewing window at the front of the box.

## Extension/variation
- Discuss which foods require water before we can eat them. Make some easy soup. A small group of children could help to chop up some vegetables. Place the chopped vegetables in the saucepan and add water to well cover the vegetables. Add a little salt and a stock cube. The practitioner should put the soup either on top of the cooker to simmer for about one hour, or in a microwave dish in the microwave for approximately 30 minutes. Invite the group to taste the result.

# I help at home

**Health and Self-care**

## Learning objectives

- To show some understanding of safety when tackling new challenges and considering risks
- To develop an understanding of good practices that contribute to good health, including exercise, eating, sleeping and hygiene
- To notice what adults do, imitating what is observed and repeating it when the adults are not there
- To accept the needs of others and understand that actions affect other people.

## Topic

Myself

## Resources

- Bed, with sheets, pillow and blanket(s) for role-play
- Table
- Cloth
- Plastic cutlery
- Plastic cups
- Plastic Plates or bowls
- Dustpan and brush
- Washing-up bowl
- Washing-up liquid
- Access to water
- Clothes (eg doll's clothes) to be washed
- Fresh peas in their pods
- Saucepan

## Preparation

- Prepare situations where the children can role-play household tasks and other things they could help with at home and in the setting.

## What to do

**Role-play activity**

- Discuss helping with the children and the types of task that they could help adults with, at home and in the setting. Suggest some of the following:
  - Go to fetch their parents to tell them if the telephone or doorbell rings when they are busy upstairs or in the garden.
  - Help to make their own beds and tidy their bedrooms. This could be practised in a 'home' role-play area.
  - Lay the table for breakfast, lunch or snack time. Practitioners could encourage children to take turns to do this at the setting, demonstrating what each person needs and where items should be placed on the tables, counting the number of people to set the table for and supporting children's efforts to remember everything. They could then suggest that they offer to help with this task at home. (Remind parents that children should not handle knives or glasses without supervision.)
  - Make their own breakfast, lunch or snack using cold ingredients that are readily available and easy to prepare.
  - Be tidy when they take off their shoes and coats and put them in the correct places, at home and in the setting. Remind them to tidy up all their possessions and not to leave items all over the house, stressing the dangers of accidents caused by people tripping on property left on floors and especially stairs.
  - Sweep up with a dustpan and brush if they spill food or make a mess while playing or taking part in craft activities. Children can take turns to do this at the setting and then offer to do it at home.
  - Help to wash up safe, unbreakable items, such as forks and spoons, plastic cups, bowls and plates. An adult should supervise the water running into the bowl or sink and remain close by to offer support when washed items are heavy or slippery.

## Extensions/variations

- Make a clothes line in the garden or playarea.
- Help the children wash small clothes and hang them on the line. Advise of the importance of clean clothes.
- Let children help to pop the fresh pea pods. Cook the peas in a saucepan so that the children can taste them.

## Links to home

- Suggest to parents that their children might help them with sweeping, dusting and cleaning around the house, watering the garden or washing the car.

# Pastry babies

## Topic
Food and shopping

## Resources
- Gingerbread man pastry cutter
- Ingredients for pastry babies:
  110g self-raising flour,
  55g margarine,
  55g sugar, currants or sultanas, water
- Ingredients for grapefruit delight: grapefruit, fresh or glacé cherries, sugar
- Ingredients for apple delight: apples, sultanas, cinnamon
- Ingredients for banana delight: 2 bananas, 100g strawberries,
  4 tsp fromage frais,
  4 tsp low-fat yoghurt
- Oven and baking tray
- Knife (for practitioner), apple corer and liquidizer

⚠ Be observant over the use of cookery materials as well as hot ovens.

## Learning objectives
- To understand and manage good hygiene and personal needs, such as handwashing, independently, especially when handling food
- To understand which foods contribute to good health, and to eat a variety of healthy foods.
- To handle equipment and tools safely and effectively, with support
- To observe and talk about the colours, textures, smells and tastes of the foods and the changes that take place during cooking

## Preparation
- Find a clean and hygienic place to work. Clean the surface to be used and ask children to wash their hands carefully. Discuss the importance of good hygiene with the children.

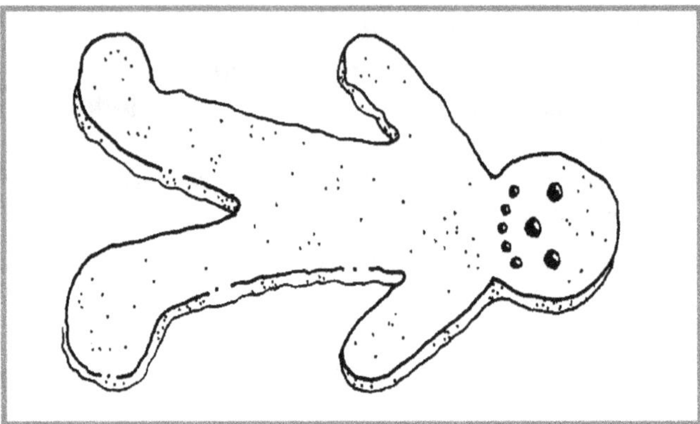

## What to do
**Cooking activity – Pastry babies**
- Preheat oven to 160°C/325°F/Gas Mark 3. Wash hands. Mix flour and margarine together. Add sugar. Mix to dough using a little water.
- Talk about how the dough feels and encourage children to describe it, using words such as *stretchy*, *elastic*, *pulling*, *sticky*, *soft*. etc
- If time, allow the dough to cool for half an hour.
- Help the children to roll out dough thinly and cut out the pastry babies using a gingerbread man cutter.
- The children can add eyes, nose and mouth using currants or sultanas. Bake for 15 minutes.

## Extensions/variations
**Grapefruit delight**
- The practitioner should cut the grapefruits in half and loosen the flesh from the outer skins. Remove any pips. Place the grapefruit halves into dishes. Sprinkle with a little sugar. Place half a cherry in the middle of each grapefruit.

**Apple delight**
- Wash the apples. The practitioner should core the apples and cut only through the skins around the middle of the apple. Fill the apple with sultanas and sprinkle with cinnamon. Put the apple in a baking dish. Pour in a little water. Bake at 200°C/400°F/ Gas Mark 6 for 30–40 minutes.

**Banana delight**
- Peel the bananas. The practitioner should cut them in half lengthwise. Mix the yoghurt and fromage frais. Place in the middle of dishes. Arrange banana halves on each side of the mixture. Use a liquidizer to liquidize the strawberries. Pour over the banana halves.

# Dressing for the weather

## Learning objectives

- To manage to put on and change clothes independently
- To develop and practise manipulative skills and to demonstrate increasing control over a variety of fastenings.
- To know when to ask an adult for help or support and to do so confidently and politely

## Topic

Weather

## Resources

- Varied clothes
- Variety of dolls
- Ice cubes
- Water
- Variety of pieces of fabric and other materials (eg plastic, vinyl, cotton)
- Card
- Paper
- Paints
- Paintbrushes
- Scissors
- Dolls template on page 191

 Supervise the use of scissors carefully.

## What to do

- Discuss with the children the many different types of weather we have, such as: hot, warm, cool, cold, windy, rainy, snowy, icy, sunny, stormy or hailing. Ask them how they protect themselves in different types of weather. Invite them to sort through the dressing up clothes and find outfits for different seasons.
- If you have a variety of dolls' clothes and accessories, children may like to dress up dolls and teddies in warm trousers or thin dresses, sun hats and sunglasses or coats and wellington boots. Talk with the children about the outdoor clothes they needed to wear today.
- Explain that materials react differently when they are in contact with water. Show them some garments or pieces of fabric in plastic vinyl and cotton and ask them to guess which would keep out the rain. Try an experiment using different materials. Take some ice cubes from the freezer. Wrap them in different materials and find out which material keeps the ice cold the longest. Try pouring a little water onto various materials to find out which let the water through and which do not. Introduce the word 'waterproof'.

## Extensions/variations

- Photocopy the Dolls template on page 191 and cut them out. Ask the children to design a complete set of clothes for the dolls, for both warm and cold weather. Add little tabs to their designs and help them cut them out. Fold the tabs over the card doll's shoulders.
- Make clothes from scraps of fabric and stick on to the dolls. Some can make summer clothes, others clothes for the rain, and others winter clothes.

Health and Self-care

# Help me put on my sari!

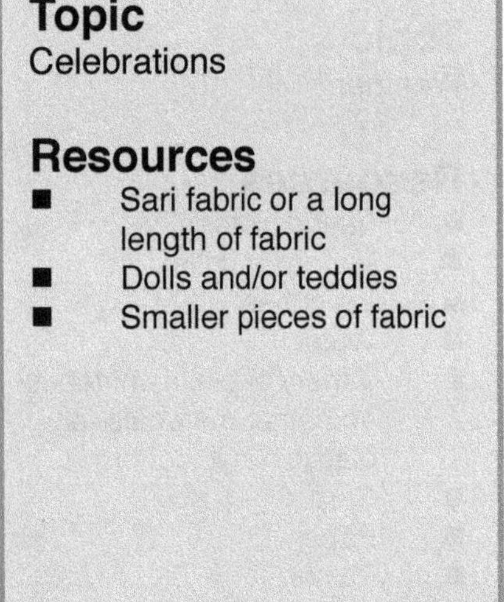

## Topic
Celebrations

## Resources
- Sari fabric or a long length of fabric
- Dolls and/or teddies
- Smaller pieces of fabric

## Learning objectives
- To understand and practise independent dressing skills
- To manipulate fabrics and learn about different types of clothing
- To develop an awareness of different cultures, communities and traditions

## Preparation
- Find a book that advises the way to put on a sari. Show pictures of saris and Hindus wearing saris to the children. Find a space where the activity can be tried out on various children.

## What to do
**Role-play activity**
- Ask the children if anyone can bring in a length of material or ask a local shop if they would have any remnants available to donate or sell very cheaply. Demonstrate the putting on of the fabric as a sari by dressing up a practitioner. Invite children to take turns to be dressed up after the demonstration.
- Tell the children that the complete dressing session is in three parts, the long petticoat, the short blouse and the sari.
- Take one end of the sari so that the higher part is at the waist. Tuck the higher part in to the waist. Wrap around the waist once. Show them how to make pleats in the remaining length (concertina fashion), take this piece (called the pallu) around the back and over the right shoulder.
- Spread it across the chest and tuck into the petticoat at the back.
- These types of saris are normally worn at weddings and celebrations. The daily sari is worn with the pallu over the left shoulder.
- Let the children practise on each other. Be careful they do not trip over the long material.

## Extension/variation
- Use smaller pieces of fabric and practise on dolls or teddies.

## Links to home
- Invite Hindu family members into the setting to demonstrate the putting on of a sari or any other traditional clothes. Extend the invitations also to those of other cultures who may have interesting traditional outfits to show and explain.

# The land of health

Health and Self-care

## Learning objectives

- To understand the importance for good health of exercise, eating, sleeping and hygiene
- To use equipment, tools and materials safely and effectively including pencils for drawing and writing
- To use imagination to create small world items appropriate to the theme
- To attempt to write words, labels, captions or short phrases and sentences
- To count reliably and write numerals in order

## Topic
Health

## Resources

- Long piece of wallpaper
- Felt-tipped pens
- Paints
- Paint-brushes
- Flour and water paste
- Newspaper
- Scissors
- Glue
- Foil
- Fabric scraps
- Craft matchsticks
- Dice
- Counters

Supervise the use of scissors carefully.

## What to do

### Circle time

- Discuss the importance of good health with the children. Talk about the benefits of sleep and rest, a good and healthy diet and the safety aspects of their lives. Ask them what happens if they don't sleep well and which foods they think are good to eat. Find out if they feel brighter after a good night's rest. Learn about their habits at home.

### Make a game

- Lay the long piece of paper across the table. Suggest that they are going to make a board game called 'The land of health'. The practitioner can pencil a very wriggly pathway across and up and down the paper, eventually ending at 'The land of health'. This can be situated wherever you and the children prefer – at one corner or in the middle.
- Work with the children to make it into a wide pathway made up of squares like a game. You can number the squares if you wish. Along the pathway invite the children to sporadically put in good things (such as fruit, fresh air) or bad things (such as lots of sweets, yawning face). Leave lots of blank spaces in between.
- Any materials may be used for effects. Here are a few ideas:
  - Papier-mâché hills or mountains (for example, 'the mountain of bad habits' or 'the good mountain')
  - Foil for lakes and rivers (for example, 'the lake of good eating')
  - Painted or fabric beds
  - Matchstick houses (for example, 'the house of fruit' or 'the house of sweets')
- The children will think of many more. When they consider it finished, the practitioner can mark some of the squares with commands like 'Go back 3 spaces' (if they have landed on bad health) or 'Go forward 3 spaces' (if they have landed on good health).
- Once the whole game is set up, play it for as long as possible.

## Links to home

- If you think there is a problem with a child falling asleep at school, have a tactful word with a parent.

Health and Self-care

# Garden by the sea

## Topic
Gardening

## Resources
- Spade
- Rake
- Garden gloves
- Garden
- Soil
- Pebbles
- Small rocks or large stones
- Rockery plants
- Marigolds or short yellow flowers
- Plastic mirrors
- Cardboard boxes
- Wire coat hangers
- Glue
- String
- Scissors
- Flour and water paste
- Newspaper, torn into small pieces
- Twigs
- Paper
- Pastel coloured tissue paper

 Wash hands after working in the garden.

## Learning objectives
- To recognize the effects of physical activity on the body
- To become aware that exercise contributes to good health
- To make an imaginative representation, using natural materials

## Preparation
- Prepare a large enough area of soil to accommodate all members of the group. Dig the square and rake over.

## What to do
### Gardening activity
- If possible ask the children to wear gloves and aprons. Make 'a garden by the sea'.

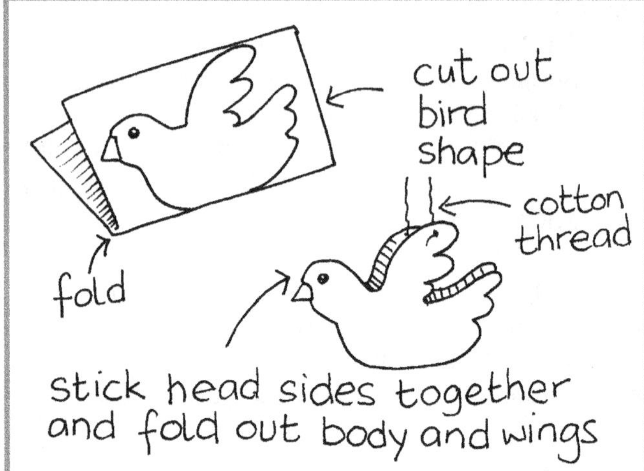


- Dig a hole and pile the soil up on one side. This will form a rock garden (resembling the cliffs). Help the children to carry and place the stones in the heaped-up soil attractively and sensibly to stop erosion. Plant small rockery plants (preferably red or orange). Press pebbles into the sides of the hole. On the flat side of the hole, plant some small yellow or orange flowers, such as marigolds (resembling the beach). Now place the plastic mirrors into the hole to form a ready-made ocean or pond.
- Talk to the children about their garden and what they had to do to make it. Encourage them to remember which tasks were hard work and how they felt after all the digging.

## Extensions/variations
- Make a nest box. Find a small cardboard box. The practitioner should cut a round hole near the top. Suspend from a wire coat hanger. Cut out paper birds, as diagram above. (The box may disintegrate if used outside in the rain.)
- Make a secret garden. Use a large cardboard box. Open one end and make a garden using papier-mâché grass, twigs with paper leaves, and crumpled pastel tissue flowers. The papier-mâché should be made into a lumpy hilly look. Paint it green. Cover the open end with tissue paper to allow light in to the garden. Cut a peephole in the cardboard side and invite the children to peep into the secret garden.

# Can you be a doctor?

Health and Self-care

## Learning objectives

- To understand that physical exercise contributes to good health
- To recognize the bodily changes caused by physical activity and exercise
- To show sensitivity to each other's differing needs and feelings
- To use counting and comparing skills

## Topic
Health

## Resources

- Heart template on page 192
- Role-play outfits and accessories for doctors and hospitals: white shirts, aprons, bandages, doctor's bag
- Stop watch
- Paper
- Pen
- Unwanted wallpaper
- Paint
- Paintbrushes
- Scissors
- Glue

## What to do

### Circle activity

- Show the children the template on page 192 and explain that the heart pumps our blood around our bodies. Talk about the lungs and how they help us to breathe and make sure that they are aware that they are breathing automatically all the time.
- Ask them to count a partner's breaths. Tell them when to begin and then tell them when one minute is over. Talk about faster breathers taking more breaths and slower breathers taking fewer breaths.
- Now try the same counting activity by counting a partner's pulse. Show them how to find the wrist pulse and count as before.
- Compare the number of beats in a minute between the fastest pulse and the slowest pulse.

### Movement activity

- If you have a hall or enough space, organize a movement session. Count pulses and breathing before and after the session.
- Help the children to make a simple block graph of their findings.

## Extensions/variations

- Make a wall frieze of 'Our hospital'. Ask the children to draw and paint a patient each, some with spots, some with happy faces, some with pale faces or red faces and some with bandages. Cut out the patients and stick to a prepared background of a ward, corridor or hospital waiting room.
- Turn the role-play area into a hospital ward or doctors surgery. Provide white shirts as doctors coats, a doctors bag and plenty of bandages.

# Exploring and using media and materials

- During the early years, children explore the world around them and this includes the media and materials that they encounter within their environment. They use their whole bodies and all of their senses to respond to and experiment with movements, actions, sounds, shapes, colours and textures.

- As they grow, they begin to take an interest in beat, rhythm and music, rhymes, songs and musical instruments. They learn to recognize and distinguish between colours, shapes and textures, to construct with various toys and materials, to make marks and mix colours and to use tools and equipment. They notice if the properties of media change and the differences between, for example, wet and dry sand or thick and watery paint.

- Practitioners should seek to encourage expression and creativity in all children and to provide a supportive enabling environment which allows them to explore, experiment, manipulate and construct with materials and to combine different media to create effects. They should also take up opportunities to introduce new vocabulary, make suggestions, ask questions, encourage thinking and planning and model skills and techniques. Some children will be naturally more creative and imaginative in art and craft work, or in dance and movement, or in drama and role play; some will be more competent in building models that move or balance; some may have highly developed manipulative skills and enjoy cutting intricate shapes and patterns; others may be less confident but fascinated by mixing colours or exploring textures. Through careful observation of their children, practitioners will learn the forms of expression that each child prefers and the levels they are working at, allowing them to treat each child as unique and to offer appropriate challenges and stimulation alongside the security of familiar materials and the time for consolidation of skills.

- Children gain confidence and independent working and playing skills when they can select resources for themselves and use simple tools and techniques that are appropriate for their own projects.

They begin to design and construct with a purpose in mind, learning to shape, assemble and join materials and adapt work to create a planned effect.

- Time, resources and encouragement must be available to children, within a large group, small groups and as individuals, to enable them to sing songs, move and dance to music and make up their own songs and rhythms with instruments. By the end of the foundation stage, children should have built up a repertoire of favourite and familiar songs and dances and be willing to perform them and to experiment with changing them to fit different purposes. They may imitate actions or beats and rhythms and be able to create their own.

- An understanding and appreciation of artistic design, form and function contributes to children's physical, creative and expressive skills, improves social and emotional awareness and self-confidence and feeds the imagination.

Exploring and Using Media and Materials

# Fire! Fire!

## Topic

People who help us

## Resources

- 'The Fireman' by Ken Blakeson and Peter Canwell from *Apusskidu* (A & C Black)
- Apparatus
- Chime bars
- Shakers
- Cardboard box
- Paints
- Paintbrush
- Coloured sugar paper
- Cotton wool
- White paper
- Glue or sticky tape

## Learning objectives

- To sing songs, make music and devise actions, and experiment with ways of changing them
- To experiment with different ways of moving, safely negotiating space
- To construct with a purpose in mind, using a variety of resources and techniques
- To understand and talk about ways to keep safe

## What to do

### Movement activity

- Choose some children to be the firemen, and others to play the musical instruments. Swap roles each time you reach the end of the song, to allow all children to take turns to act and to play the music.
- Play and sing the song 'The Fireman'. During the first verse, ask the children to pretend to climb up high. They might move their arms and legs as though climbing a pipe or a rope. Ring bells or use chime bars for bells.
- Encourage them to pretend to spray water from hoses to put out the fire. Use shakers for water noise (either maracas or tins filled with buttons or rice).
- Now try miming these verses to the tune of 'She'll Be Coming Round the Mountain':

*The firemen are sliding down the pole*
(gradually crouch down to the floor)
*The firemen are sliding down the pole*
*Now they're climbing on the engine*
(stand up and move arms and legs as if climbing on the engine)
*Climbing on the engine*
*The firemen are rushing to the fire.* (run up and down on the spot)
*They are climbing up their ladders very tall*
(make climbing movements)
*They are climbing up their ladders very tall*
*They are climbing up their ladders*
*Climbing up their ladders*
*Climbing up their ladders very tall.*
*The water from their hoses goes swoosh swoosh*
(swing arms about)
*The water from their hoses goes swoosh swoosh*
*And they're putting out the fire*
(wave arms around)
*Putting out the fire*
*The firemen are putting out the fire.*

## Extensions/variations

- Make a house on fire using a strong cardboard box. Cut out flame shapes and stick around the windows. Use cotton wool for smoke.
- Arrange for a local firemen to talk to the children about the dangers of fire.

## Related activity

- Catch the robber (see page 22)

# Summer means holidays



## Learning objectives

- To join in with songs and music, dance and movements and to experiment with ways of changing them
- To use and explore a variety of materials, tools and techniques and to experiment with design and function
- To represent ideas, thoughts and feelings through art, music and role-play

## Topic

Seasons

## Resources

- Some pieces of small apparatus
- Two large, very strong, cardboard boxes
- Summer or seaside music, eg 'Take Me to the Seaside' by Kenneth Leaper, from *Harlequin* (A & C Black)
- Soft balls
- Percussion instruments: chime bars, triangles, shakers, etc
- Sand
- Tray
- Powder paint or food colouring
- Cardboard
- Glue
- Pencil
- Paintbrushes

## Preparation

- Arrange a few pieces of small apparatus across a safe space. Have a couple of large very strong cardboard boxes in the middle of the floor. Tell the children that they are small rocks on a sandy beach.
- Get the music ready.

Observe children carefully when balancing on apparatus. Be alert to the safety of each child.

## What to do

### Movement activity

- Ask the children about summer and most of them will think of holidays and the seaside. Ask them to jump on and off the rocks.
- Tell them that the sand is hot and ask how they would walk. Encourage them to lift up their feet quickly.
- Make up movements to match the song. For example, shake toes to feel the shingle, fill the buckets with sand or pebbles, cup hands to lift up the shingle.
- Give the children soft balls to bounce upon the rocks. Ask them to throw the balls gently to each other and try to catch them. Younger children could sit on the beach and roll the balls across the sand to each other.
- Another possible seaside activity is donkey-riding. The children could sit astride the boxes and pretend to jog along the beach.

## Extensions/variations

- Ask the children what noises they hear at the seaside or on any summer holiday.
- Invite them to try to create summer noises using percussion instruments. Bang the triangles for a gull's cry. Use chime bars to hear the sound of an ice cream van. Slide and shake shakers to hear the tide coming in across the shingle.
- Make sand pictures in a tray. Have a tray of sand. Draw pictures with fingers. If you have any coloured sand (you could add food colouring or powdered paint to the sand), make a sand collage picture on a piece of cardboard. Draw the picture first, with a brush full of glue and stick the sand to the drawing.

Exploring and Using Media and Materials

# The Grand Old Duke of York

**Topic**
Homes

**Resources**

- Simple, safe stairs, steps or climbing equipment

## Learning objectives

- To move rhythmically
- To imitate movements in response to music
- To begin to build a repertoire of songs and dances
- To travel with confidence up and down stairs, steps or climbing equipment
- To create intended movements

## Preparation

- Organize some climbing equipment or rope netting to form steps, or simply find some safe steps.

## What to do

**Movement activity**

- Ensure that the apparatus or steps are safe. Invite two children to climb carefully up and down in time to the song. Ask the other children to march up and down on the spot, singing and using relevant actions to the verses while the climbers concentrate on climbing.
- If using apparatus, again allow two children at a time, inviting them to use both feet to climb upon the relevant equipment. Ask them to climb slowly and carefully.

*O, the Grand Old Duke of York*
*He had ten thousand men*
*He marched them up to the top of the hill* (climb upwards)
*And he marched them down again* (climb back down).

***Chorus***
*And when they were up they were up* (climb upwards)
*And when they were down they were down* (climb back down)
*And when they only half way up, they neither up nor down.*

- In the second verse, invite another two children to make their climb:

*O, the Grand Old Duke of York*
*He had ten thousand men*
*They beat their drums to the top of the hill*
*And they beat them down again.*
***Chorus***

- In the last verse allow the last two children to take part to:

*O, the Grand Old Duke of York*
*He had ten thousand men*
*They piped their pipes to the top of the hill*
*And they piped them down again.*
**Chorus**

## Links to home

- Ask the parents to help the children to count the steps/stairs in their house and elsewhere.

# Time to go home

**Exploring and Using Media and Materials**

## Learning objectives

- To identify, explore and compare a variety of materials
- To take an interest in describing and naming colours and textures
- To choose particular colours for a purpose

## What to do

**Circle time**

- Invite the children to sit in a circle.
- The practitioner chooses groups of children to put on their coats by describing the colour/texture of what they are wearing. For example, he/she might say that the children who are wearing red may put their coats on first, then the person wearing a fluffy jumper, and so on.
- Ask the children to feel their clothes and describe the texture.

## Extension/variation

- Invite children to take turns to be the leader and choose the colours.

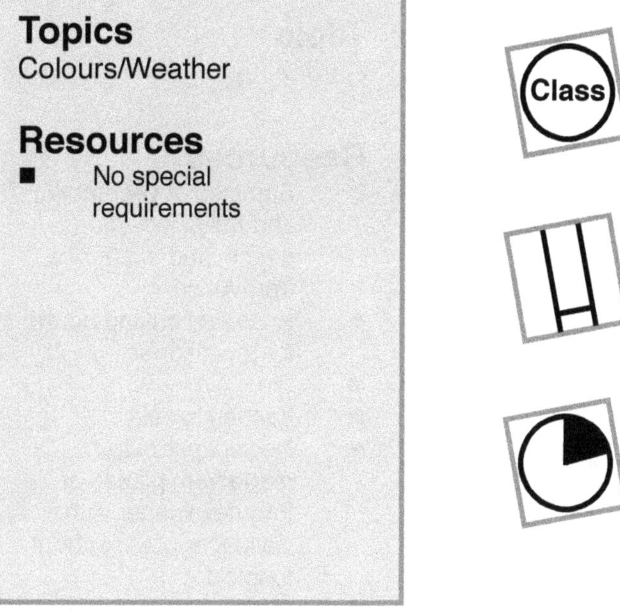


## Topics

Colours/Weather

## Resources

- No special requirements

## Links to home

- Ask parents to reinforce the names of colours.

## Exploring and Using Media and Materials

# Fruitful

### Topic
Gardening

### Resources
- Samples of vegetables and fruits, including a peach, and examples from Africa
- Knife and cutting board for practitioner
- Bin
- Kitchen towels
- Newspaper pulp made from pieces of torn newspaper with wallpaper glue (without fungicide)
- Tray
- Thin white tissue paper
- Paintbrushes
- Ready-mixed paints in suitable colours for fruits and vegetables
- Wicker basket for display
- Books: *Oliver's Vegetables* and *Oliver's Fruit Salad* by Vivian French (Hodder Children's Books)

## Learning objectives
- To combine different media to create new effects
- To use simple techniques competently and appropriately
- To choose particular colours to use for a purpose
- To create simple representations of familiar objects

## What to do
**Circle time**
- Pass round the whole fruit and vegetables.
- Let the children examine them and describe what they see, smell and feel.
- Cut up the fruit and vegetables and let the children see what they look like inside.
- Invite the children to taste the fruits and vegetables and say which they like or dislike
- Introduce new vocabulary by describing colours, textures, sizes, shapes and tastes with the children and naming the various fruits and vegetables.
- Read *Oliver's Vegetables* or *Oliver's Fruit Salad.*

**Art activity**
- Support moulding the papier mâché pulp into the correct shapes for fruit and vegetables.
- Cover the shapes with white tissue paper.
- Allow them to dry, then invite the children to paint them in the appropriate colours of their choice.

## Extensions/variations
- Display the African fruit and vegetables in the basket for the Kwanzaa feast (see page 124–125).
- Peach fruit made in this way could be used for The Selfish Giant project (see page 132–133).

## Links to home
- Ask parents to talk about the names of vegetables and if they grow on top of the ground or in the soil.
- Ask parents to talk about the names of fruits and how they develop from flowers.

## Related activities
- Banananana (see page 92)
- Kwanzaa (see pages 124–125)
- The Selfish Giant (see pages 132–133)

# Quiet as a mouse



## Learning objectives

- To explore the different sounds of instruments and to tap out simple repeated rhythms
- To sing songs and make music and experiment with ways of changing them

## Topic

Animals

## Resources

- Nursery rhyme/song: 'Three Blind Mice'
- Range of percussion instruments, enough for one each
- Song: 'Mouse', from *Start with a Song* by Mavis de Mierre (Brilliant Publications)

## What to do

**Music activity**

- Show each type of instrument and ask what kind of sound it could make.
- Ask if the children can be as 'quiet as a mouse'. Challenge the class to hand out the instruments without making any sound.
- Allow the children to examine the percussion instruments and find out what sound they do make.
- Sing 'Three Blind Mice' and ask the children to clap to the beat (pulse) of four.
- Suggest that the children try to add a percussion accompaniment only on the first beat, then be silent for the other three. The children can whisper 'two, three, four'.

## Extension/variation

- Learn the song 'Mouse'.

## Related activity

- Tick, tock, hum, click (see page 116)

Exploring and Using Media and Materials

# Statues

## Topic
Shapes

## Resources
- Music: any chart dance music
- CD player

## Learning objectives
- To move rhythmically
- To make up dance movements and experiment with ways of changing them
- To create movements in response to music
- To negotiate space safely within a group
- To move, stop and balance with good control and coordination

## What to do
**Dance activity**
- Play the music and let the children dance to it. When the music stops they must remain still like statues. Play the game for as long as you wish, challenging children to stop and freeze in different positions, such as balancing on one leg, or with arms held above head. As long as all of the children are trying their best to freeze every time the music stops, there is no need to introduce the rule that anybody who moves accidentally must sit down and be out of the game, unless the children wish to play in this way.

## Extension/variation
- Children have to stay still like a statue while the music is playing, then move about on the spot when the music stops.

# Paint the town red



## Learning objectives

- To manipulate tools and materials to achieve a planned effect
- To use simple tools and techniques competently and appropriately

## Topic

Colours

## Resources

- Clean paintbrushes (to fit in toy buckets)
- Toy buckets
- Water
- Plastic aprons
- Camera
- Coloured plastic blocks (or other small coloured items)

## What to do

**Outside activity**

- Invite children to paint outside and create their own designs on the walls, fences or ground.
- Offer them the toy buckets of water. Ask what colour they want to paint.
- Put plastic blocks (or any other items) of that colour into the bucket.
- Hold a conversation with each child about what they are painting on the wall/fence, and what colour they are using.
- Take a photograph of the children and their work.
- Leave the water to dry and return to the area later, with the children, to look at their paintings.

## Extensions/variations

- A suitable time after the activity go outside.
- Ask what they think has happened to their paintings. Talk about evaporation.

## Links to home

- Warn parents that the children are especially encouraged to play with water and ensure that they are all providing enough spare clothes for their children.

Exploring and Using Media and Materials

# Making biscuits

## Topic
Food and shopping

## Resources
- Ingredients for biscuits:
  225g flour,
  1 teaspoon baking powder,
  175g butter or margarine,
  110g caster sugar,
  water or milk to mix
- Kitchen scales
- Rolling pins
- Baking tins
- Pastry cutters

## Learning objectives
- To manipulate materials to achieve a planned effect
- To use simple tools and techniques competently
- To handle malleable materials safely and with increasing control
- To understand the need for good hygiene when preparing food
- To manage basic hygiene needs, such as handwashing, independently
- To experience the activity through a variety of senses, such as sight, touch and smell (and later, taste)

## Preparation
- Prepare a clean, safe and tidy area with enough space for each participating child and adult to sit and work at a surface.
- Provide aprons and washing facilities and ensure that everyone washes their hands carefully before beginning the cooking activity.

## What to do
### Cooking activity
- Support the children in taking turns to measure out the ingredients and mix up the dough. Divide the dough into small pieces and give one piece to each child.
- Invite the children to knead and squeeze their dough and talk about how it feels. Model appropriate vocabulary, such as stretchy, soft, sticky, cold, hot, etc.
- Offer them the pastry cutters and invite the to choose shapes to cut out and place on a baking tray.
- The practitioner should put the trays in the oven to bake at 160°C/325°F/Gas Mark 3 for 15 minutes.

# Make Christmas decorations

Exploring and Using Media and Materials

## Learning objectives

- To combine different media to create new effects
- To use simple tools and techniques competently
- To experiment with colour, design, texture, form and function

## Topic

Celebrations

## Resources

- Cardboard
- Scissors
- Glue
- String
- Flour and water paste
- Strips of newspaper
- Paints
- Paintbrushes
- Glitter
- Gold or silver thread
- Scissors
- Oranges
- Foil
- Candles
- Skewers
- Cocktail sticks
- Sweets
- Black sugar paper
- Yellow or orange paper
- Cotton wool
- Paper clips

## What to do

### Art activity

- Make papier-mâché Christmas decorations. Help the children draw and cut out shapes from cardboard of the moon and stars, Christmas trees, diamonds, circles and squares.
- Make a shape with paste on the card and stick string to the sticky part or cover each shape with papier-mâché.
- Allow to dry and paint in bright colours.
- When all the shapes are dry, paint the string patterns in a contrasting colour
- Put a little glue onto the shape. Scatter some glitter on it.
- Make a hole in the top of each decoration and thread through a paper clip. Tie some thread through the paper clip to hang.

Supervise any scissor usage and be aware of the points on the cocktail sticks.

## Extensions/variations

- Make Christingles. Make holes in the tops of oranges. Cut foil to fit and push inside the hole. Insert candles into the holes. The practitioner should push four cocktail sticks into the orange. Push sweets on to the cocktail sticks to decorate.
- Houses in the snow. Cut out the shapes of houses from black sugar paper. Cut out the windows. Behind windows stick yellow or orange paper to resemble a glow. Paint a background frieze of grey. Stick on the houses. Stick on tiny pieces of cotton wool to resemble snow.

Exploring and Using Media and Materials

# Sponge prints

## Topic

Shapes

## Resources
- Scissors
- Several sponges
- Paper
- Paints
- Foil dishes
- Card
- Thread
- Wire coat hangers
- White paper
- Leaves
- Soft pencils

Beware sharp edges of any materials used. Use scissors with care.

## Learning objectives
- To explore and experiment with materials to experience colours and textures
- To manipulate materials and use simple techniques to achieve a planned effect
- To select appropriate resources and particular colours and adapt work for a purpose
- To represent ideas and feelings imaginatively through art and design

## Preparation
- Provide a large table with plenty of materials.

## What to do
### Investigation activity
- Help the children to cut the sponges into different shapes. Make simple shapes such as squares, circles, rectangles and triangles.
- While the sponges are clean and dry, discuss the shapes and allow the children to poke and press the sponges.
- Introduce new vocabulary to support language development by using words such as: *squashy*, *squishy*, *spongy*, *mushy*, *soft, foamy and pressed*.
- What happens when the sponges are pressed? Do they become thinner the harder they are pressed?

### Craft activity
- Pour the prepared paints into foil dishes. Lay the card or paper on the table.
- Dip the sponges in the paints and print by pressing the sponge on to the card.
- The shapes can be cut out and used to make a shapes mobile. Attach thread to the sheets and hang from wire coat hangers.

## Extensions/variations
- Sponge-print on to paper to make an attractive wall display or covers for books.
- Collect some leaves. Dip them into paint and print the shape on to white paper.
- Alternatively, place the leaves beneath the paper and gently rub with a soft pencil over the top of the leaf shape.

# Marble painting



## Learning objectives

- To combine different media to create new effects
- To manipulate materials to achieve a planned effect
- To use and explore a new technique, experimenting with colour and design

## Topic

Toys

## Resources

- White paper
- Baking tray
- Paper or foil dishes
- Marbles
- Paints
- Kitchen tongs
- Dry beans, peas or rice
- Plastic containers with lids
- Sticky tape

## What to do

### Art activity

- Put a piece of white paper on a baking tray.
- Put two or three different paint colours in paper or foil dishes. Put a marble into each colour.
- Carefully take out the marbles one by one and place them on the white paper. See if the children can pick up the marbles with kitchen tongs.
- Ask the children to tilt the tray backwards, forwards and sideways to make a swirling pattern. Carefully remove the marbles with the kitchen tongs.

## Extension/variation

- Be a shaker maker. Ask the children to measure out a small quantity of dry beans, peas or rice and to pour them into clean plastic containers and secure the lid firmly with sticky tape. Ask the children to slide the instruments from side to side, then shake them up and down, and listen to the different sounds.

Exploring and Using Media and Materials

# Mehendi hand

## Topic
Celebrations

## Resources
- Photocopies of drawings of hands with patterns marked on them with dotted lines
- Brown or dark red crayons, pencils or pens
- Plain paper
- Pictures of mehendi designs on hands
- Internet: www. mehendiart.com

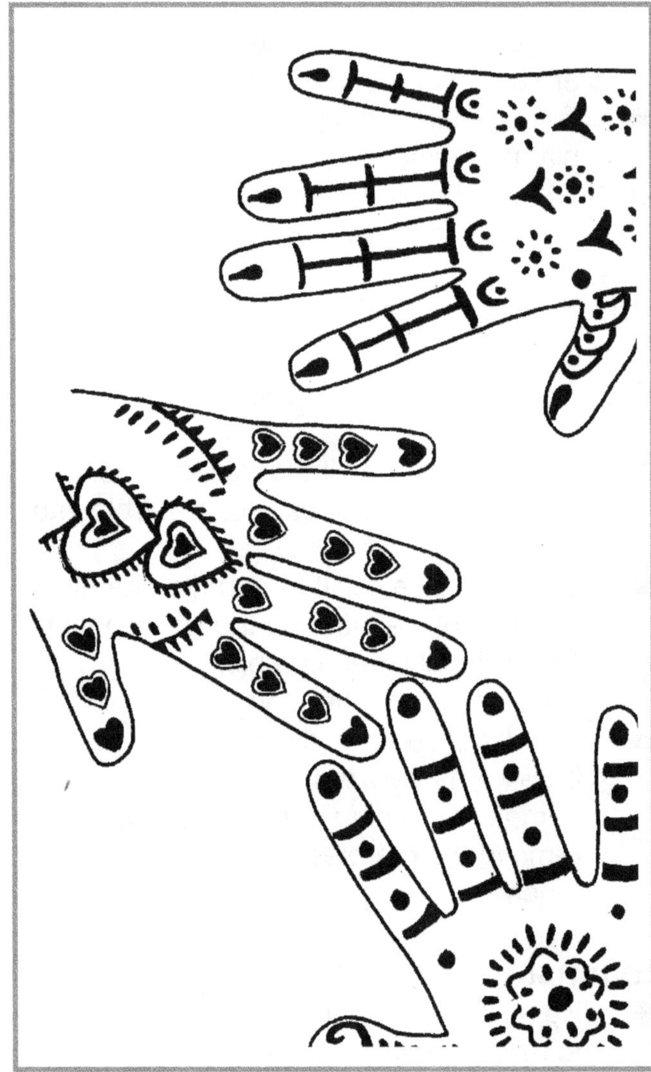

## Learning objectives
- To explore materials, tools and techniques, experimenting with colour and design
- To represent ideas, thoughts and feelings through art and design
- To learn about the traditions of a particular culture and community

## Preparation
- Prepare copies of outline drawings of a hand for children to practise designs on.

## What to do
### Circle time
- Explain that the day before a Hindu girl gets married her girl friends and family decorate her hands and feet with a red plant dye called henna or mehendi.
- Show the children some pictures of mehendi designs on hands as examples.
- The bride's wedding designs usually include the groom's name hidden amongst the patterns on her palm.

### Art activity
- Let the children trace around the shapes on the pictures of mehendi designs of hands.
- Offer each child a copy of a hand outline and encourage them to draw designs on it with a brown or dark red crayon, pencil or pen. They can practise in this way until they have made some designs that they are pleased with.
- Offer the children sheets of plain paper and support them in drawing around their own or each other's hands. Ask them to fill in the outlines of these hands with their chosen designs.

## Extension/variation
- Suggest that children write their names on the hand drawings, then draw around the names to hide them (but do not draw over the names).

## Related activity
- Wedding (see pages 126–127)

# Porridge



## Learning objectives

- To identify, explore and compare a variety of materials
- To take an interest in describing texture
- To experiment to create different textures
- To understand that different media can be combined to create new effects and substances

## What to do

**Circle time**

- Read the story of Goldilocks And The Three Bears. Suggest that the children make some porridge.

**Cooking activity**

- Support children as they measure and stir the ingredients.
- Put porridge oats into the casserole dish. Ask how the porridge feels as well as looks (eg soft, makes a scrunchy noise when rubbed together).
- Add water and milk and stir. Ask if the porridge dissolves (no).
- Cook in a microwave oven at 850W for three minutes. An adult should remove the porridge from the microwave.
- Stir and return to oven for two more minutes.
- Ask what the porridge looks like now. Stir the cooked porridge.

**Snack time**

- Serve and add milk and sweetener as required.

## Extensions/variations

- Make some porridge too sweet and too salty.
- Encourage a role-play conversation between the children as if they are the bears or Goldilocks as they eat the porridge.

## Related activity

- Goldilocks and the Three Bears (see pages 168–169)

## Topic

Food and shopping

## Resources

- Book: *Goldilocks and the Three Bears* (Ladybird does a nice edition)

**For 3 or 4 portions of porridge**

- 1 cup porridge oats
- 1 cup water
- 1 cup milk
- Milk to add
- Sugar or syrup
- Salt
- Teaspoon
- Glass casserole dish with lid
- Wooden spoon
- Cup or beaker
- Cereal dishes
- Spoons
- Microwave oven

Check records for diabetes. Although the microwave oven does not feel hot, the heat from the porridge will be conducted to the glass.

Exploring and Using Media and Materials

# Bananananana

## Topic
Food and shopping

## Resources
- Resources
- Poem: 'Bananananananana' by William Cole, from The Orchard Book of Funny Poems (Orchard)
- Fruits and vegetables
- Pale coloured chalks
- Coloured wax crayons
- Candle
- Water colours
- Water-based black ink or dark coloured dye
- Paintbrush
- Paper towel
- White paper
- Scissors

## Learning objectives
- To combine different media to create new effects
- To use simple techniques competently and appropriately
- To choose particular colours to use for a purpose
- To create simple representations of familiar objects

## What to do
### Circle Time
- Read the poem and show the fruits and vegetables
- Ask for names of fruits and extend the word eg peachhhh, plummmm. Encourage everyone to say the words.

### Art activity
- Explain to the children that they will be making special chalk and crayon resist pictures of fruits and vegetables.
- Encourage them to try out ideas on small sheets of paper first.
- Write the words and draw the shapes of the fruits and vegetables several times over the paper using the chalk thickly.
- Thickly colour around the drawings and words with different coloured wax crayons, leaving no paper showing.
- Support brushing the ink or dye over the whole picture. The chalk should suck up the ink, and the wax resist it.
- Support mopping off excess ink with the paper towel.
- The children could trim the paper to the shape of the fruit or vegetable for display

## Extension/variation
- Write words using a candle, then draw lines across the page. Colour using water colours which will shrink from the wax.

## Links to home
- Ask parents to reinforce names of fruits and vegetables.

## Related activity
- Fruitful (see page 82)

# Bricks

## Learning objectives

- To join construction pieces together to build and balance, making enclosures and creating spaces
- To construct with a purpose in mind, manipulating materials to achieve a planned effect
- To use and explore materials and techniques, experimenting with colours, design, form and function

## What to do

### Circle time

- Read The Three Little Pigs. Ask the children whether their homes are made from bricks or wood or other materials.
- Encourage the children to describe their homes, supporting the use of appropriate vocabulary such as: roof, wall door window, chimney, corner and stairs.
- Make references to the wall display.

### Construction activity

- Ask the children to build a home using the construction bricks.
- Talk with the children about what they are making. Encourage the construction of walls and a roof.

## Extensions/variations

- Ask them how the bricks are arranged in the wall. Look at a wall outside if possible, and copy the pattern.
- Demonstrate that interlocking bricks make a strong structure, while bricks stacked in columns fall over.

## Topics

Homes/Shapes

## Resources

- Book: The Three Little Pigs (Ladybird does a nice edition)
- Wall display: photographs of homes in different environments (city, town, countryside, suburban), and of different styles (flat, maisonette, bungalow, semi-detached, detached, terraced) and from different ages (Tudor timber-framed, Georgian with sash windows, Victorian terrace, present day estate house)
- Construction bricks and base

## Related activities

- Lines (see page 136)
- Stuck up the chimney (see page 162)

**Exploring and Using Media and Materials**

# Changing pitch

## Topics
Health/Toys

## Resources
- Poem: 'Ned' by Eleanor Farjeon, from *The Oxford Treasury of Children's Poems* (Oxford University Press)
- Rhymes: 'Diddle, Diddle Dumpling, My Son John'; 'Through the Day'; 'There Were Ten in the Bed', from *This Little Puffin* compiled by Elizabeth Matterson (Puffin)
- Wooden xylophone
- High-pitched percussion instruments such as bells and triangles
- Low-pitched percussion instrument such as drums
- Music: *Clair de Lune* by Claude Debussy (1862–1918)
- Clay pots of different sizes
- Rhythm sticks or wooden spoons
- Rope
- Wood 2.5cm x 4cm x 150cm
- Cup hooks
- Two chairs

## Learning objectives
- To recognize, explore and learn how the pitch of sounds can be changed
- To make music with percussion instruments and experiment with making instruments from other media and materials

## Preparation
- Screw cup hooks, well spaced out, into the 4cm side of the length of wood.
- Tie a large knot at one end of the rope and thread through the hole of a plant pot. Tie a loop at the other end of the rope.
- Set up at least three different sized plant pot bells.

## What to do
**Circle time**
- Read one of the poems or rhymes about bedtime and getting up.
- Read one of the books about gardening.
- Suggest finding out whether an instrument could be made from plant pots.

**Music activities**
- Stand the xylophone on its end with longer (low-pitched) notes at the bottom.
- Ask the children to make a high-pitched sound like mice squeaking at the top of the stairs. Play the high notes on the xylophone.
- Ask for a low-pitched note like growling lions at the bottom of the stairs. Play the low notes on the xylophone.
- Ask the children what they notice about the size of the xylophone bars and the pitch of the note. (Longer bars, lower pitch.)
- Hand out the percussion instruments. Let the children experiment to determine the pitch.
- Tell the children that when you play a high note, the children with high-pitched instruments (eg the bells and triangles) should respond. Similarly, when you play the low notes, the children with low-pitched instruments (eg the drums) should respond.
- Secure the length of wood between two chairs and suspend the plant pots, like bells, from the hooks. Make it easy to rearrange the pots.
- Ask the children to arrange the pots with the deepest (lowest) pitch on their left and highest notes to the right.
- Ask the children whether they notice anything as regards the size of the pot and the pitch. (The smallest pot will have the highest pitch.)

## Extensions/variations
- Play 'Going to bed, getting up'. The children describe climbing up the stairs by making their voices rise in pitch, and fall when going downstairs. Sing to the notes of a scale: eg *C D E F G.*
- Suggest that the children make up a tune with their pots.

# Dicing with colour



## Learning objectives

- To develop a repertoire of actions by putting a sequence of movements together using colours as the stimulus
- To experiment with different ways of moving
- To move confidently in a range of ways, safely negotiating space
- To follow instructions involving several ideas and actions

## Topic

Colours

## Resources

- Sponge die with colours
- Large flash card with illustrations of movements
- Easel (optional)

## Preparation

- Prepare a large sponge die. Stick a different colour to each face, ie white, black, red, green, blue, yellow.
- Make a large card showing the colours matched against simple movements, eg white = arms above the head, black = jump up and down.

## What to do

**Outside or hall activity**

- Explain the game and some suggested actions or movements for each colour.
- Display the card so that all the children can see it and ensure they can all see the die when it lands.
- Throw the die and call out the colour that it lands on. Encourage the children to remember and perform the appropriate action or movement.
- Let the children take turns to throw the die.

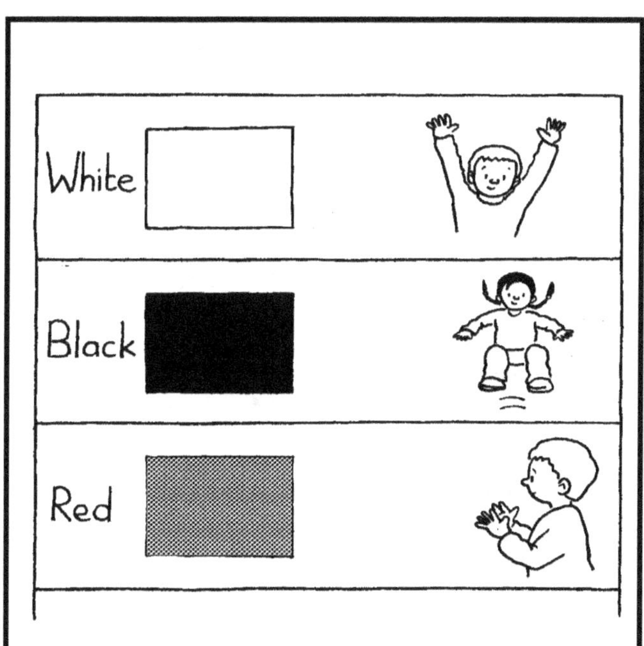


## Extensions/variations

- Invite the children to choose which actions and movements they could perform for various colours. Support them by offering some suggestions, such as: stretch high, crouch low or take little running steps.
- Ask which movements would fit best with each colour, eg red is warm = stretch out, blue is cold = curl into a ball, yellow is sunny = skip.
- Encourage the children to try to link the movements smoothly.

Exploring and Using Media and Materials

# Pebble pet

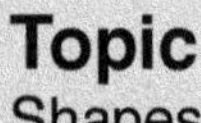

## Topic
Shapes

## Resources
- Smooth hand-sized pebbles
- String
- PVA glue
- Thick paints
- Paintbrushes
- Playdough
- Fabric
- Varnish (for use by practitioner)

## Learning objectives
- To understand that different media can be combined to create new effects
- To manipulate materials to achieve a planned effect
- To choose particular colours to use for a purpose
- To represent own ideas through art and craft

## Preparation
- Collect enough pebbles for the group.

## What to do
### Art activity
- Make a pebble pet by painting the stone, adding ears and tail with paint, fabric or playdough.
- When the pet is dry, the practitioner can varnish it to stop the paint from rubbing off.

### Show and tell activity
- Show the pets, and talk about what they like, what kind of animal they might be, and their name, what they eat, etc.

## Extensions/variations
- Encourage small groups of children to play with their pebble pets together.
- Talk about how water has worn down stone to make it a pebble.

## Links to home
- Ask any parents visiting the seaside to bring back some pebbles.

## Related activity
- Seaside (see page 102–103)

# Under my umbrella



## Learning objectives

- To develop a repertoire of actions by putting a sequence of movements together
- To imitate movements in response to music
- To sing songs and create dances and experiment with ways of changing them
- To represent thoughts and feeling through role-play
- To remember and discuss features of the environment and how they are affected by weather

## Topics

Water/Weather

## Resources

- DVD: *Singing in the Rain* – excerpt of Gene Kelly dancing in the rain
- DVD player and television
- Painting: *The Umbrellas* Pierre-Auguste Renoir
- Book: *Alfie's Feet* by Shirley Hughes (Red Fox) – alternative resource
- Umbrellas, raincoats, Wellington boots
- Song: 'Raindrops Keep Falling on My Head' by Burt Bacharach
- CD player
- Songs: 'In the Puddles' and 'Umbrella', from *Start with a Song* by Mavis de Mierre (Brilliant Publications)
- CD and book: 'Singing in the Rain' from *I Can Sing, I Can Colour* (IMP)

## Preparation

- If appropriate, find Gene Kelly dancing in the rain on the DVD.
- Have on view the painting *The Umbrellas*.

## What to do

**Indoor playtime activity**

- Watch *Singing in the Rain* – excerpt of Gene Kelly dancing in the rain. Alternatively, read *Alfie's Feet.*
- Ask whether the children have ever been caught in the rain. Ask if they had an umbrella.
- Ask how it felt. Talk about the differences between warm summer rain and cold winter rain.

**Dance activity**

- Play 'Raindrops Keep Falling on My Head'.
- Ask the children to pretend it has started to rain and to put up their umbrellas, and skip around the room.
- Pretend that the rain has stopped and invite children to close their umbrellas and stand in the sunshine

**Role-play activity**

- Encourage dressing up and role-play the experience of being out in the rain.
- Support the children's language development by introducing new vocabulary, such as: *pouring*, *drizzle*, *shower* and *soaked.*

**Music activity**

- Play any of the songs and encourage the children to mime to the music.

## Extension/variation

- Learn the words to 'Singing in the Rain'.

## Links to home

- Ask to borrow umbrellas for the dance.

## Related activities

- Storm (see page 144)
- Running water (see page 117)
- Freezing cold (see page 134–135)

Exploring and Using Media and Materials

# Creepy-crawly mini-beasts

## Topics

Animals/Gardening

## Resources

- CD player
- Non-fiction books about insects
- Craft and junk materials
- Card
- Scissors
- Pencils and crayons
- Paints and paintbrushes
- PVA glue and spreaders
- Playdough
- Magnifying glasses
- Pasta or cotton reels for threading
- String
- Scrapers or sandblocks
- Live snails in clear box
- Live earthworms in clear boxes or jars
- Lettuce and other green leaves
- Soil and sand
- Rhymes: 'Little Miss Muffet' and 'Incy Wincy Spider' from *This Little Puffin* compiled by Elizabeth Matterson (Puffin) Poems: 'The Spider and The Fly' by Mary Hewitt 'The Fly' by Walter de la Mare and 'Animal Houses' by James Reeves from *The Oxford Treasury of Children's Poems* (Oxford University
- Song: 'The Snail' by Mary O'Hara (Levi-O'Hara) from *Music Speaks Louder than Words* Press)
- Music: 'Flight of the Bumble Bee' by Nikolas Rimsky-Korsakov

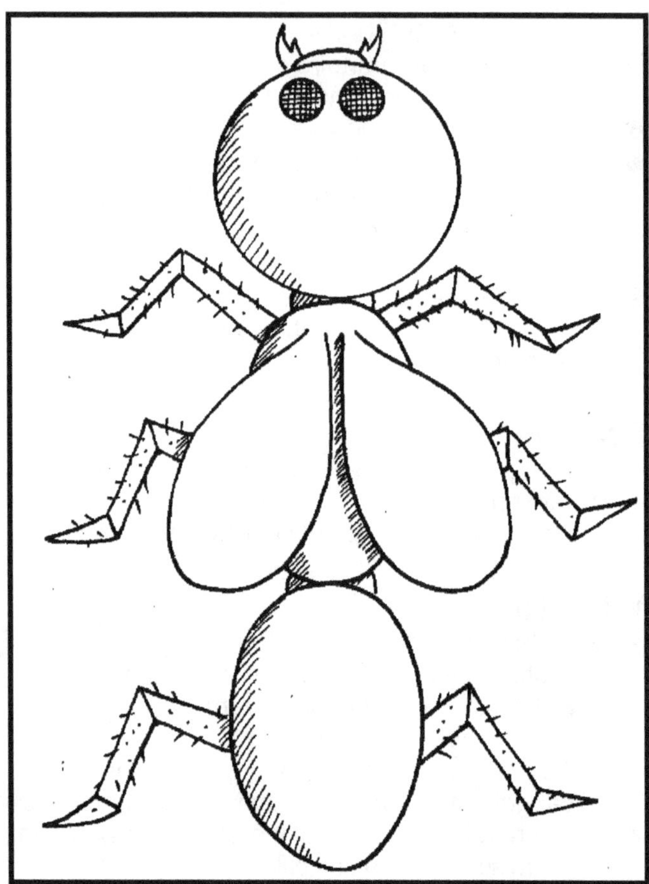

## Learning objectives

- To imitate movements and actions in response to music or verse
- To use lines to enclose a space and shapes to represent an object
- To use and explore a variety of materials, tools and techniques, experimenting with colour, design, texture and form
- To observe and talk about animals in the natural environment
- To represent idea through art and design, music, dance and stories

## Preparation

- Collect some snails and some worms in the garden. Put the snails temporarily into clear containers and give them some lettuce leaves to feed on.
- Pour layers of soil and sand into other clear containers to make wormeries and put some green leaves and some worms on top.

## What to do

### Circle time

- Observe the snails with the children and talk about them. Encourage them to use descriptive language such as: *shell mollusc, slow, slime* and *spiral.*
- Look at the snails and the worms with magnifying glasses.
- Look at the worms at intervals to see how they are mixing up the soil and sand.
- Read 'The Fly', which describes a fly's eye view of the world, ie everything looks very big. Suggest to the children that they imagine a very large insect. Ask them to describe their insect and what it would do.

### Music activity

- Sing the nursery rhymes 'Little Miss Muffet' and 'Incy Wincy Spider' and read the poem. Perform appropriate actions and talk about spiders.
- Play the song 'The Snail' and ask the children whether the music is fast or slow.
- Dance to the song, moving each limb slowly. Then offer contrast by dancing to a fast piece of music, such as 'Flight of the Bumble Bee'.
- Make sounds representing the movements of a worm using scrapers or sandpaper block, then make up a wriggly worm dance using the instruments to keep the beat.

### Art activity

- Make a pop-up spider card by folding a thin piece of card three times to make eight columns, then opening it out and drawing half a spider with its body at the centre fold and four legs touching one edge (see diagram).
- Cut out the spider, then fold it again to make the legs bent and stick the eight feet down onto another piece of card, so that, when the card is opened, the spider can pop up.
- Encourage children to make or paint monster insects to their own designs. Offer picture books and posters for ideas.
- Remind them that insects always have six legs and three body parts, but may have two, four or no wings.
- Suggest to the children that they make up stories about their monster insects

### Art activity

- Make worms from playdough, or thread pasta or cotton reels on to string.

## Extensions/variations

- Read the poem 'Animal Houses'.
- Make snails from coiled playdough.

## Links to home

Ask parents to look for spiders' webs and mini-beasts with their children.

Return any creatures to the environment from which you found them after you have finished with them.
Care with hygiene – do not handle snails.
Wash hands before and after working outside.
Check children have had a tetanus inoculation.

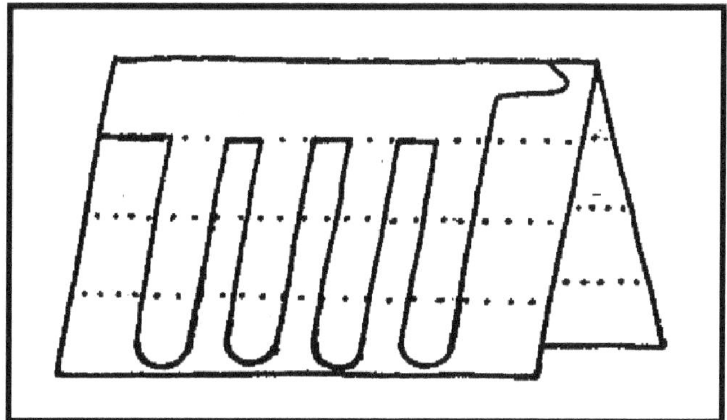

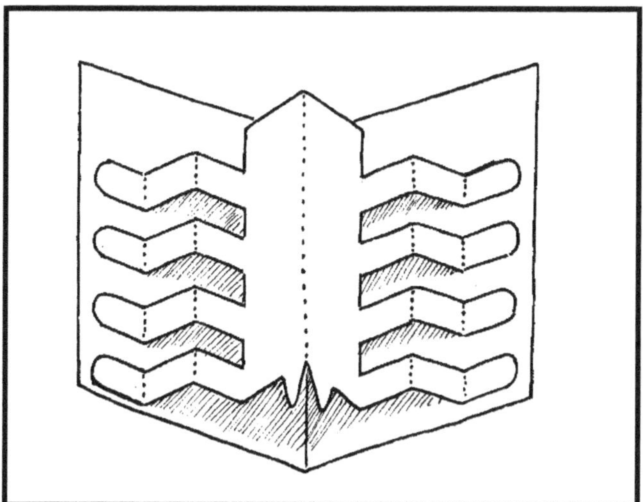

Exploring and Using Media and Materials

# Growing up

## Topics

Families/Myself

## Resources

- *The Last Noo-Noo* by Jill Murphy (Walker Books)*New Born* by Kathy Henderson (Frances Lincoln) *When I was a Baby* by Catherine Anholt (Picture Mammoth)
- Rhyme: 'Baby Games' from This Little Puffin compiled by Elizabeth Matterson (Puffin)
- Songs: 'Rock A Bye Baby' from The I Can't Sing Book by Jackie Silberg (Brilliant Publications) 'We've Grown So Tall' from Start with a Song by Mavis de Mierre (Brilliant Publications)
- Collection of toys and equipment items used by babies
- Teddies and dolls
- Plastic dolls for bathing
- Towels, flannels and soap
- Digital cameras
- Scissors
- Paper
- Paints and paintbrushes
- Playdough
- Wire coat hangers
- Thin string or thread

 Supervise the water tray activity and the use of scissors.

## Learning objectives

- To explore a variety of objects and materials, describing and comparing colour, texture, shape, form and function
- To combine different media and construct with a purpose in mind, selecting appropriate resources
- To sing familiar songs and perform appropriate actions
- To remember and represent own ideas, thoughts and feelings through role-play and stories
- To show and talk about favourite things and make models to represent them

## Preparation

- Make a collection of baby toys and equipment and display them on a table for children to look at, handle and talk about.

## What to do

### Circle time

- Read *The Last Noo-Noo* and talk about the things that the children do not use any more. Ask the children for examples.

- Show the children items from the collection table. Let them examine the items and talk about them, eg *dummy*, *rattles*, *potty*, *feeding bottle*.
- Ask if anyone has a younger brother or sister. Ask how they felt when they first saw their new brother/sister.
- Read *When I Was a Baby* and discuss each picture. Compare what the children can do now, with what they could not do as a baby.
- Ask the children if they could describe their earliest memory. Begin, 'I can remember when …'
- End the session with the song 'We've Grown So Tall'.
- Ask what the children think they will be able to do next year.

**Art and craft activities**

- Suggest that children choose some of the baby items and talk about their colours, textures and functions.
- Ask them to arrange the items on the table or floor and take photographs of them from different angles, observing the shapes made by the items touching each other and the spaces between them.
- Print out the photographs and encourage children to compare them with the actual arrangement of objects.
- Invite children to look carefully at the arrangement and the photographs and paint pictures of the items they have chosen.
- Invite children to use their photographs or to make playdough models of their favourite items and to hang them from a coat hanger, to make a mobile. Support them as they attach the items and decide how to make the mobile balance.

**Music activity**

- Discuss with the children the songs that they learned when they were babies and the songs they sing to younger brothers and sisters.
- Invite children to sing songs and demonstrate accompanying actions to the group.
- Learn and sing some baby game songs together. Offer dolls and teddies and suggest that the children sing the songs to them.

**Role-play activity**

- Encourage imaginative play and support language development as the children play with dolls. Suggest that they give the babies a bath, feed them, dress them and put them into bed.

## Extensions/variations

- Invite a parent with a young baby to come into the setting and show the children how to bath the baby or feed her with a bottle. Support the children as they ask questions about what the baby can and cannot do and sing a lullaby to her as she goes to sleep.
- Talk with the children about how to care for a baby and how to keep a baby safe.

## Links to home

- Ask if they would like to lend any baby items for the collection. (Make sure they are clearly labelled with a name.)

## Exploring and Using Media and Materials

# Seaside

## Topics

Transport and travel/ Weather

## Resources

- Book: *The Bears Who Went To The Seaside* by Suzanna Gretz and Alison Sage (A&C Black)
- Poem: 'maggie and milly and molly and may' by e e cummings from *Verse Universe* (BBC Publications); 'Seaside' and 'Sand' from Out And About Through The Year by Shirley Hughes (Walker Books)
- Songs: 'Heat Wave' by Irving Berlin; 'We're All Going on a Summer Holiday' sung by Cliff Richard; 'Surfin' USA' by The Beach Boys; 'Oh I Do Like to be Beside the Seaside' by John A. Glover-Kind
- CD player
- Seashells
- Grout
- Powder paint
- Teaspoon
- Plastic pot and spatula
- Flat-sided tin with no sharp edges or circular cheese box with lid or clay pot
- Dried beach flotsam
- Junk materials including fabric and string
- Paint and paintbrushes
- Cardboard
- Clean sand and plastic sheet or sandpit
- Buckets, spades moulds, sticks, pebbles
- Paddling pool
- Ice-lolly moulds, diluted fruit juice, freezer
- Scissors
- PVA glue and spreaders

## Learning objectives

- To show interest in and describe textures
- To enjoy joining in with dancing and ring games
- To imitate and create movement in response to music
- To safely use and explore a variety of materials, tools and techniques, experimenting with colour, design, texture and form
- To capture experiences with a range of media
- To create simple representations of events, people and objects
- To represent ideas and feelings through engaging in imaginative role-play based on own first-hand experiences
- To play cooperatively as part of a group to develop and act out a narrative or storyline

## Preparation

- Mix grout with water, if required.
- Make ice lollies.

## What to do

### Circle time

- Read 'maggie and milly and molly and may'.
- Ask which children have been to the seaside for their holiday.
- Pass round the seashells. Ask for descriptions of colour, shape (spiral or bivalve) and texture. Draw attention to the differences between the smooth inside and the rough outside of the shells.
- Read *The Bears Who Went To The Seaside* and talk with the children about what they would take to the seaside.
- Read the poems 'Seaside' and 'Sand' and ask the children which they like best.

### Craft activities

- Add a teaspoonful of paint to the grout and mix to a paste in a plastic pot.
- Spread over the tin, pot or lid. Keep the base clean.
- Press the seashells into the grout in a pleasing arrangement.
- Make a collage from beach flotsam.
- Work with the children to create a large display of a beach scene. Help by suggesting appropriate materials and techniques.
- Encourage the children to paint a picture of their holiday on the beach.

- Ask questions about their paintings, and how it relates to their holiday.

### Music activity

- Discuss and explain going on holiday, feeling hot and surfing in the sea and practise mimes and acting with the children.
- Play the songs 'Heat Wave', 'Surfin' USA' and 'We're All Going on a Summer Holiday' and encourage the children to mime, act and dance to them.
- Teach the song 'Oh I Do Like to be Beside The Seaside'.

### Role-play activity

- Use a large outdoor sandpit or spread a plastic sheet over the grass and tip clean sand onto it. Provide a paddling pool close by.
- Encourage children to dress in bathing costumes or shorts and to imagine that they are at the seaside.
- Share the ice lollies
- Experiment with building sandcastles and discuss the textures of wet and dry sand and which is best for building.

## Links to home

- Ask parents about holidays they have taken with their children and request that they supply bathing costumes or beach outfits for their children, along with towels, sunhats and sun screen.

Exploring and Using Media and Materials

# The Farmer's in his Den

## Topic
People who help us

## Resources
- A large safe space indoors or outdoors

Please ensure the children do not become too excited and make certain that the patting part is done gently.

## Learning objectives
- To join in with dancing and ring games
- To imitate movement and actions in response to music
- To begin to build a repertoire of familiar songs and sing them confidently as a member of a group
- To negotiate space successfully when playing with other children

## What to do
**Movement activity**
- Show the group how to form a circle and join hands. Choose one child to stand still, in the centre of the circle. This child will be the farmer. The others dance around him or her in a ring as they all sing. If you are not familiar with the words, here they are:

  *The farmer's in his den, the farmer's in his den,*
  *E, I, E, I, O, the farmer's in his den.*
- The second verse is sung and the farmer chooses a wife, who stands with 'him' in the middle of the circle.

  *The farmer wants a wife, the farmer wants a wife.*
  *E, I, E, I, O, the farmer chooses a wife.*
- After each verse, the last child to enter the circle chooses another child to join the ones in the middle of the circle:

  *The wife wants a child.*
  *The child wants a nurse.*
  *The nurse wants a dog.*
  *The dog wants a bone.*
- The last verse begins:

  *We all pat the dog.*

  Everyone usually finds it very comical as they pat the 'dog's' head. Make sure that this is done very gently!
- An alternative ending is to go on to 'The dog wants a bone' and then to sing 'We all clap the bone', which is equally funny but avoids the physical contact of the 'patting' and can be more appropriate for less confident or more boisterous children.
- Ensure that the children understand that, although the traditional words of the song are old-fashioned, either a boy or a girl may be chosen to take on any of the roles.

## Related activity
- The farmer grows our food (see page 176)

# Spring is here

**Exploring and Using Media and Materials**

## Learning objectives

- To take part in imaginative active experiences within a group, remembering and following the actions of a story or song
- To tell stories, sing songs and make music, dance or movements and experiment with ways of changing them
- To listen to stories and songs, accurately anticipating key events and responding with relevant actions

## Topic
Seasons

## Resources
- *Over in the Meadow* by Jane Cabrera (David & Charles)

## What to do

**Circle time**

- Discuss the season of spring with the children. Explain that new flowers and blossoms grow. Tell them that baby animals are born. Read the story *Over in the Meadow*. If you also know it as a song, sing it with the children, using the pictures in the book.

**Movement activity**

- Allow plenty of space for the activity. Read the story a page at a time. As each page has a different number of animals from one to eleven (counting the mother animals), the children need to be patient until you call and count them in. If preferred the whole class could join in, but keeping to the book will add to mathematical skills.
- **Page 1**: Ask Mother Turtle to show the baby turtle how to dig in the sand. Show the children digging movements using their hands and feet as they lie on the floor.
- **Page 2**: Mother Fish and her two baby fishes could make swimming movements, using their arms and legs.
- **Page 3**: Ask the children to stand up, look all around like owls and call 'Tu-whoo!'
- **Page 4**: The rat family should try to make gnawing movements by moving their jaws around. They might also run around or scratch for food.
- **Page 5**: Ask the baby bees to run quickly around the hive, buzzing with Mother Bee.
- **Page 6**: The baby ducks should waddle around the room and quack with Mother Duck.
- **Page 7**: Encourage children to jump up high as Mother Frog's babies.
- **Page 8**: Introduce the children to the word 'bask'. Ask them to lie stretched out like lizards as though sunbathing with Mother Lizard.
- **Page 9**: There are lots of worms in the soil. Ask the children to wriggle and slither with Mother Worm.
- **Page 10**: Suggest that the children sit on the floor and twitch their whiskers like the rabbits. They can also hop, skip and jump in their burrow with Mother Rabbit.
- **Last page**: Tell the children who have role-played mothers to lie asleep on the floor. Ask the baby animals to come out to play and to run around, dance, hop, skip and make any other movements that they can think of.

## Related activity

- Spring plants and animals (see page 27)

Exploring and Using Media and Materials

# From tadpole to frog

## Topic
Animals

## Resources
- Books and pictures of frogs and tadpoles

The RSPCA regards frogs and tadpoles as endangered species and does not recommend the collection of frog spawn from public areas. Frog spawn may be collected from private ponds, but should be returned to the pond in due course.

## Learning objectives
- To move rhythmically and to imitate movements in response to music
- To take part in active imaginative experiences, finding different ways of moving and experimenting with ways of changing them
- To develop control and coordination in large and small movements
- To improve balance skills

## What to do
### Circle time
- Offer details of metamorphosis and development from a tadpole to a frog. Discuss the concept and the process with the children and encourage them to ask and answer questions. Use books and pictures and, if possible, take children to a local pond at intervals to see frogspawn, then tadpoles and then frogs.

### Movement activity
- Find a large space and ask the children to pretend to be tadpoles. Encourage them to think about how tadpoles grow.
- First ask them to lie on their tummies, gradually pushing out one leg then two, followed by one arm and then the other arm.
- Ask the children to get up from their prone positions and squat like frogs on the floor. Encourage them to move around like frogs, jumping and leaping from squatting positions, trying to maintain their balance and not fall over. Invite them also to try to balance while moving in different ways, such as hopping on one leg.

# Jewels in the crown

**Exploring and Using Media and Materials**

## Learning objectives

- To understand that different media can be combined to create new effects
- To manipulate materials to achieve a planned effect
- To safely use and explore materials, tools and techniques, experimenting with colour, design, texture, form and function

## Preparation

- Cover a large table with used newspaper.

## What to do

### Art activity

- Ask the children which shapes of bead they wish to make. Cut strips of coloured paper or white paper for long beads, and triangles for oval beads. Paste both sides. Roll paper around a knitting needle or skewer.

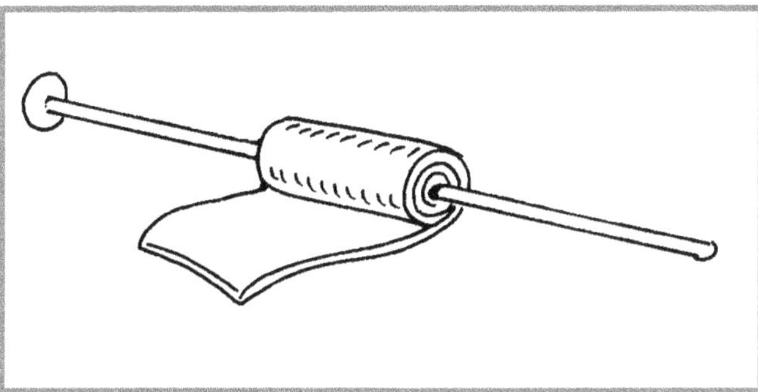

- Slide the beads off and leave to dry.
- The white beads can be painted different colours.
- Help the children thread the string through the holes made by the needle or skewer. Tie in a double knot to finish.

## Extension/variation

- Cut a strip of cardboard to make a crown. Measure it around the child's head. Staple or glue the sides of the crown together. Allow the children to decorate the crowns with their beads, glitter and other craft pieces.

## Related activity

- The Queen's palace (see page 21)

## Topic

Celebrations

## Resources

- PVA glue
- Knitting needles or skewers
- Coloured paper
- White paper
- Paint
- Paintbrushes
- Strong cotton, string or thread
- Cardboard
- Stapler
- Glue
- Glitter

Supervise the use of needles and skewers carefully, keeping the points away from the children's eyes.

**Exploring and Using Media and Materials**

# Texture collages

## Topic
Colours

## Resources
- Different shaped objects
- White paper
- Crayons
- Candle
- Paints
- Paintbrushes
- Straws
- Wood shavings
- Wool
- Milk bottle tops
- Sponge
- Plain craft matchsticks
- Glue or paste
- Scraps of fabric with different textures

Avoid using feathers as a tactile source as some children may have an allergy to feathers.

## Learning objectives
- To select appropriate resources and adapt work where necessary
- To experiment with colours, design and texture
- To safely use and explore a variety of materials, tools and techniques

## What to do
### Art activity
- Put an interestingly textured object under a piece of paper. Rub the surface of the paper with a wax candle.
- Paint a weak solution of paint across the design. The design magically appears under the paint.
- Encourage the children to use as many different things as possible.

## Extensions/variations
- Make a complete wall frieze with separate panels organized by each child. Each panel can contain as much texture and colour as wished. There will need to be a great variety of tactile bits and pieces. Stick them in swirls and whirls and make exciting patterns.
- Textile pictures: Find some scraps of fabric with different textures. Ask the children to lightly draw a scene, such as houses in a street, a garden with pets, or a beach in summer or a park in winter and then to choose suitable fabric pieces to stick to the picture. Talk with the children about the colours and the textures they have chosen.

# Noah's animals

**Exploring and Using Media and Materials**

## Learning objectives

- To create movements and dances in response to music and to experiment with ways of changing them
- To use simple tools and techniques competently and appropriately
- To choose particular colours to use for a purpose
- To create simple representations of animals

## Preparation

- Draw or copy a variety of animal face masks in the right sizes and shapes for the children.

## What to do

### Circle time

- Read a story about Noah, eg *Professor Noah's Spaceship.*
- Suggest that the children make masks so that they can role-play the story.
- With the children, list the animals in the story.
- Show the children pictures and photographs of the animals. Explain that the male and female animals look different in some species and similar in others. Offer new vocabulary such as: *lion* and *lioness*, *bull* and *cow* or *ram* and *ewe.*

### Art activity

- Offer the children a choice of animal face masks and invite them each to cut out one and adapt it in any way they choose.
- Talk about the colours they might use. Suggest that they look at a picture of the animal if they would like to choose realistic colours.
- Support colouring in the masks. Help the children to tie elastic through the holes at each side and make the masks fit.

## Extension/variation

- Perform *Professor Noah's Spaceship* while dancing to Carnival of Animals.

## Links to home

- Invite parents to watch the performance of *Professor Noah's Spaceship.*

## Topic

Animals

## Resources

- Book: *Professor Noah's Spaceship* by Brian Wildsmith (OUP)
- Books and photographs of male and female animals
- Music: Carnival of Animals suite by Camille Saint-Saëns
- CD player
- Paint or crayons as required
- Paintbrushes
- Stiff cardboard animal masks
- Elastic
- Stapler
- Scissors

Supervise the use of scissors and staplers.

## Related activity

- Noah's music (see page 149)

# Hats

## Topic

People who help us

## Resources

- Books: *ABC I Can Be* by Verna Allette Wilkins and Zoë Gorham (Tamarind Books); *What Am I?* by Debbie MacKinnon and Anthea Sieveking (Frances Lincoln)
- Photographs of people who help us, showing their hats

**For making hats**

- Small plates
- Card
- Crêpe paper
- PVA glue and spreaders
- Sticky tape
- Newspaper
- White lining paper
- String
- Fabrics, yarns, ribbons, foil, coloured papers, tissue paper, artificial flowers, beads, sequins, feathers, tassels and fringes
- PVA glue and spreaders
- Papier mâché materials (optional)
- Paint and paintbrushes
- Scissors and pinking shears

⚠ Supervise the use of scissors and any sharp tools.

## Learning objectives

- To select appropriate resources, tools and techniques and to shape, assemble and join materials to achieve a planned effect
- To use and explore materials and techniques, experimenting with balance, colour, design, texture, form and function

## What to do

**Circle time**

- Read *ABC I Can Be* and/or *What Am I?*
- Most people who help us wear special hats.
- Ask children to describe hats of police, firefighters, the lollipop person, etc.
- Suggest that the children copy a hat, or design one of their own, for someone who helps us.

**Craft activity**

- Encourage the children to think about which materials suit the character.
- Select the style of hat, cap or helmet, and create the basic shape using card for a headband and a brim or peak. (For a hard helmet, consider using papier mâché on a balloon and cutting the top half to shape once the balloon is dry, then adding a card brim or peak.)
- Support the children in making a hat to fit to their head. Paint or cover with coloured materials. Adjust the headband or brim to fit and stick or staple in place. Make the top of the hat or cap by gathering a large circle of crêpe or tissue paper into the band and sticking or stapling it in place.
- Ask the children whether their finished hat balances and fits, and if they have achieved their intended designs, adapted them or improved upon them.

## Extensions/variations

- Let younger children decorate an existing hat.
- Make hats for the Pied Piper project and the Wedding project. Encourage the children to add a range of materials appropriate to the character. Discuss the qualities and use of: fabrics, yarns, ribbons, foil, papers, tissue paper, artificial flowers, beads, sequins, feathers, tassels and fringes, and paint.

## Links to home

- Ask if the setting could borrow some hats to decorate or copy.

## Related activities

- The Pied Piper (see page 164–165)
- Wedding (see page 126–127)

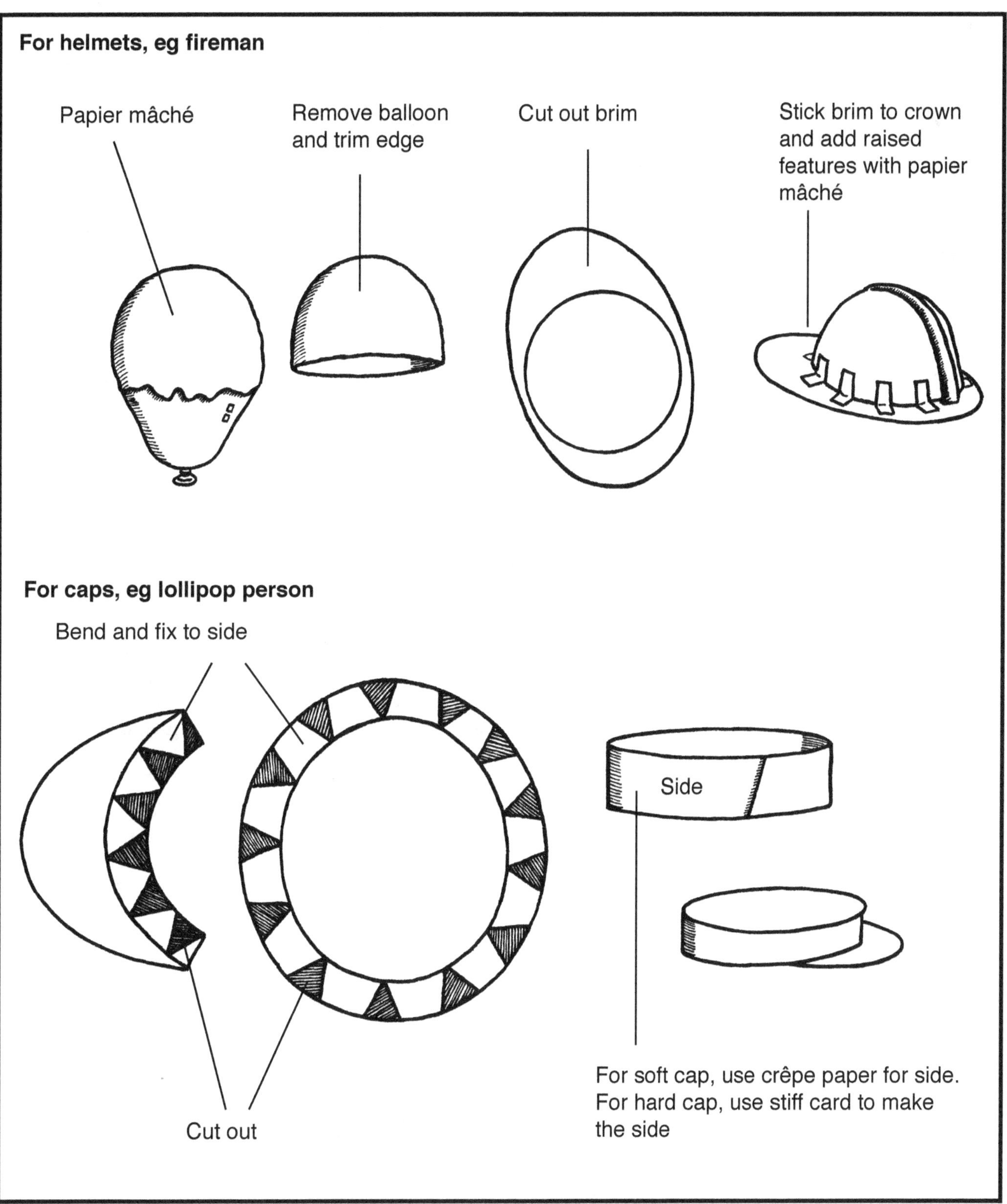
For helmets, eg fireman
Papier mâché
Remove balloon and trim edge
Cut out brim
Stick brim to crown and add raised features with papier mâché
For caps, eg lollipop person
Bend and fix to side
Side
Cut out
For soft cap, use crêpe paper for side. For hard cap, use stiff card to make the side

**Exploring and Using Media and Materials**

# Spring flowers

## Topics
Seasons/Gardening

## Resources
- Paintings: *Flowers in a Vase* by Rachel Ruysch; *Hebridean Roses, Eigg* by Winifred Nicholson; *Vase of Flowers* by Odilon Redon; *Flowers in Glass Vase* by Ambrosius Bosschaert; *Sunflowers* by Vincent van Gogh
- Paints
- Paintbrushes
- Thick paper for base
- Coloured tissue and crêpe papers
- Junk materials
- Coloured pipe cleaners
- Glue and glue spreaders
- Scissors

Supervise the use of scissors and any sharp tools.

## Learning objectives
- To safely use and explore a variety of materials, tools and techniques, experimenting with colour, design, texture and form
- To construct with a purpose in mind, using a variety of resources
- To create simple representations of objects

## What to do
### Circle time
- Show two different paintings of a vase of flowers. Ask whether the paintings look dark or light.
- Invite the children to count how many colours have been used and point to different ones
- Ask whether the painting has been painted with thick (oil) or thin (water colour) paint.
- Ask which painting they like best. Encourage them to give reasons.

- Suggest that the children make their own picture of the fresh flowers.
- Ask for ideas on how they could make a picture of flowers. For example, they could use tissue paper or make a collage of petal shapes using different fabrics. Encourage children to explore ideas that use a mixture of media.

### Art activity
- Allow those children who have expressed how they wish to proceed to choose their own materials.
- When they have made a variety of flowers, invite them to choose whether to keep their pictures or cut them out and arrange them in vases as 3D models. Display the pictures and the models together.

## Extension/variation
- Make flowers for the Kwanzaa and The Selfish Giant projects.

## Links to home
- Ask parents to allow their child to dismantle a flower to explore its structure.

## Related activities
- Kwanzaa (see page 124–125)
- The Selfish Giant (see page 132–133)

# Autumn leaves

**Exploring and Using Media and Materials**

## Learning objectives

- To safely use and explore a variety of materials, tools and techniques, experimenting with colour, design, texture and form
- To manipulate materials to achieve a planned effect
- To select appropriate resources and adapt work as necessary
- To observe and talk about plants found in the natural environment

## Topics

Seasons/Gardening

## Resources

- Collection of different coloured leaves
- Painting: *Autumn Leaves* by John Everett Millais
- Coloured paper: white, brown, red, green and orange paper
- Stiff paint brushes
- Toothbrushes
- Small sponges
- Selection of thick paints including brown, orange, green and red
- Trays for paint
- Plastic aprons
- Newspaper
- Cereal box card
- Scissors
- Songs: 'Let Us Dance' and 'Conker, Conker', from Start with a Song by Mavis de Mierre (Brilliant Publications)

## Preparation

- Take the children to visit a park with a variety of trees to collect autumn leaves before offering this activity.

## What to do

### Circle time

- Share the children's experiences of the visit to the park.
- Examine the collected leaves. Talk about the texture, colour, number of leaflets (ash leaf, chestnut leaf), the shape of the edges.
- Encourage children to sort and match the leaves.
- Show the painting *Autumn Leaves*. Ask what the children in the picture are doing.

### Art activity

- Encourage the children to choose their own colours.
- Support different techniques to make leaf prints:
- Spread paint on the leaf and make a print by pressing it on to a sheet of paper.
- Place the leaf on clean paper and splatter or dab paint round the edge.
- Draw round a leaf on to card. Cut out the inside of the shape to make a stencil. Use different techniques to fill the space, eg splattering paint using different colours
- Point out the colours and textures created when different colours are mixed.

Take care with scissors.

## Extension/variation

### Music activity

- Sing the songs about autumn trees.

## Related activities


- Fruitful (see page 82)
- Trees (see page 128)
- The Selfish Giant project (see pages 132–133)

# Tiles

## Topics
Homes/Shapes

## Resources
- Cardboard template 7cm x 7cm (for size of tile)
- Clay, modelling clay or playdough
- Knife
- Kiln if required
- Rolling pins
- Tools to model material
- Wooden base board to stick tiles on
- Strong adhesive (for use by practitioner)
- Poster paints
- Paintbrushes
- PVA glue
- Newspaper
- White lining paper
- Thick cardboard
- Damp cloths
- Polythene

Take care with sharp tools.

## Learning objectives
- To safely use and explore a variety of materials, tools and techniques, experimenting with colour, design, texture and form
- To handle malleable materials with increasing control
- To recognize, create and describe patterns

## Preparation
- Prepare cardboard templates.
- Wedge the clay to remove air.

## What to do
**Craft activity**
- Encourage the children to roll out a square of clay about 1.5cm thick. Support trimming it to size, using the template.
- Ask them to make shapes, patterns and textures on the surface of the tile by pressing shapes into the surface, engraving or adding material to make a raised shape. If bits of clay are added as decoration they should be joined using 'slip' (clay mixed with water to a liquid consistency).
- The clay can be kept moist by keeping it covered with damp cloths and wrapping it in polythene.
- Ask the children to describe the shapes and patterns they have made. Encourage confident use of descriptive language and introduce new vocabulary, such as: *shape, pattern, decoration, triangular, rectangular, circular, raised, swirling, straight, curved, repeating*.
- When the clay is 'leather hard', the surface can be painted with different coloured clay 'slips' and then fired in a kiln.
- If the clay tile is not going to be fired, it can be decorated with paint mixed with PVA glue. Playdough can be used instead of clay.
- On completion, the tiles should be treated with a coat of diluted PVA to make them water-resistant.

## Extensions/variations
- Mount the tiles together to make a group mural. Discuss how the blocks could be arranged to emphasize the effects of shape, pattern and decoration.
- Shapes can be cut from thick cardboard, then glued on top of the template. Apply white poster paint as a base, then paint.

## Related activity
- Bricks (see page 93)

# Add water



## Learning objectives

- To experiment with colour and design
- To explore what happens when colours mix and how colours can be changed

## Preparation

- Try the Extension activity first to ensure that your felt-tipped pen colour is a mixture of two or more different colours.

## Notes for practitioner

- Paintings by Morris Louis such as *Saf Gimmel* are created by running diluted colour down the canvas.

## What to do

### Circle time

- Show the children the painting. Discuss how it could have been created.

### Snack time

- Pour some concentrated fruit drink into a clear plastic beaker. Ask for predictions of what will happen when you add water.
- Support children in learning and using new vocabulary, such as: *diluted*, *concentrated*, *strong*, *weak*, *wet*, *dry* and colour names.
- Dilute some of the fruit drink, gradually adding water a little at a time. Invite children to talk about what they can see happening and then to taste what is happening.

### Art activity

- Fasten a piece of kitchen towel to the sloping easel with masking tape.
- Show the children how to make a wet painting. Paint diluted paint along the top of the kitchen towel and let it drip down the paper.
- Add water by squeezing the sponge.
- Encourage experimentation with thicker colour and varying the amount of water.
- Let different colours drip on to each other and mix together. Discuss the colours.
- Dry and mount the pictures.

## Extension/variation

- Mark a piece of kitchen towel with felt-tipped pens. Drip water on to the colour, and let it run. The water will separate the mixture of colours in the felt pen.

## Topic

Water

## Resources

- Painting: *Saf Gimmel* by Morris Louis or similar
- Plain white kitchen towels
- Masking tape
  Thin paints in primary colours (red, yellow, blue)
- Paintbrushes
- Easels
- Sponges
- Water in plastic pot
- Blackcurrant or other concentrated fruit drink
- Clear plastic beakers
- Drinking water
- Coloured felt-tipped pens

 Note any child with diabetes or allergies to E numbers.

## Related activity

- Bananananana (see page 92)

Exploring and Using Media and Materials

# Tick, tock, hum, click

## Topic
Homes

## Resources
- Book: *Clocks and More Clocks* by Pat Hutchins (Bodley Head Children's Books)
- Poem: 'Bleep' by Michael Rosen, from *Michael Rosen's Book of Nonsense* (Hodder and Stoughton)
- Percussion instruments
- Collection table with a variety of clocks, including one with a loud tick and a pendulum clock
- Long pendulum of string with bob at end
- Song: 'The Clock', from *Start with a Song* by Mavis de Mierre (Brilliant Publications)
- Song: 'My Grandfather's Clock', see www.kididdles.com
- Metronome
- Two wood blocks of different size with beater

## Learning objectives
- To learn about long and short sounds
- To learn to control and play a percussion instrument
- To tap out simple repeated rhythms
- To explore and learn how sounds can be changed

## What to do
**Circle time**
- Read *Clocks and More Clocks.* Ask why it appeared that the clocks gave the wrong time.
- Show children examples of clocks from the collection table.
- Show the pendulum clock (or a picture of one). Demonstrate with string and bob how a pendulum can swing steadily. Count the swings with the class: 1, 2.
- Shorten the string to make the beat go faster, and ask everyone to count again. Ask if the beats are faster or slower.
- Read the poem 'Bleep'.
- Ask the children to suggest sounds they can hear in the home.
- Ask them to think of some sounds that are long, eg spinning washing machine, hum of fridge, a hair dryer, running water in the bath, lawn mower. Make sure they understand the difference between a sound that continues without a break (sustained) and a succession of short sounds that follow on from each other so quickly that they give the impression of one long sound.
- Ask the children to make a long sound with their voices.
- Ask for some short sounds, eg tick of a clock, beeping of a computer, snipping scissors.

**Music activity**
- Sing 'My Grandfather's Clock' using the metronome if available. Explain it helps everyone to keep to the same beat.
- Hand out the instruments and ask the children whether their instrument makes a short or long sound.
- Demonstrate how the head of a beater will bounce off a vibrating surface (eg a drum head) if you use a loose wrist.
- Ask the children to make either a long or short sound, and to say which it is.
- Ask how a sound can be shortened (eg by touching the vibrating surface). Touching a triangle will prevent it from vibrating.

## Extensions/variations
- Play the two wood blocks as tick-tock as the children sing.
- Divide the children into two groups – long and short sounds. Agree on signals for each group to play in turn. Count to four beats, and get those instruments with short duration, eg tone blocks, maracas, to play each beat.
- Continue counting four beats and ask the children playing instruments with a long duration, eg cymbal or triangle, to make their sounds last for a full four beats.

# Running water

**Exploring and Using Media and Materials**

## Learning objectives

- To begin to move rhythmically
- To make movements and dance and experiment with ways of changing them
- To imitate and create movement in response to music
- To represent ideas through movement and dance
- To negotiate space safely while moving as part of a group

## Topics

Water/Weather

## Resources

- Book: *The Story of Running Water* by Joanna Troughton (Cambridge University Press)
- Non-fiction books about water, rivers, the sea
- Music: 'Winter', from *The Four Seasons* by Antonio Vivaldi; *Arabesque 1* by Claude Debussy); 'Orinoco Flow', from the Watermark album by Enya; The overture from *The Hebrides* 'Fingals Cave' by Felix Mendelssohn
- CD player
- Sand tray
- Watering cans, sieves, jug, bucket of water

## Preparation

- Find the appropriate excerpts on the CDs.

## What to do

### Circle time

- Read *The Story of Running Water*, which is a folk tale. Ask the children whether it is a true story.
- Tell them that rain falls and runs down the mountain to the rivers, lakes and then to the sea. The water evaporates into clouds. The rain falls from the clouds.
- Introduce new vocabulary and support the development of descriptive language by using new words such as: *flowing*, *liquid*, *sea*, *river*, *lake*, *pond*, *running*, *falling*, *clouds*, *evaporating*, *meandering*, *stormy*.
- Illustrate this by using the sand tray – water a mound of sand until water runs from the sand.

### Dance activity

- Using the suggested music, tell the story of the rain reaching the sea.
- Encourage the children to dance to each section, imagining that they are the drops of water.
- 'Winter' from *The Four Seasons* sounds like falling rain with 'plop, plop' sounds. Have the children dance separately.
- *Arabesque 1* sounds like water running – down the mountain. The children should begin to move faster and closer to each other into a stream.
- 'Orinoco Flow' sounds like the river 'sailing' into the sea. Encourage the children to move slower and wind around like a meandering river.
- 'Fingals Cave' sounds like a stormy sea. Ask the children to hold hands in groups of four, and imagine that they are waves. Suggest that they run forwards and run backwards or/ and lift their arms up and down.

## Extension/variation

- Encourage groups of children to make up a sequence of movements to the music.

## Links to home

- Invite the parents to a performance.

## Related activity

- Freezing cold (see pages 134–135)

Exploring and Using Media and Materials

# The Nutcracker

## Topic

Toys

## Resources

- DVD: *The Nutcracker* performed by the Kirov Ballet (Philips Video Classics); 'The Nutcracker Suite' in *Fantasia* (Walt Disney)
- Book: *The Nutcracker* by Alexander Dumas, translated by Douglas Munro (Oxford University Press)
- Music: *The Nutcracker Suite* by Peter Tchaikovsky
- DVD player and television or computer
- CD player
- Photocopier
- Paper fasteners
- Scissors
- Small hole punch
- Craft pieces for decoration
- Glue and spreaders
- Pencils
- Drums and drumsticks
- Percussion instruments
- Mechanical toys

⚠ Supervise the use of scissors.

## Learning objectives

- To tap out simple repeated rhythms and move rhythmically, observing a beat
- To make music and dance and experiment with ways of changing them
- To manipulate materials to achieve a planned effect
- To safely use and explore a variety of materials, tools and techniques, experimenting with design and functions

## Preparation

- Read story of *The Nutcracker* to simplify it before telling it to the children.
- Photocopy the next page on to card, one for each child.
- Make up one toy to show the lever movement.

## What to do

### Circle time

- Ask the children to imagine that their toys could come alive. Discuss what the toys might say or do.
- Watch a DVD of *The Nutcracker* performed as a ballet with the children. Explain what is happening in the story to them as they watch.
- Watch 'The Nutcracker Suite' section in the DVD *Fantasia* (14 minutes).

### Music and dance activities

- Let each child examine and play with a mechanical toy.
- Hand out the percussion instruments.
- Ask the children to make up a rhythm to copy the movement of the toy.
- Provide some drums and encourage children to take turns to play a steady beat while others march to it as soldiers.
- Play the 'Dance of the Flowers' from *The Nutcracker Suite* and invite children to dance freely to the music.

### Craft activity

- Support cutting out of the shapes. Punch holes in the shapes for the split pins.
- Overlap the tops of the arms and tops of the legs and join to strip with split pin.
- Connect second set of holes to the body.
- Fit together so the strip can move freely up and down.
- Stick the head on to the top of the strip.
- Decorate the front. Add hair or a hat.
- Encourage the children to discuss how each clown looks different because of the decoration.

## Extension/variation

- Watch 'The Nutcracker Suite' section in the video *Fantasia* (14 minutes) and 'The Nutcracker' performed as a ballet. Ask which video the children liked best, giving reasons.
- Ask if there are any parents who have ballet training or experience and would like to come in to talk to the children or demonstrate some dance steps.

## Links to home

- Find out which children go to ballet or other dance classes and ask whether anyone could bring in a ballet uniform or tutu and shoes for the other children to see.

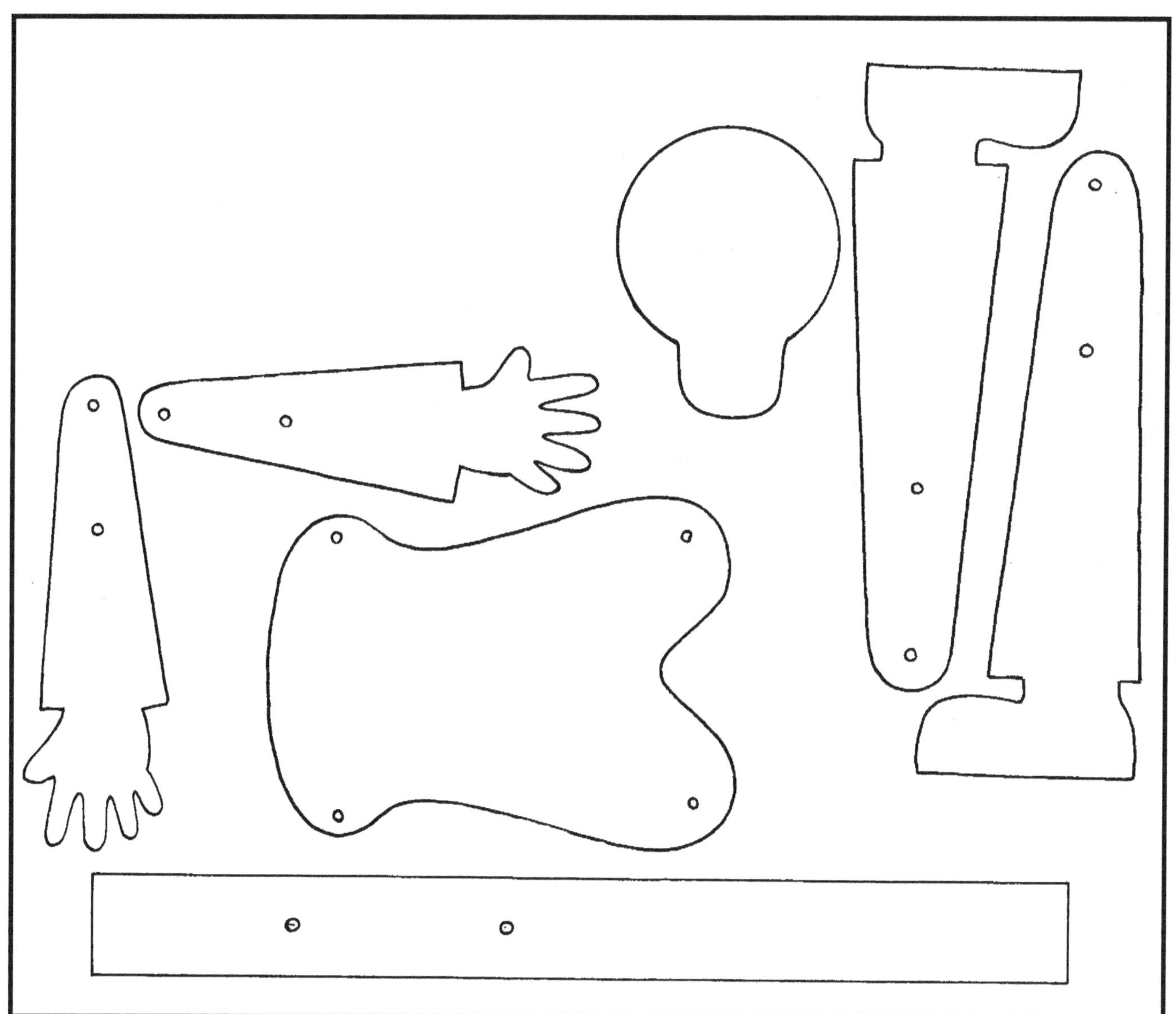

Exploring and Using Media and Materials

# The Hokey Cokey

**Topic**
Health

**Resources**
- Card or paper
- Glue
- Glitter

Watch the children do not bump each other when rushing into the middle of the circle.

## Learning objectives

- To enjoy joining in with dancing and ring games
- To begin to build a repertoire of songs and dances
- To combine and repeat a range of movements
- To create intended movements with all limbs
- To move with control and coordination

## What to do

### Movement activity

- Explain the game of Hokey Cokey. Gather the children into a circle. Intersperse younger children with older children and space adults around the circle, so that everyone can learn the movements more easily and remain calm and in control when moving the whole circle. Ask the children to do exactly what the rhyme advises. Begin with the verse:

*You put your right arm in, your right arm out, your right arm in and you shake it all about*
*You do the Hokey Cokey and you turn around*
*That's what it's all about.*
***Chorus***
*O! The Hokey Cokey!* (join hands, hold them upwards, all run forwards into the centre of the circle, and backwards to the outside circle again)
*O! The Hokey Cokey!* (repeat actions)
*O! The Hokey Cokey!* (repeat actions)
*Knees bend, arms stretch. Rah! Rah! Rah!*

- The dancing game is repeated with left arm, right leg, left leg and whole self.

## Extensions/variations

- Show the group some simple letters. Ask the children if they can form the letters on the floor by curling their bodies into the correct position. Use one or more children to form the letter. For example, for Y = lie down, feet together, arms outstretched above; C = curl up in this shape.
- Paste the same letter shapes on to a piece of paper or thin card. Sprinkle glitter on the shapes to make glitter letters.

# Let's travel by plane

**Exploring and Using Media and Materials**

## Learning objectives

- To construct with a purpose in mind, using a variety of resources
- To handle tools, objects and construction materials safely and with increasing control
- To use a range of one-handed tools and equipment with confidence
- To show interest in different occupations and ways of life

### Topic

Transport and travel

### Resources

- Pictures of aeroplanes
- Large and small boxes
- Cardboard
- Foil
- Pens
- Paints
- Paintbrushes
- Scissors
- Glue
- Paper
- Yoghurt pots
- String

## What to do

**Circle time**

- Discuss travel with the group and ask them to think of different ways of travelling. Ask how many children have travelled in an aeroplane to go on holiday or to visit relatives. Talk about bus or train journeys that they may make, as well as places that they walk or drive to.

**Design and technology activity**

- Make an aeroplane. Find some pictures of aeroplanes and invite the children to make a big one.
- Two long boxes should be sufficient for the body of the aircraft with a smaller one on top for the cabin. Long pieces of cardboard can be used for the wings. Help them draw or cut out the windows and door. Attach a further piece of cardboard for the tail. Covered with foil this model will look most realistic.
- Perhaps they can think of some names for the airline. Consider using the name of the setting, street or area as a starting point, but encourage more imaginative ideas too.
- Talk about the staff who work on aircraft, such as stewards and pilots and ask children whether they might like to wear a uniform and work on an aeroplane when they grow up.

## Extensions/variations

- Make small paper aeroplanes, and see how far they will fly across the room.
- Make hot air balloons from yoghurt pots suspended by string.

## Related activity

- Let's ride the train (see page 48)

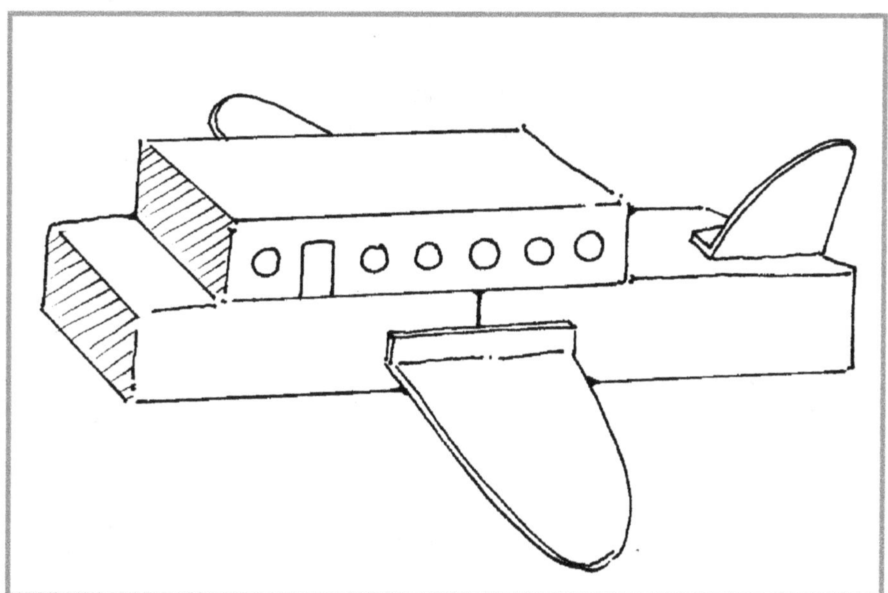

Exploring and Using Media and Materials

# Cheese straws

## Topic
Food and shopping

## Resources
For cheese straws:
- 50g grated cheese
- 1 teaspoon salt
- 100g plain flour
- 50g margarine
- 1 egg
- 1 tablespoon water
- Pastry cutters
- Baking tray
- Oven

For wheels:
- 85g flour
- 40g margarine
- Marmite or jam
- Water
- Baking tray
- Oven

 Be careful using cutting tools and oven.

## Learning objectives
- To use simple tools and techniques competently and appropriately
- To manipulate materials to achieve a planned effect
- To handle malleable materials with increasing control
- To appreciate the need for good hygiene practices and to manage personal hygiene independently

## Preparation
- Prepare a clean, safe area for the cooking activity.

## What to do
### Cooking activity
- Wash hands.
- Rub margarine into cheese, salt and flour until the mixture resembles breadcrumbs. Mix in 1 egg and 1 tablespoon of water.
- Let the children work with their hands until it is a dough mixture. Add more water if necessary. Roll out the dough into a rectangle 2mm thick.
- Help the children cut the dough into finger shapes or use a pastry cutter. Put the shapes on to a greased baking tray.
- Bake for 10 minutes until light brown, 200°C/400°F/Gas Mark 6.

## Extension/variation
- Make wheels. Rub in margarine and flour. Add water to form dough mixture. Roll into a rectangle. Spread with marmite or jam, according to preference. Roll up into a cylinder shape. Cut into thin slices (like wheels). Bake at 200°C/400°F/Gas Mark 6 for approximately 15 minutes until light brown in colour. Double the quantities if there are several children.

# Hip hip hooray



## Learning objectives
- To clap simple repeated rhythms
- To sing a familiar song
- To express ideas and opinions effectively

## Topic
Celebrations

## Resources
- Painting: *Hip Hip Hooray* by Karel Appel
- Song: 'If You're Happy and You Know It (Clap Your Hands)', from *This Little Puffin* compiled by Elizabeth Matterson (Puffin)
- Book: *If You're Happy and You Know It* illustrated by Annie Kubler (Child's Play)

## What to do
### Circle time
- Show the children the painting *Hip Hip Hooray* of bright figures and animals.
- Ask the children what they think of the painting and what kind of mood it conveys
- Tell them the title. Ask what they do when they are happy.
- Look at the book *If You're Happy and You Know It.*

### Music activity
- Sing 'If You're Happy and You Know It (Clap Your Hands)' with the actions.
- Ask on what other occasions people clap their hands.
- Ask the children to clap as giving applause.
- Tell them that you are going to clap to the rhythm of the words of the song, that is, one clap for each word, or each part of a word (syllable), and include the rests. Clap as you sing.

## Extensions/variations
- Clap different rhythms and ask the children to copy.
- Ask the children to clap a short four-beat rhythm over and over again. This is an *ostinato.*

**Exploring and Using Media and Materials**

# Kwanzaa

## Topic

Celebrations

## Resources

- Book: *Too Much Talk* by Angela Shelf Medearis (Walker Books)
- Examples of African art - carved statuettes and masks
- African thumb piano
- African fruits and vegetables
- Modelling clay, rolling pins, knives and tools
- Black, green and red paints
- Cake candles and holders - 1 black, 3 red and 3 green
- Notched plastic lids
- Black, green and red wool
- Strips of black, green and red paper or fabric
- Scissors
- Sticky tape
- Laminator
- Drums of different sizes
- CD of Zulu warrior dancers and drummers
- CD Player
- Internet Source: www.officialkwanzaawebsite.org

## Preparation

- Wedge the clay to remove air.
- Make notches around the outside edges of plastic lids.
- Find a suitable piece of music on the CD
- Read and discuss the story *Too Much Talk* with the children

## Notes for practitioners

- Creativity (*Kuumba*) is one of the seven basic values of African culture reinforced during Kwanzaa.
- The language used during the festival is Swahili.
- The sixth day of the festival of Kwanzaa celebrates creativity (*Kuumba*).
- The seventh day celebrates faith (*Imani*) and there is a feast (*Karamu*) when the children are given gifts that must include a book and an item representing African heritage, eg a carving.
- The festival of Kwanzaa, celebrated during the seven days between 26th December and 1st January, was created to celebrate and strengthen the family, community and culture of African-American people as well as Africans throughout the world through the seven basic principles or values (*Nguzo Saba*). These are: Unity (*Umoja*), Self-determination (*Kujichagulia*), Collective Work and Responsibility (*Ujima*), Cooperative Economics (*Ujamaa*), Purpose (*Nia*), Creativity (*Kuumba*) and Faith (*Imani*).
- Kwanzaa has seven basic symbols and two supplemental ones.

## Learning objectives

- To use media and materials in original ways, thinking about uses and purposes
- To represent ideas, thoughts and feelings through art and design, music, dance, imaginative role-play and stories
- To experience and respond to a celebration using all the senses

## What to do

### Role-play activity

- Talk about shock and surprise, running uphill and downhill, belief and disbelief. Mime and act out the characters' expressions and responses.
- Play the thumb piano rising and falling in pitch as the children pretend to run uphill and downhill.

### Music activity

- Play the music and ask the children to clap or stamp to the beat. (Zulu music has a strong repeating beat with a solo singer who sings a refrain to which the ensemble replies in harmony.)

### Craft activity

- To make a *Kinara*, roll clay into a fat sausage shape and flatten the sides and base so that it is stable. Push the seven candles with holders into the clay and decorate the outside by pressing in shapes. After it has hardened, paint in red, black and green.
- To make a *Mkeka tablemat*, wind wool around a plastic lid, pushing it into the notches. Weave in and out of the stretched wool using green, black and red lengths of wool or strips of paper or fabric (see diagram).

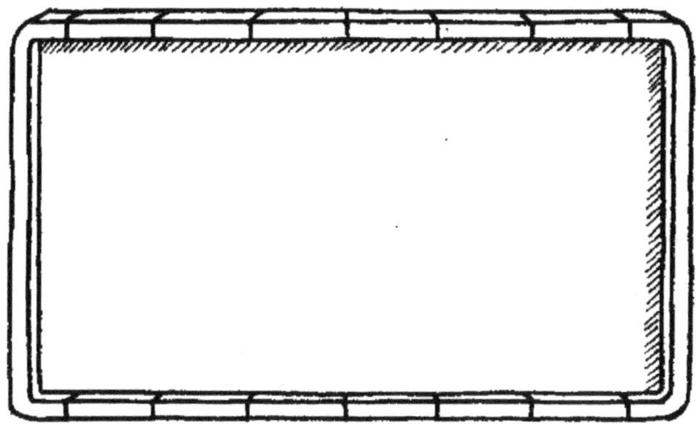

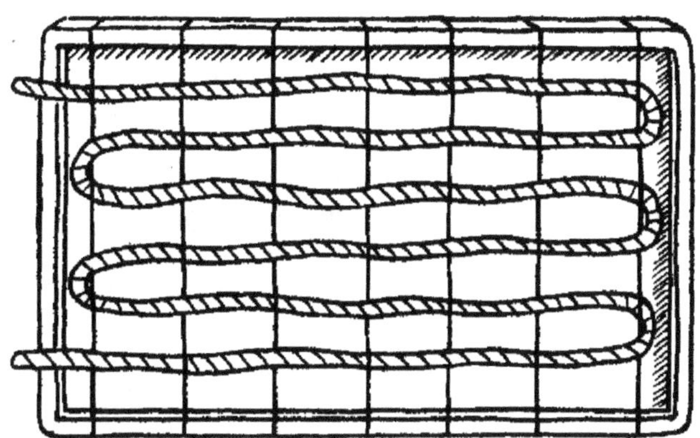

## Extensions/variations

- Weave a large brown 'straw' mat as a centrepiece for fruit and vegetables and laminate it.
- Provide drums for children to explore sounds and make up their own rhythms
- Discuss African art, patterns, costumes and illustrations in the story.
- Make a display on the green, red and black flag (Bendera) in front of a poster listing the seven principles (see Internet site).

## Links to home

- Invite parents, carers and families to join in with the celebrations.

## Exploring and Using Media and Materials

# Wedding

### Topic
Families

### Resources
- Books: *When Willy Went to the Wedding* by Judith Kerr (Picture Lions); *Maisie Middleton at the Wedding* by Nita Sowter (Picture Lions); *Who do you love?* by Martin Waddell (Walker Books); *Guess How Much I Love You* by Sam McBratney (Walker Books)
- Music and songs: 'Wedding March' by Felix Mendelssohn 'Magic Moments' sung by Perry Como, by Burt Bacharach; 'Congratulations' sung by Cliff Richard
- CD Player
- Wedding pictures and photographs
- 3 pieces of thick card longer and wider than the photographs
- Pencils, rulers and scissors
- PVA glue and spreaders
- Pasta in different shapes
- Cardboard boxes of different sizes
- Paints, pens or crayons
- Craft materials for decorating
- Dressing-up outfits

## Learning objectives
- To safely use and explore materials, tools and techniques
- To construct with a purpose in mind
- To build a repertoire of songs appropriate to the theme
- To communicate thoughts and feelings using songs, poems and stories
- To engage in imaginative role-play based on own experiences

## Preparation
- Collect photographs of weddings. Ask practitioners and families to donate any spare or duplicate pictures or take pictures of the children dressed up in wedding outfits for role-play.

## What to do
### Circle time
- Read stories: *When Willy Went to the Wedding* and *Maisie Middleton At The Wedding.*
- Discuss how people can keep memories of an event by taking photographs.

- Talk about the food at weddings and show pictures or photographs of wedding cakes.
- Ask if any of the children have attended a wedding and if anyone has been a bridesmaid or a page boy. Encourage them to talk about their experiences (especially if anything funny happened), the special clothes, food and presents and the significance of the occasion.

**Craft activity**

- Ask the children to place a photograph in the centre of the first of three pieces of card and draw round it with a pencil and a ruler. Support them in cutting out the rectangle they have drawn.
- Glue pasta shapes onto the card around the hole. Name the shapes and introduce new vocabulary and language, such as *repeating pattern, sequence* and *arrangement.*
- Glue the photograph into the centre of the second piece of card.
- Draw two diagonal lines up from the base of the third piece of card, to form a triangle. Cut along one line and fold along the other, to make a stand.
- Glue the three pieces of card together to make a photograph in a frame.

**Music activity**

- Play the songs 'Magic Moments' and 'Congratulations'.
- Ask when the songs should be played – at the beginning or end of the ceremony?
- Let the children choose two hymns for the wedding ceremony, then teach them to the group so they can sing them from memory.
- Play Wedding March ('Here Comes The Bride'), 'Magic Moments' and 'Congratulations'. Talk about the music being played at the beginning of the ceremony and the songs being sung at the end.
- Explain that the bride and groom can choose hymns or songs, music and poems for a Christian church wedding ceremony.

**Role-play activity**

- Talk about the key people attending a wedding, such as the bride, the groom, the vicar, priest or registrar, bridesmaids, page boys, best man, ushers, parents and witnesses.
- Involve all the children in dressing up and re-enacting a Christian wedding. Record the role-plays by taking photographs.

## Extensions/variations

- Read the stories *Who Do You Love?* and *Guess How Much I Love You.*
- Support children in making up poems and speeches for weddings.
- Invite parents or visitors into the setting to describe weddings in other faiths or cultures.
- Make a three-tier weddiing cake using cardboard boxes. Encourage the children to work together and to decorate each box using different materials. Discuss how the three tiers will balance.

## Links to home

- Ask parents to talk to their child about the parents' or relatives' wedding if appropriate.

**Exploring and Using Media and Materials**

# Trees

## Topic

Seasons

## Resources

- Non-fiction books or posters showing trees
- Thick paints: green, russet, orange, brown
- White paper
- Thick cardboard
- Black or brown crayons
- Brown fabric or brown wrapping paper
- Brown jumpers/T shirts etc for children
- Glue and glue spreaders
- Newspaper
- Scissors
- Elastic bands
- Painting: *Four Trees* by Egon Schiele

A high ratio of helpers to children is required if working near water or in public parks. Take note of any poisonous plants. Take care with scissors.

## Learning objectives

- To safely use and explore a variety of materials, tools, and techniques, experimenting with colour, design, texture, form and function
- To select tools and techniques to shape, assemble and join materials
- To select appropriate resources and adapt work where necessary
- To work cooperatively with other children

## Preparation

- Visit the park in advance to check health and safety, and to plan activities. It may be necessary to write up a risk assessment.

## What to do

**Circle time**

- Talk about the changes in appearance of trees through the seasons.

**Visit**

- Visit an environment that has different trees.
- Repeat the visit through different seasons.
- Make bark rubbings on brown wrapping paper and with brown crayons.
- Collect fallen leaves and twigs.

**Artwork**

- Look at the painting *Four Trees* and talk about the shape of the trees.
- Invite children to use their bark rubbings and to create leaves, blossoms and fruit to attach to clothing to make tree costumes. Remind them that costumes must be easy enough to put on and take off.

## Extension/variation

- Discuss how to attach leaves and blossoms so they can be dropped in the play *The Selfish Giant.*

## Links to home

- Ask parents to join the class in a walk round a suitable park or an ecology centre that has trees.

## Related activities


- Fruitful (see page 82)
- Autumn leaves (see page 113)
- Decorate a tree (see page 179)
- The Selfish Giant (see pages 132–133)

# Morris dancing

**Exploring and Using Media and Materials**

## Learning objectives

- To move rhythmically and imitate movement in response to music
- To make music and dance and experiment with ways of changing them
- To initiate new combinations of movement to expresss feelings and ideas
- To move with control and coordination
- To handle tools and materials safely and with increasing control

## Topic

Celebrations

## Resources

- Musical instruments, such as triangles or wood blocks
- Milk bottle tops
- String
- Coloured paper
- Wallpaper paste (without fungicide)
- Skewers or knitting needles
- Wire rack
- Scissors
- Thread

## Preparation

- Explain to the children that Morris dancing often takes place at Easter or spring festivals and carnivals.
- Collect and wash some milk bottle tops. Cut across one half and bend into a bell shape.
- Collect a number of small 'jingle bells' available from craft shops and catalogues
- For younger children or stronger costumes, you could use the bells on straps with velcro fastenings that are available from toy shops.

Take care with skewers and/or knitting needles.

## What to do

### Making the bells

- Help the children to make holes through the milk bottle tops 'bells' or to see the holes at the tops of the jingle bells, thread string through them and tie them around their ankles (not too tightly).

### Movement activity

- A large safe space will be required for this. Ask some of the children to play triangles or wood blocks while the others in the group perform Morris dancing, then allow the groups to swap places.
- Invite the children to march around in a procession and then to form a circle and move clockwise (to follow the path of the sun). While the music players bang loudly, the dancers jump into the air (this is to remind the wheat to grow high) and stamp their feet.

## Extension/variation

- Make jewels for a celebration. Cut out rectangles of coloured paper. Paste both sides with PVA glue. Wrap the pasted papers around skewers or knitting needles. Remove and place them on a wire rack to dry. Help the children to thread the beads on to a strong thread. Fasten with a double knot. Wear them with pride.

Exploring and Using Media and Materials

# Today's weather

## Topic
Weather

## Resources
- Book and CD of songs: *Start with a Song* by Mavis de Mierre (Brilliant Publications)
- Instruments
- Weather symbols on cards

## Learning objectives
- To build a repertoire of songs about the weather and sing them from memory
- To explore the different sounds of instruments

## Preparation
- The children should know the meaning of the weather symbols.

## What to do
### Music activity
- Ask the children what the day's weather is.
- Let a child select the appropriate symbol to display.
- On the back of the card list the appropriate songs. Ask the children which song they should sing from the list, eg:
  - Rain: 'In the Puddles'
  - Cold weather: 'It's a Cold Day' or 'On a Frosty Morning'
  - Snow: 'Snow Play' and 'Snowflakes'
  - Wind: 'Wind Song'
  - Sun: 'Sunshine'.

## Extension/variation
- Encourage the children to choose an instrument that makes a sound like the rain or wind, or evokes the feeling of sunshine or cold. Let them demonstrate their chosen instrument to the rest of the group.

## Related activity
- Freezing cold (see pages 134–135)

# The Alley Alley O

**Exploring and Using Media and Materials**

## Learning objectives

- To sing songs, create movements and experiment with ways of changing them
- To begin to build a repertoire of songs and dances
- To demonstrate control and coordination in large movements

## Preparation

- Prepare a large safe space against a wall. Be sensitive to any child who is not capable of joining in.

## What to do

**Movement activity**

- Ask the children to hold hands and form a long line. Sing the entire action song as the game progresses.
- **1st verse**

  *The big ship sails on the alley alley o,*
  *The alley alley o, the alley alley o.*
  *The big ship sails on the alley alley o,*
  *On the last day of September.*

  The child on the end nearest the wall puts his hand on the wall to make an archway. The child at the far end of the line (the leader) runs through the archway pulling all the others behind him/her. When the last child runs through the arch, the child touching the wall is twisted round and his/her arms are crossed.
  The leader runs through the next archway formed by the child touching the wall and the next child. He too will now have his arms crossed.
- Repeat this until all the line of children have their arms crossed. Join the ring by holding hands with the first and last child.
- **2nd verse**

  *The Captain said, 'It will never, never go', etc.* (all shake their heads sternly)

## Topic

Transport and travel

## Resources

- No special requirements

- **3rd verse**

  *The big ship sank to the bottom of the sea, etc.* (all crouch down and then get up again)
- **4th verse**

  *We'll dip our heads in the deep blue sea, etc.* (all bow their heads down as low as possible)

## Extension/variation

- Rowing boats. Invite the children to sit on the floor, in pairs, facing each other, as though they are in rowing boats. Ask them to hold hands and sway backwards and forwards as they sing the song: 'Row, row, row your boat ...' Sing any other verses that the adults or children know, or make up some of your own.

Exploring and Using Media and Materials

# The Selfish Giant

## Topics

Seasons/Gardening

## Resources

- Book: *The Selfish Giant* by Oscar Wilde (Puffin)
- Song: 'Here is My Head', from *Start with a Song* by Mavis de Mierre (Brilliant Publications)
- Music: Debussy Piano Works Volume
- CD Player
- Pink and white tissue paper
- PVA glue and spreaders
- Stapler and staples
- Scissors
- Cardboard boxes/card
- Paints and paintbrushes
- Chopping board
- Knife for practitioner
- 150g yoghurt pots with hole in base
- Old saucers
- Compost
- Medium sized plate
- Fork
- Tablespoon/teaspoon
- Rolling pin
- Mixing bowl
- 50g yoghurt pots for measuring
- Fresh peaches: 1 per tart
- 4 yoghurt pots plain flour (= 200g)
- 1 yoghurt pot sunflower margarine (= 60g)
- 1/4 teaspoon salt
- 3/4 full pot of cold water (= 50ml)
- 1 tsp sugar to sweeten
- Cooking tray
- For meringue: 1 egg white per tart, 1 yoghurt pot caster sugar (= 60g)

## Learning objectives

- To explore and compare peaches, pastry and meringue, using all the senses
- To imitate movement and dance in response to the music and story
- To create simple representations of events, people and objects
- To play cooperatively as part of a group to act out a storyline

## What to do

**Circle time**

- Read *The Selfish Giant* and tell the children that they are going to act out the story to music.
- Play the music and talk about how it can fit into the story. Then play the music and read the story at the same time.

**Role-play, music and dance activity**

- Play the CD and prompt and support the children in imitating and creating movements and dances for each part of the story:
- **Scene 1**: Children in garden – 'Passepied' from *Suite Bergamasque*
- **Scene 2**: Giant returns – 'Danse Bohemienne' played loudly with bass turned up, then turn down for children playing in the road

- **Scene 3**: Winter in the giant's garden – 'Danse'
- **Scene 4**: Spring has come and giant gets out of bed – 'Arabesque 2'
- **Scene 5**: Giant knocks down the wall – children's percussion
- **Scene 6**: Children come to play – 'Passepied'
- **Scene 7**: The giant is old, and sees the Christ child for the last time – 'Nocturne'.

**Art and craft activities**

- Make masks of the giant's face.
- Make a wall using decorated cardboard boxes or large construction kits.
- Draw tree shapes onto large pieces of card, cut them out and decorate them. Make stands for them with smaller pieces of card, or lean them against the wall.
- Make blossom for the trees, using pink and white tissue paper circles. Pinch them together in the centre and glue or staple them. Attach them to the trees using sticky tape for 'spring' and take them off for 'winter'

**Cookery activities**

- Read *The Selfish Giant* up to the part that describes the peach trees in the garden.
- Pass round the peaches and let the children examine them.
- Ask them to describe them, how they feel, smell and their colour and texture.
- Ask what they think is inside the peach.
- Cut the peach in half. Keep the stones (the seeds) to plant.
- Let each child taste a piece. Ask them what it tastes like.

**Method**

- Peel the peaches and chop them.
- Mix the salt into the flour and rub in fat. Stir in water and knead until smooth.
- Roll out the pastry and cut out a circular base.
- Put peaches and some sugar onto the base and cover the top by folding the pastry over them, or cut strips for a lattice or another circle as a lid.
- Cook on a greased baking tray in a moderate oven 175°C/375°F/Gas Mark 5 for 10-15 minutes.
- To make meringue, separate the egg yolks from the white and whisk the whites until stiff while adding caster sugar. Top the tart with the meringue and cook in a slow oven 150°C/300°F/Gas Mark 2 for about 15 minutes.

## Extensions/variations

- Plant the peach seeds into compost.
- Let the children take turns in looking after the seeds/plants.
- Sing 'Here is My Head' but change 'apple' to 'peach'.

## Links to home

- Ask parents if they would like to come in to help with the cookery or try the recipe with their children at home.
- Plan and create a performance of *The Selfish Giant* with the children. Invite parents to supply costumes and to come to watch the performance.

An adult should put food in and out of the oven.

Check for wheat allergy.

Supervise the use of scissors and staplers.

**Exploring and Using Media and Materials**

# Freezing cold

## Topics

Water/Weather

## Resources

- Poem: 'Cold', from *Out and About Through the Year* by Shirley Hughes (Walker Books) 'Ice' by Walter de la Mare from *The Oxford Treasury of Children's Poems* (Oxford University Press)
- Songs: 'The North Wind Doth Blow' and 'Here We Go Round the Mulberry Bush' from *This Little Puffin* compiled by Elizabeth Matterson (Puffin); 'It's a Cold Day', from *Start with a Song* by Mavis de Mierre (Brilliant Publications)
- CD Player
- Computer with draw program, printer and paper
- Books or photographs showing the Antarctic continent at the South Pole
- Dressing up outfits suitable for cold weather
- Ice cubes/blocks of ice
- Fabrics and threads
- Cardboard
- Stiff paper
- PVA glue and spreaders
- Paints and paintbrushes
- Scissors

⚠ Do not use ice straight out of the freezer. Let it warm up first.
Supervise the use of scissors.

## Learning objectives

- To safely use and explore a variety of materials, tools and techniques, experimenting with colour, design, texture, shape, form and space
- To combine different media to create new effects in collage
- To select and use technology for a particular purpose
- To sing familiar songs and build a repertoire of favourite songs
- To intiate new combinations of mime, movement and gesture in order to express and respond to feelings, ideas, thoughts and experiences
- To move rhythmically and imitate movement in response to music
- To represent ideas, thoughts and feelings through engaging in imaginative role-play

## Preparation

- Load the draw program on to the computer.
- Listen to the CD to find the relevant part of the music (2 minutes after the beginning). In the second movement of the 'Prelude' the

soprano begins to sing and a wind machine can be heard. The music begins to swirl into a crescendo.

## What to do

### Circle time

- Read the poem 'Cold' and look at the illustrations. Talk with the children about how they feel in cold weather and what they do when they are cold.
- Ask the children whether they have been outside in a snowstorm and, if so, how they walked and whether they shivered.
- Tell the children that the piece of music was written for a film called *Scott of the Antarctic.*
- Listen to the music with the children and ask them what kind of place they think the Antarctic would be. After discussion explain that it is very cold and dangerous with nothing there but ice, snow and wind.
- Show some photographs of the Antarctic to the children.
- Pass round the small block of ice.
- Ask the children to describe its texture and how they feel touching the ice.
- Read the poem 'Ice'. Ask if the poem is a good description of ice.

### Art activity

- Talk with the children about icicles and how they hang down in 'spiky' shapes. If it is cold enough, find some outside for them to look at.
- Encourage the children to draw 'spiky' shapes on to cardboard, then connect them so the card looks like a jigsaw. The design could be made with a draw program on the computer.
- Cut out the shapes and cover some with fabric and threads. Paint some of the shapes.
- Stick the shapes back together like a jigsaw.
- Encourage the children to talk about what they are making.

### Music and dance activities

- Ask the children to pretend that they are in a snowstorm. Encourage them to mime pushing against the cold wind.
- Suggest that they be the wind, and mime how it swirls around.
- Play the music and ask them to move to the music this time.
- Learn and sing 'The North Wind Doth Blow'.
- Ask them to pretend to shiver like the cold robin.
- Sing 'Here We Go Round the Mulberry Bush' and do the actions.

### Role-play activity

- Encourage the children to dress up for cold weather and pretend they are walking in a snow storm or on a very cold freezing day.
- Support them by introducing new descriptive vocabulary for language development, such as: *chilly*, *frozen*, *icy*, *snowstorm* and *blizzard.*

## Extensions/variations

- Sing 'It's a Cold Day' and do the actions.
- Encourage the children to add more verses, eg flap arms, put on gloves.
- Encourage the children to make up a story or poem about being cold.

## Related activities


- Add water (see page 115)
- Storm (see page 144)


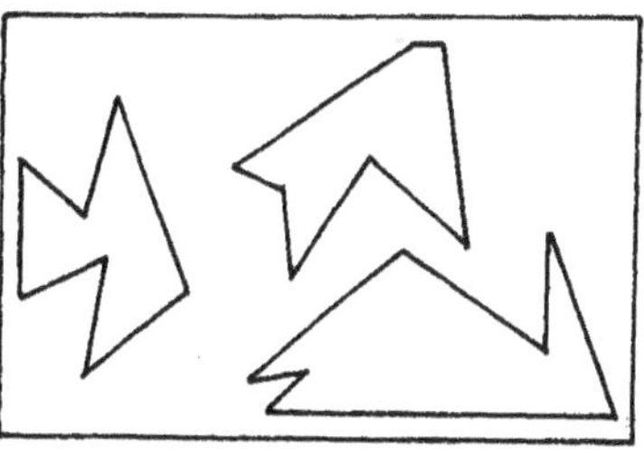

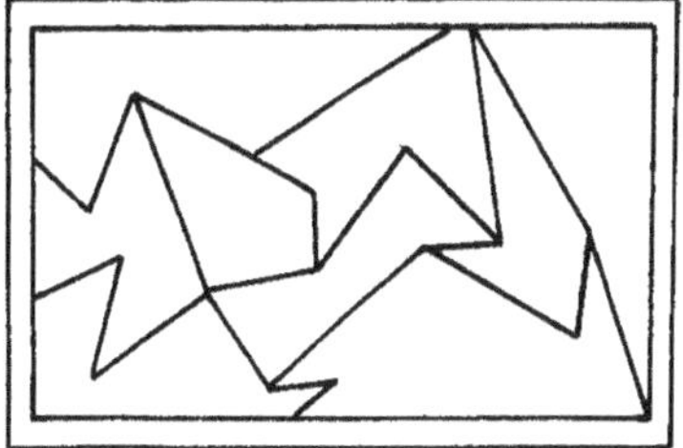

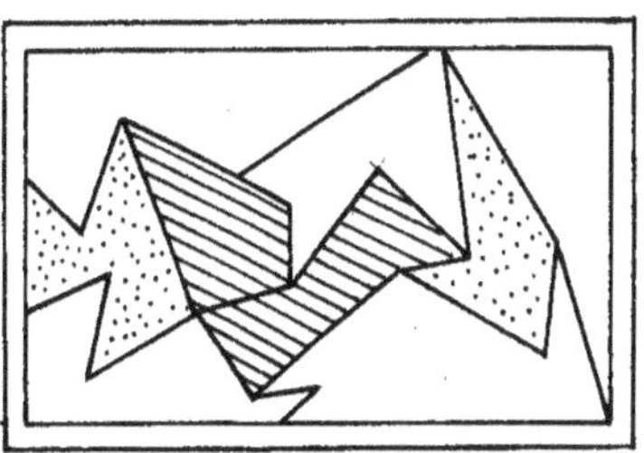

Exploring and Using Media and Materials

# Lines

## Topics

Shapes/Transport and travel

## Resources

- Paintings: *Untitled #10* by Agnes Martin; *½x Series (Blue)* by Robert Mangold; *Onement III* by Barnett Newman
- Paints
- Paintbrushes
- Trays for mixing colours
- Paper
- Straight-edged objects, eg rulers
- Pencils
- Coloured construction bricks and base

## Learning objectives

- To construct with a purpose in mind
- To use simple tools and techniques competently and appropriately
- To experiment with colour, design and form
- To recognize, create and describe patterns

## Notes for practitioner

- *Untitled #10* is composed of a repeating pattern of straight thick grey and medium thickness white lines divided by a thin graphite line.
- *½ x Series (Blue)* is made up of panels, the shadows creating straight lines, as well as diagonal pencil lines.
- *Onement III* shows a vertical straight red line through the middle of a maroon background

## What to do

**Circle time**

- Ask where the children have seen straight (parallel) lines, eg railway lines, on the middle of the road, zigzag lines on the road by school, edges of the pavement, parking restrictions, etc.
- Show painting(s) and ask if they can see any patterns.

**Art activity**

- Suggest they make pictures to show straight lines.
- Encourage the children to mix colours to show contrasts between the lines.

## Extension/variation

- Build constructions with coloured bricks to show straight lines.

## Links to home

- Ask parents to point out straight and parallel lines in the environment.

## Related activities

- Bricks (see page 93)
- Crossing the road (see page 147)

# Marzipan play

**Exploring and Using Media and Materials**

## Learning objectives

- To manipulate materials to achieve a planned effect
- To use simple materials competently and appropriately
- To experiment with colour, design, texture and form
- To appreciate the need for good hygeine

## What to do

### Craft activity

- Make marzipan sweets for Christmas, or any other celebration (such as bazaars, festivals, parties or birthdays). Ensure that the children wash their hands before touching the food.
- Give each child a small piece of marzipan and ask them to roll it out with a rolling pin. Suggest that they squeeze and roll the marzipan into balls or shapes of fruits for example, apples, oranges or pears.
- Encourage new vocabulary and language development by using a variety of descriptive words, such as *squeeze*, *poke*, *twist*, while playing alongside the children.
- Offer additional resources and tools as required.
- Brush the shapes with food colouring to form blush on apples, oranges.

### Circle time

- Talk about the activity and invite the children to say what they enjoyed most. Encourage them to remember the colours, smell and texture of the marzipan.

## Extensions/variations

- Cut coloured cellophane into strips and wrap the marzipan sweets. Twist the edges like crackers.
- Make boxes for the sweets. Line them with tissue paper and decorate with patterns made with paint or gummed shapes.

## Related activity

- Make Christmas decorations (see page 87)

## Topic

Celebrations

## Resources

- Aprons
- Ready-made marzipan
- Rolling pins
- Pastry cutters
- Scissors
- Food colouring: red, green, yellow, orange
- Clean paintbrushes
- Coloured cellophane
- Paints
- Paintbrushes
- Small boxes
- Tissue paper
- Gummed shapes

Ensure children wash hands before touching food. Be watchful of scissors and tools. This activity is not suitable if any children in the group have a nut allergy

# Expressive Arts and Design

# Being Imaginative

From a very early age, most children begin to pretend. They may 'drink' from an empty toy cup, hold a building block to their ear as though it is a telephone, run to pick up a doll, saying 'The baby's crying!', or squirm across the floor to be a worm or a caterpillar. If adults join in with the play and offer further ideas to enhance the make-believe, the children will develop confidence in inventing imaginary worlds, characters and scenarios and in acting out familiar experiences and stories.

If a variety of interesting resources are made available, children will begin to represent and communicate their ideas through drawing and mark making, learning to choose colours and develop preferences and eventually creating representations of people, animals, objects, vehicles, buildings, events and experiences.

Children should be encouraged to use movement to express their ideas and feelings and to create movements in response to music and rhythm. Practitioners can offer opportunities for them to learn and sing songs and encourage them also to make up their own songs, tunes and rhythms. Actions and gestures, miming and acting contribute to imaginative role-play and can help children to imitate and practise the things that adults do, re-create their own experiences and favourite stories, or introduce new narratives and storylines into their play. Drama activities should be initiated and led by confident practitioners whenever appropriate and the children encouraged to extend the ideas in their own chosen directions..

Confidence in speech, vocabulary and social skills are developed when children play cooperatively within a group to create and act out a scenario, experience, narrative or story. Less confident children can be encouraged to play alongside others at first, following the same theme, and supported as they gradually learn to join in and offer ideas too.

Practitioners must allow children time and opportunities to develop competence in using media and materials. They may then seek to encourage them to think of how to use their skills and experiences in original ways, to create satisfying projects, explore challenging ideas or make items for a purpose, such as props for their role-play.

It is vital that children in the foundation stage are encouraged to develop their imaginations and feel able to express their ideas, thoughts and feelings creatively through design and technology, art and crafts, music and dance, role-play and drama.

# Miss Polly had a Dolly

**Being imaginative**

## Learning objectives

- To create new combinations of movement and gesture in order to express and respond to ideas, stories, rhythm and music
- To represent their own thoughts and ideas through music, dance and role-play

## What to do

**Movement activity**

- Read or sing the song 'Miss Polly Had a Dolly'. Explain the actions to the children. They may stand up or sit on the floor together.
- Now change the words and perform the relevant actions:

  *Miss Polly had a dolly who was not any better* (rock dolly)
  *So she wrote to the doctor with a letter, letter, letter* (writing movements on hand)
  *The doctor came and rang the bell, bell, bell* (ring bell)
  *'Please help my dolly to be well, well, well.'*
  *The doctor took her temperature* (put thermometer in dolly's mouth)
  *And he said, 'There's really not much wrong with her*
  *She just wants to stay in her bed, bed, bed*
  *And she should start to walk around instead.'* (walk around, or make walking movements with fingers)
  *Miss Polly took her dolly out of bed, bed, bed* (lift out dolly)
  *She looked at her dolly and she said, said, said* (wag fingers at her)
  *'You're playing a naughty game, game, game*
  *But I love you, dolly, just the same, same, same.'* (rock dolly)

- Suggest that the children make up other verses of their own or similar songs for other toys. Encourage all original ideas and support children to adapt them as necessary to fit the activity.

### Topic
Health

### Resources
- 'Miss Polly Had a Dolly' from *Okki-tokki-unga* (A & C Black)
- Photos of family people or pictures cut from magazines
- Scissors
- Card
- Drinking straws
- Glue
- Egg boxes
- Ribbon
- Paints
- Paintbrushes

## Extensions/variations

- Make a dolly on a stick. Cut out photos or magazine figures and stick to card. Stick each figure to the top of a straw. Use them as you would use puppets.
- Make doll's hats. Use individual egg carton portions. Paint and decorate. Thread ribbon through the sides to tie on to the doll.

Being imaginative

# Hairdressing salon

## Topic
Myself

## Resources
- Unbreakable mirrors
- Hairbrushes
- Combs
- Old shirts or aprons
- Empty plastic bottles
- Wool in 'hair colours'
- Glue
- Paper
- Pencils
- Crayons

## Learning objectives
- To engage in imaginative role-play based on own first hand experiences
- To use available resources to create props to support role-play
- To play cooperatively as part of a group to develop and act out a theme
- To use and manipulate one-handed tools and simple techniques competently and appropriately
- To understand the need to keep hair in a clean and healthy condition and begin to manage personal needs by brushing or combing hair
- To take turns and show sensitivity to other's needs and feelings

## What to do
**Role play area**
- Offer the children the opportunity of a hairdressing session. Provide clean combs, brushes and plastic (unbreakable) mirrors. Use aprons or old shirts for gowns. Provide clean, washed, empty plastic containers for pretend shampoo and conditioner.
- Talk about hair and how important it is to keep hair brushed and clean. Invite children to take turns to visit the hairdressing salon. Make sure that they each have a turn to be a hairdresser if they wish to.
- Provide sufficient time for the children to find out everything they would like to know.
- Children may brush or comb a friend's hair, if the friend is willing, using that person's comb and/or brush, or ask the adults to join in with the role-play and be customers in the salon. Ensure the children act gently.
- Be sensitive to cultures where the hair is permanently covered.

## Extensions/variations
- Invite children to learn to make plaits. Teach them first with several strands of wool separated into three sections.
- Encourage children to watch each other as they move their heads, to see how some hair sways as the head moves, while some (very short or very curly) hair does not appear to move. Outside, observe how hair blows in the wind.
- Ask children if they can draw the shapes of their friends' hair. Some will be straight, some curly, some longer and some shorter. Some may be worn in plaits, bunches, pony tails or other variations such as dreadlocks.
- Using wool, make a textured portrait of someone's hair shape and style, matching the colour as far as possible.

## Links to home
- Ask children to bring in their own combs and brushes (labelled with their names).

## Related activity
- Hygiene in role-play (see page 65)

# Can you be a tree?



## Learning objectives

- To introduce a narrative into imaginative role-play
- To use creative movement and actions to express experiences
- To move with confidence in a range of ways, safely negotiating space within a group of other children
- To handle materials and tools effectively in creative art work
- To experiment with colour and design

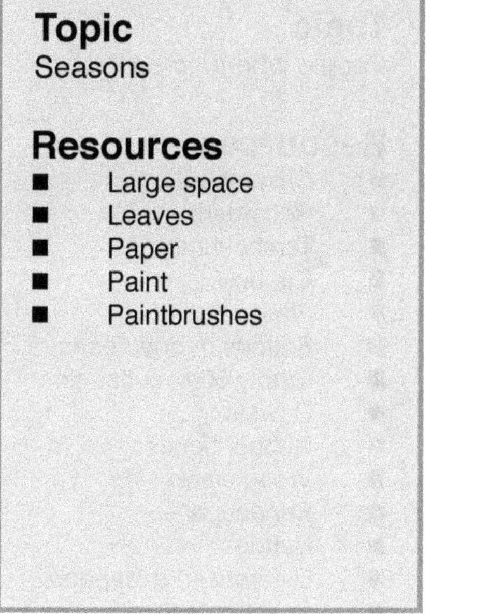

### Topic
Seasons

### Resources
- Large space
- Leaves
- Paper
- Paint
- Paintbrushes

## What to do

**Circle time**

- Discuss the seasons and how you could represent them as trees and creatures. Talk about the differences between the seasons and what grows in spring, summer, autumn and winter. Mention weather, temperatures, food, clothes and animals being born, living, feeding and hibernating.

**Movement activity**

- Invite the children to pretend to be trees, growing from acorns or seeds curled up in the ground and stretching up to be very tall. Suggest that they become bees, buzzing around and looking for flowers.
- Ask them to imagine that they are trees in autumn, swaying in the wind, and leaves falling to the ground.
- Encourage them to act out some of the young animals who are born in the spring. They could pretend to be baby birds standing on the edge of a nest and then flying away, or baby lambs skipping and hopping in a field.
- Ask them to be trees on a hot summer day, spreading their leaves to the sunshine, and people or animals lying in the shade under the trees.
- There will be many young animals born in the spring. Pretend to be baby birds and stand nervously on the edge of the nest. Flap arms and pretend to fly away. Pretend to be baby lambs and skip and hop.

## Extension/variation

- Collect some leaves and use them for printing. Gently paint one leaf at a time and press it onto paper to make a print of its pattern. Allow children to mix colours and create their own designs. They might try to match the shades of the leaves and make a picture of a tree, or they might prefer to make up imaginative colours and abstract patterns.

Being imaginative

# Thank you for the music

## Topic
People who help us

## Resources
- Chime bars
- Recorders
- Tambourines
- Cat bells
- Plastic bottles
- Buttons or dried peas
- Empty 500g coffee tins
- Dowels
- Rubber bands
- Wood blocks
- Sandpaper
- Buttons
- Different sorts of paper
- Foam or felt
- Glue
- CD player
- Variety of types of music, including lively music and peaceful music
- Kitchen implements

## Learning objectives
- To express and respond to experiences through making music
- To respond to music by creating movements
- To play alongside other children who are engaged in the same theme
- To represent ideas, thoughts and feelings through sounds and music
- To sing songs, make music and dance and experiment with ways of changing them
- To participate in craft activities to enhance the music theme, using a range of media and experimenting with design and function

## Preparation
- Make a display of an assortment of sound makers.

## What to do
**Circle time**
- Discuss music with the children and talk about how it can make them feel happy or sometimes sad. Ask them to imagine living in a world with no music and to consider the teachers and musicians who make beautiful sounds to give us pleasure. Ask children if they listen to music at home and if they would like to learn to play an instrument.
- Ask whether any of the children have ever been to a concert or a musical show.
- Discuss which types of music make them want to tap their feet or hands or to dance. Ask whether they prefer loud or soft music.

**Music activities**
- Have a music-making session. Help them to explore what happens to their minds and bodies when performing or listening to music.
- Begin by clapping out the rhythm of the children's names and asking if they can guess the names from the beats. Sing simple nursery rhymes, clapping along to the rhythm.
- Play them some simple music, either on the piano or a CD. Ask them to choose which percussion instruments they would like to use to accompany the music.
- Introduce new descriptive vocabulary by thinking of words to describe the music, such as: *calm*, *peaceful, soothing, sad*, *happy*, *lively, exciting* or *loud*
- Play some lively music and invite the children to move to it as they interpret the sound. Do the same with peaceful music.

**Art activity**
- Fill some plastic bottles with buttons or dried peas and shake them. Use empty coffee tins for drums. Use pieces of dowel for the drumsticks. Cover wooden blocks with sandpaper.

## Extensions/variations
- Crumple up paper for sounds, for example newspaper, cellophane, tissue paper.
- Tap two dowels or sticks together. You could decorate the sticks with designs.
- Add some foam and felt pieces to cover the ends of the dowels for a softer effect and a safer activity.
- Use kitchen implements to provide accompaniment.

## Links to home
- Invite any family members who play instruments to come into the setting to play and talk to the children.

# A foggy day



## Learning objectives

- To engage in imaginative role-play based on first-hand experiences
- To create representations of events
- To introduce a storyline into play
- To represent ideas, thoughts and feelings through music, movement and role-play
- To negotiate space, adjusting speed or changing direction to avoid obstacles

## Topic

Weather

## Resources

- Wheeled vehicle toys
- Chairs
- Boxes
- 'Fog' by the Scunthorpe and Teachers' Centre from Harlequin (A & C Black)
- Pictures of foggy scenes. If possible have some from long ago, showing streets shrouded in mist
- Dolls or soft toys
- Fluorescent paper
- Paper
- Grey paint
- Paintbrushes
- Wax crayons
- Thin fabric (eg chiffon scarf or a thin, gauzy veil)

## Preparation

- Place several obstacles, such as chairs, boxes, wheeled vehicles, in a large, safe space.
- Teach the children the song 'Fog'.

## What to do

### Circle time

- Talk about fog and ask the children if they can remember experiencing it. Show them some pictures of fogs long ago when the streets were completely shrouded in mist. Ask them what it must have felt like trying to find their way through the traffic and what might have happened if the traffic had tried to drive too fast. Ask them whether they think that there were any traffic lights and whether people would have been walking amongst the traffic.

### Movement activity

- Ask the children to hold hands with their doll or toy (their 'pretend' child) and find their way to school. Play or ask them to sing the song 'Fog'. Tell them that the obstacles you have placed around are cars, buses and lorries stuck in the fog. The children should walk very slowly through the fog from one side of the room to the other, avoiding the obstacles on the way and keeping their child safe beside them.
- Discuss how they could make it easy for the drivers to see them. For example, they could wear bright luminous or fluorescent clothing, bands, tabards or waistcoats.

## Extensions/variations

- Make a foggy picture. Ask one half of the group to draw a street scene and the other half to draw a country scene using wax crayons. When the pictures are completed, use a thin wash of pale grey paint and brush it across the coloured pictures.
- Peer through the fog. Has anyone a chiffon scarf or a thin gauzy veil? Look through the material and find out what can be seen. Ask the children if they can identify anything or anyone in the room through the material and if they can tell who is speaking just by identifying their voice.

Being imaginative

# Storm

## Topics
Seasons/Weather

## Resources
- Book: *Chimp and Zee and the Big Storm* by Catherine and Laurence Anholt (Frances Lincoln)
- Thick paints: blue, dark green, white, black
- Spoons
- Combs
- Toothbrushes
- Sponges
- Printing roller
- White lining paper
- Pale blue sugar paper
- Paintings: *Pont Neuf in Paris* by Louis Anquetin; *Sea and Light Clouds* by Emil Nolde; *Starry Night* or *Road with Cypress and Star* by Vincent van Gogh
- Music: Overture from *The Hebrides* 'Fingal's Cave' by Felix Mendelssohn
- Glue and spreaders
- Cardboard boxes
- Collage materials
- CD player

## Learning objectives
- To choose particular colours to use for a purpose
- To use media and materials in original ways
- To represent thoughts and feelings through art and design
- To experiment with colour and texture
- To handle equipment and tools effectively

## What to do
**Circle time**
- Read *Chimp and Zee and the Big Storm.*
- Show the paintings and ask how the children can tell the pictures show a storm.
- Talk about:
  - the composition (in *Pont Neuf in Paris*)
  - the horses' manes and woman's cloak and scarf are flying; the woman grips her hat
  - clouds and colours used (*Sea and Light Clouds* uses stormy colours and a lot of movement in the sky and sea)
  - the texture of the paint (in *Starry Night* or *Road with Cypress and Star* the paints are thick and have been vigorously painted).

**Art activity**
- For finger painting, support spreading the paint on a plastic surface. A plastic-topped table is ideal.
- The children can comb through the paint to make waves.
- Support making a monotype by laying paper on top of the paint. Press over gently at first, then try further prints by pressing harder.
- Show how mixing with black or white alters the tone of the colour.
- Encourage experimentation to get different textures, eg using a toothbrush to splatter paint.
- Play 'Fingal's Cave' while painting.

## Extension/variation
- Paint or make a collage of a large wave on cardboard for a seaside project.

## Links to home
- Ask for old combs.

## Related activities
- Under my umbrella (see page 97)
- Weather dance (see page 175)
- Windy weather (see page 183)
- Running water (see page 117)

# Family fingers

**Being imaginative**

## Learning objectives

- To initiate new combinations of movement and gesture to express ideas
- To sing to self and make up simple songs
- To join in and play cooperatively as part of a group to develop role-play and singing

## What to do

**Circle time**

- Read *Toby's Doll's House* and talk about the titles of relatives (uncle, aunt, etc) and who's who.

**Music time**

- Learn some finger play games and songs.
- Make up a finger play song based upon a family, eg starting at the thumb:

*Here comes Mum on her way*
*Here comes Dad lots to say*
*Here comes Brother very tall*
*Here comes Sister not so small*
*Here comes Baby…*(children add their own words)

*Here comes Grandma fat and jolly*
*Here comes Grandad driving a lorry*
*Here comes Uncle very smart*
*Here comes Auntie with home-made tart*
*Here comes Cousin…*(children add their own words)

## Extension/variation

- Encourage the children to role-play and sing using finger puppets.

## Links to home

- Ask parents to talk about who's who among their relatives.

## Topic

Families

## Resources

- Book: *Toby's Doll's House* by Raynhild Scamell and Adrian Reynolds (David & Charles Children's Books)
- Song: 'Tommy Thumb', from *This Little Puffin* compiled by Elizabeth Matterson (Puffin)
- Book: *Clap Your Hands Finger Rhymes* compiled by Sarah Hayes (Walker Books)
- Finger puppets

**Alternative books**

- *First Verses: Finger Rhymes* edited by John Foster (OUP)
- *Finger Fun and Action Rhymes: Big Book* by Wendy Body (Longman)

# Hello Grandma

## Topic
Families

## Resources
- Book: *The Monster Who Loved Telephones* by John Agard (Longman Book Project)
- Toy telephones

Children should have some understanding of how to use a telephone and practise while playing, but should not use one alone.

## Learning objectives
- To notice what adults do, imitating what is observed, and then doing it spontaneously when the adult is not there
- To introduce a storyline or narrative into play
- To play cooperatively with another child to develop a narrative.

## What to do
**Circle time**
- Read *The Monster Who Loved Telephones*.
- Invite the children to say why they think using the telephone can sometimes make people happy or discuss telephone conversations that would be happy ones.
- Ask if there is anyone that they talk to on the telephone, such as a family member who does not live with them.
- Explain how to make an emergency telephone call, but make it very clear that children must never do this other than in an absolute emergency and that they should not try to telephone anybody without an adult's help.

**Table activity**
- In pairs, the children could talk to each other on the toy telephones and pretend that they are talking to a relative such as Grandma.
- Discuss what the children could talk about.

## Extension/variation
- Act as a scribe and encourage the children to dictate stories about when their grandma (or other relatives) came to visit.

## Links to home
- Ask parents to teach stranger safety, but also to teach their child to know their name, address and telephone number.

# Crossing the road



## Learning objectives

- To engage in imaginative role-play based on own first-hand experiences
- To play cooperatively as part of a group to develop and act out storylines and narratives
- To represent thoughts and feelings through music, role-play and stories
- To understand safety features within the local environment
- To understand why and how people must behave safely near roads

## Preparation

- Draw a road on the playground using chalk. The road should be big enough for use by the outdoor wheeled toys. Include a road crossing.

## What to do

**Outside activity**

- Play at crossing the road. Teach the children the Green Cross Code.
- Support the children as they learn and use new vocabulary and develop language skills by using words such as: *stop, look, listen, go*, *wait*, *left*, *right*, and *cross*.

**Imaginative play activity**

- Use the play mat and/or construction toys and vehicles to role play crossing the road.

**Visit**

- Organize a trip out of the setting to use a pelican crossing, and observe the traffic lights.

**Music activity**

- Learn a road safety song (see Resources).

## Extensions/variations

- If there is a local crossing patrol person, invite him/her to speak to the children in the setting.
- Read 'Lollypop Lady'.

## Links to home

- Ask parents to reinforce the use of pelican crossings, and the Green Cross Code.
- Invite parents and carers to volunteer to come into the setting and practise the Green Cross Code with the children during role-play, or to accompany practitioners and children to use a local pelican crossing.

## Topics

People who help us/
Transport and travel

## Resources

- Chalk
- Outdoor wheeled toys
- Traffic lights
- Construction kit to make wheeled vehicles, roadways, traffic lights
- Play mat with town streets
- Toy vehicles
- Songs: Safety songs from *This Little Puffin* compiled by Elizabeth Matterson (Puffin)
- Poem: 'Lollypop Lady' by John Agard, from *The Oxford Treasury of Children's Poems* (OUP)

⚠ Ensure proper adult:child ratio for visit.

## Related activities

- Hats (see page 110–111)
- Lines (see page 136)

Being imaginative

# A nice cup of tea

## Topics

Food and shopping/Water

## Resources

- Book: 'Mad Hatter's Tea Party', from *Alice in Wonderland* by Lewis Carroll
- Song: 'I'm a Little Teapot', from *This Little Puffin* compiled by Elizabeth Matterson (Puffin)
- Soft chairs
- Table
- Plates, cups and saucers
- Teapot, milk jug and sugar bowl
- Spoons
- Brown paper cut in squares to look like sliced bread
- Yellow, pink, green, red paper (to make sandwiches)

## Learning objectives

- To pretend that one object represents another, especially when objects have characteristics in common
- To notice what adults do, imitating what is observed and then doing it spontaneously when the adult is not there
- To play alongside other children who are engaged in the same theme

## Preparation

- Set up the role-play area as a room in a house with table and chairs.

## What to do

**Circle time**

- Read the excerpt 'Mad Hatter's Tea Party' from *Alice in Wonderland.*

**Home corner activity**

- Ask for a cup of tea, and encourage the children to pretend making a cup of tea.
- Encourage the children to pretend to make and serve sandwiches.

## Extension/variation

**Music activity**

- Learn the action song 'I'm a Little Teapot'.

## Links to home

- Suggest to parents that they allow their child to help put out crockery and cutlery on the table.

# Noah's music



## Learning objective

- To create movement in response to music
- To represent ideas and feelings through music, dance and role-play

## Topic

Animals

## Resources

- Book: Any Noah story such as *Professor Noah's Spaceship* by Brian Wildsmith (OUP)
- Music: *Carnival of Animals suite* by Camille Saint-Saëns
  Select:
  1 Royal March of the Lion
  2 Hens and Cocks
  4 Tortoises
  5 The Elephant
  6 Kangaroos
  7 Aquarium
  8 Rabbits and Hares
  19 Aviary
  23 Finale
- CD player

## What to do

### Circle time

- Read a story about Noah and his ark.
- Talk to the children about how the animals went into the ark, two by two. Discuss how the animals may have arrived at the ark. Compare how the children arrive at the setting, and then walk into the room.
- Go through the different animals represented in *Carnival of Animals* and ask how the animals would move as they make their way to the ark.

### Dance activity

- Play *Carnival of Animals* and ask the children if they can work out which pieces of music describes the elephant, the lion and the tortoise. Encourage them to explain how they know.
- Ask, 'How are the animals moving?' Ask the children to move like each of the animals.

## Extensions/variations

- Ask how shoals of fish move. Choose three leaders for the children to follow. Point out that they need to be aware of the other children around them, and not to bump into each other. Play 'Aquarium' and ask the children to move to the music.
- Encourage the groups to move in the space individually and as a team imaginatively, eg moving across the room in an 'S' shape while swaying their bodies.

## Related activity

- Noah's animals (page 109)

**Being imaginative**

# Rockin' Robin

## Topic
Celebrations

## Resources
- Song: 'Rockin' Robin' by J. Thomas, sung by Jackson 5 or Bobby Day. For the words search 'rockin robin' on the Internet
- CD player
- Bird masks
- Bird wings and tails made from brown paper
- Red jumpers/T shirts
- Brown or black or pink tights

## Learning objectives
- To capture experiences and responses with music and dance
- To play cooperatively as part of a group
- To represent ideas, thoughts and feelings through dance

## Preparation
- This activity is most appropriate during the Christmas period.
- Make bird masks, wings and tails.

## What to do
### Music activity
- Play the song to the children and discuss making up a dance to the music.
- Ask the children to clap to the beat, then sway to the beat.

- Teach the chorus and when to sing 'Tweet'.
- Go through each verse and ask for suggestions on what movements they should make to the music.
- Draw a line on the floor for the children to stand on.
- Ask the children to do their own dance to the music on the spot as if they are robins perched on a branch.
- Give them time to practise.

## Extension/variation
### Performance
- Dress up as robins and dance!

## Links to home
- Ask to borrow clothes to make up costumes.
- Invite parents to attend the performance.

## Related activities
- Stuck up the chimney (see page 162)

# Sing to your pet

**Being imaginative**

## Learning objectives

- To sing to self and make up simple songs with animals sounds and humming
- To represent ideas and thoughts by including animal sounds and humming
- To explore and use the different sounds of percussion instruments to accompany the songs

## Topic

Animals

## Resources

- Choral and orchestra music: *African Sanctus* by David Fanshawe
- Percussion instruments
- Song: 'I Went to Visit a Farm One Day', from *This Little Puffin* compiled by Elizabeth Matterson (Puffin)
- CD player

## Preparation

- Find 'Chants' (Track 10) on the CD, Masai Milking Song (Kenya, 1972) and Turkana Cattle Song (Northern Kenya, 1970).

## What to do

### Music activity

- Explain to the children that the women believe that if they do not sing to the cows, then the cows may not give them enough milk.
- Play the music and ask whether the men sound like cattle lowing.
- Ask how many different instruments can be heard within the music (eg horns, tin whistles, drums and bells).
- Talk with the children about their pets. Encourage them to make up a song to sing to their pet. It does not have to rhyme or even have words.

## Extensions/variations

- Encourage the children to make up an accompaniment to their song with a percussion instrument of their choice.
- Sing 'I Went to Visit a Farm One Day'.

## Related activities

- Tra-la (see page 154)
- Kwanzaa (see pages 124–125)

# Sing a song of soap

## Topic
Food and shopping

## Resources
- Book: *Teddybears Go Shopping* by Susanna Gretz (A & C Black)
- Flip chart
- Felt-tipped pen
- Picture dictionaries
- Percussion instruments

## Learning objectives
- To sing to self and make up simple songs to a beat with words
- To make up rhythms
- To understand and appreciate rhyme

## Preparation
- Make a list of items you can buy that rhyme, eg:
  - Boiled beef and lettuce leaf
  - Sherbet pips and crinkly chips
  - Sudsy soap and fluffy coat

## What to do
### Circle time
- Read *Teddybears Go Shopping.*
- Support children as they learn new vocabulary and develop languages skills through naming shops, such as *grocery*, *greengrocery*, *bakery*, *chemist*, *supermarket*, *butcher* and *supermarket.*
- Further develop languages skills by talking about what each shop might sell.
- Robert Teddybear suggests that the shopping list sounds like a song. Ask why he thinks this. (It rhymes and has a rhythm.)
- Ask the children to make up a song with pairs of rhyming products, like the Teddybears' song, during the session (while they are doing other tasks).
- Suggest using the dictionaries.
- Suggest that the children ask you to write down any ideas they have during the session on to the flip chart.
- Share the ideas at the end of the session.

## Extension/variation
- Ask children to decide how the song should be sung, which instruments should accompany it and how they should be played.

## Links to home
- Ask that parents play rhyming games with their child.

# Rattle those pans

Being imaginative

## Learning objectives
- To use what has been learnt about media and materials in original ways for particular purposes
- To make up rhythms
- To explore the different sounds of instruments and items used as instruments

## Preparation
- Watch the DVD for ideas. The performers use everyday things to make music to which to dance.

## What to do
**Circle time**
- If appropriate, watch *STOMP Out Loud*.
- Discuss with the children what they have seen and support the learning of new vocabulary, such as *vibrate* and *timbre*. Introduce words describing the qualities of sounds, such as *rattling*, *smooth*, *tinkling*, and words relating to sound production, such as *hitting*, *shaking*, *scraping*.

**Collection table activity**
- Encourage the children to experiment and explore the sounds that are made by everyday items by hitting them with a variety of different materials, shaking them and blowing on them.
- Put balls of paper on to a drum. Watch the paper jump as you tap the drum. Tell children they do not need to hit things very hard or rapidly – encourage them to allow items to vibrate.

## Extension/variation
- Encourage the children to make up their own rhythms.

## Links to home
- Warn parents that children will want to hit different materials in the home, and to guide them to try appropriate items.
- Ask children to find objects that make particular sounds, eg high tinkling sounds, and bring them into school. These could be grouped on the collection table with the describing words written above the objects.

## Topic
Food and shopping

## Resources
- DVD: *STOMP Out Loud*
- Television and DVD player
- Bubble wrap
- Cutlery
- Wood blocks
- Different sized tins
- Cardboard boxes
- Pipes
- Car wheel hubs
- Plastic and metal buckets
- Metal dustbins and lids
- Brooms and brushes
- Saucepans
- Frying pans
- String
- Drum
- Small balls of paper

## Related activities
- Tick, tock, hum, click (see page 116)
- The park in the dark (see page 160)

# Tra-la

## Topic
Toys

## Resources
- Book: *Winnie-the-Pooh* by A. A. Milne (Methuen Children's Books)

## Learning objectives
- To sing to self and make up simple songs with melody and nonsense words
- To experiment with words and sounds, including nonsense and rhyme

## What to do
**Circle time**
- Read from Chapter 2 of *Winnie-the-Pooh.* Winnie is doing his 'Stoutness Exercises' and making up a song with invented words. (This is called scat singing and is often used as an accompaniment to a song, eg *doo be wap.*)
- Ask the children to make up their own song during the session.
- At the end of the session ask volunteers to sing their song to the group.
- Discuss the sounds of the nonsense words when praising their efforts.

## Extension/variation
- Suggest that the listeners copy the phrases sung.

## Related activity
- Sing to your pet (see page 151)

# Moving house

## Learning objectives

- To engage in imaginative role-play based on first-hand experiences
- To play cooperatively with other children to develop a storyline or narrative
- To express questions and answers effectively, showing an awareness of listeners' needs
- To connect ideas and events and understand past, present and future forms in speech

## Topic

Homes

## Resources

- Book: *Moving House* by Anne Civardi and Stephen Cartwright (Usborne First Experiences)
- Poem: 'The New Neighbour' by Rose Fyleman, from *Friends Sense and Nonsense Poems for Young Children* compiled by Suzanne and Jane Bottomley (Macdonald)
- Internet: search Marie Lloyd and 'music hall' for words to song: 'My Old Man Said Follow the Van'

## What to do

### Circle time

- Read *Moving House.* Ask if anyone remembers moving home. Talk about moving home and what has to be planned.
- Read 'The New Neighbour' and ask who has had a new neighbour.

### Role-play activity

- Ask what other things the children might ask a child when they meet for the first time.
- In pairs, ask the children to make conversation with each other by asking questions as though they have just moved in next door.
- If the children have not moved house, they could make up what might happen.

## Extension/variation

- A practitioner could sing the song 'My Old Man Said Follow the Van', and ask the children to listen to the words and decide what the song is about. Explain that the family moved house because they did not have the money to pay the rent, but the van was full and the woman tried to follow it on foot and got lost. (Be very sensitive if there might be any children in the group whose families have had or are having difficulties with paying for their housing.)

## Links to home

- Be sure that you are aware of any children who have recently moved home or are preparing to move, so that you can decide whether the activity would be appropriate at this time and talk about it with some children in advance.

Being imaginative

# The King's Breakfast

## Topic
Food and shopping

## Resources
- Poems/Chants/Songs: *The King's Breakfast* by A. A. Milne (Egmont Children's Books); 'Slice, Slice The Bread Looks Nice' and 'Yellow Butter' by Mary Ann Hoberman, from *This Little Puffin* compiled by Elizabeth Matterson (Puffin)
- Toaster
- Bread
- Plates, knives and bread board
- Margarine
- Choice of spreads
- Brown and coloured playdough, rolling pins and tools
- Percussion instruments
- Art and craft resources and found materials for modelling

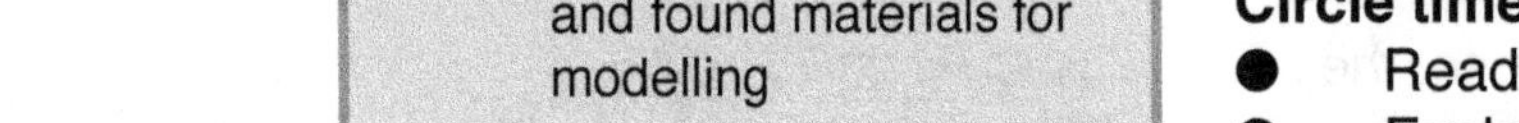

## Learning objectives
- To represent ideas, thoughts and feelings through art, design, music and role-play
- To create simple representations of objects
- To choose particular colours, textures and materials to use for a purpose
- To play cooperatively as part of a group to act out a narrative
- To tap out simple repeated rhythms and make some up
- To explore the different sounds of percussion instruments and how they can be changed.

## What to do
### Circle time
- Read *The King's Breakfast.*
- Explain that an Alderney is a breed of cow and a dairymaid milks a cow.
- Talk about favourite fast foods such as burgers and chips.
- Support the children in making their own toast or sandwiches with margarine and a choice of savoury and sweet spreads. Talk about the textures and colours.
- Encourage good manners at the table.
- Recite 'Slice, Slice, The Bread Looks Nice', altering the words to include the spreads you are using.

**Art activity**

- Roll out brown playdough and use other colours and tools to create different spreads.
- Invite children to make paintings, drawings, collages and models of their favourite meals. Discuss the shapes, textures, colours and forms of the resources they choose and encourage the mixing of media, eg use real uncooked pasta, rolled paper for sausages, foam strips for chips and string for spaghetti.

**Music activity**

- Learn and say the chant 'Yellow Butter' and clap with the beat, slowly at first and gradually speeding up.
- Ask children to choose instruments to represent the four foods (butter, jelly, jam and bread) and experiment to make the sounds fit the beats.
- Divide into four groups and play the instruments appropriately while a practitioner reads the chant.
- Gradually read more quickly and encourage the children to keep up.

**Role-play activity**

- Ask the children to imagine wanting something and how they would feel and behave if they were told that they could not have it.
- Invite them to say the words from the poem expressively and use their arms, hands and faces to act out the feelings. Model an example of this if necessary.
- Read the poem and ask the children to join in with the words or to mime the feelings.

## Extensions/variations

- Arrange models attractively and take photographs of favourite meals.
- Play instruments to the rhythms of different food words.
- Try speaking in different character voices.

## Links to home

- Ask parents to talk with their children about colours and textures of foods and to encourage them to spread their own bread and help with food preparation

# Messing about in boats

## Topics
Transport and travel/Water

## Resources
- Poem: 'A Good Play' by R. L. Stevenson from *The Oxford Treasury of Children's Poems* (OUP)
- Props for making a boat
- Song: 'We Sail the Ocean Blue', from *HMS Pinafore* by W. S. Gilbert and Arthur Sullivan
- CD player
- Water tray
- Objects that float, sink
- Small pots and polystyrene trays
- Empty washing-up liquid bottles
- Plasticine

## Learning objectives
- To use available resources to create props to support imaginative play
- To play cooperatively as part of a group to develop and act out a storyline or narrative in role-play, taking account of others' ideas about how to organize the activity
- To represent own ideas, thoughts and feelings through imaginative role-play and stories and show sensitivity to others' needs and feelings
- To speak confidently about ideas, choose the resources needed and say when help is needed or not needed
- To observe similarities and differences between materials in water and explain why some float and some sink

## What to do
**Imaginative play activity**
- Read the poem 'A Good Play'. Ask the children what they could use to make a pretend boat.
- Support collecting the props, and the children's imaginative play in the boat.
- Play the song 'We Sail the Ocean Blue' as the children play.

## Extensions/variations
**Water tray activity**
- Put objects that float and sink into the water: such as plastic toys and Plasticine, leaves and stones. Add small pots and polystyrene trays as model boats and offer empty washing up liquid bottles (Squeezing out a jet of water can push a boat along.)
- Support the children's use of new vocabulary and developing understanding of language with words such as: *sink*, *float*, *heavy*, *light*, *sail* and *mast*.

## Related activity
- Seaside (see pages 102–103)

# Lollipop person

Being imaginative

## Learning objectives

- To engage in imaginative role-play based on first hand experiences
- To play cooperatively as part of a group to develop and act out experiences
- To use available resources to create props to support role-play.
- To show interest in different occupations and the lives of familiar people
- To ask for help from adults when it is needed.

## Preparation

- Arrange for a lollipop person to visit if possible.

## What to do

**Circle time**

- Talk to the children about their daily journeys. Explain why they should hold hands with a grown-up. They should be aware that traffic is sometimes unable to stop quickly and that they may be hard to see if they are dressed in dark clothes, particularly on dark mornings or dark winter afternoons.
- A visit from a lollipop person would be beneficial. Allow him/her to become a familiar and reliable person.

**Role-play**

- Suggest that children take turns to dress up as a lollipop person (or a Road Crossing Patrol) in a commercially obtained outfit or a white coat or reflective jacket. Sets of 'People who help us' tabards for children's role-play are widely available.
- Make a 'road lollipop' using a broom handle with a large circle of cardboard on the top.
- Work with the children to create a zebra crossing. Help them to paint black and white stripes across the back of a piece of left-over wallpaper.
- Let the children take turns in taking the 'road lollipop' home to practise crossing the road with siblings and parents.

## Extension/variation

- If you don't have a lollipop person near to your setting, take the children out for a walk to see one, if possible, or to use whichever type of zebra, pelican or pedestrian crossing is locally available.

## Topic

People who help us

## Resources

- White coat
- Broom handle
- Cardboard circle
- Glue
- Unwanted wallpaper
- Black and white paint
- Paintbrushes

## Links to home

- Ask parents to donate unwanted pieces of wallpaper and to support the children's interest in crossing the road safely.

Being imaginative

# The park in the dark

## Topic
Toys

## Resources
- Book: *The Park in the Dark* by Martin Waddell (Walker Books)
- Book: *The Very Noisy Night* by Diana Hendry (Little Tiger Press) – alternative title
- Bought percussion and home-made instruments
- Junk materials

 Ensure proper adult:child ratio per visit.

## Learning objectives
- To represent ideas, thoughts and feelings through music and sound effects
- To work as part of a group to develop a storyline or narrative
- To use available resources to create props and instruments to support a storyline
- To listen to a story, accurately anticipating key events and responding with appropriate actions.

## What to do
### Music activity
- Read and show *The Park in the Dark.*
- Discuss what kind of sound effects (instruments and voice/body) could be made for each part of the story, eg old creaking swing, tiptoe downstairs, dustbin alley with cat and mice, Little Gee frightened, witches and goblins, howling tree, playground sounds, the train, running, back upstairs to bed. Let the children experiment with the instruments and make any needed.
- Ask for ideas and invite children to choose different parts to play with their instruments. All of the children could say 'Whoopee!' and 'Yaiooee!'
- Encourage the children to play the instruments while you read the story.

## Extension/variation
- Ask what was 'the thing' in the story (a train). Ask the children if they could suggest something else that would be frightening in the dark. Ask them to make a sound like their frightening thing.

## Links to home
- Ask parents to take their child to a playground and a park.
- Ask for volunteers to support a visit to an adventure playground.

## Related activities
- Rattle those pans (see page 153)
- Tick, tock, hum, click (see page 116)

# Down on the farm

**Being imaginative**

## Learning objectives

- To engage in imaginative and role-play based on own first-hand experiences
- To play alongside other children who are engaged in the same theme
- To use available resources to create props to support role-play and small-world play
- To create simple representations of objects
- To introduce a storyline or narrative into play

## Preparation

- Organize a visit to a small farm that is open to the public. Staff should visit first and check its suitability.

## What to do

**Circle time**

- Read *Dora's Eggs* and ask where the farm animals lived.

**Music activity**

- Sing 'Old Macdonald Had a Farm'.

**Small-world activity**

- Encourage children to set up a farm with the animals, improvising with scrap materials (eg, corrugated cardboard for ploughed fields, green twisted tissue paper as hedges, blue paper as pond).

## Extensions/variations

**Outside activity**

- Encourage the children to set up a farmyard, using the boxes as sty, hen house, stable and cowshed, and place the animals in appropriate places, deciding what they need to live comfortably.
- Suggest they ride round the farm to feed the animals (using the buckets).

## Links to home

- Ask for volunteers to support a visit to the farm.

## Related activity

- Sing to your pet (see page 151)

### Topic

Animals

### Resources

- Book: *Dora's Eggs* by Julie Sykes (Little Tiger Press)
- Song: 'Old Macdonald Had a Farm', from *This Little Puffin* compiled by Elizabeth Matterson (Puffin)
- Small-world farm
- Small pieces of scrap materials
- Large boxes for animal pens
- Toy farm animals or cardboard models
- Buckets (for feed)
- Large wheeled sit-on toys

⚠ Check regulations for visits. Insist upon hygiene rules – washing hands after handling animals and before eating.

# Stuck up the chimney

## Topic
Celebrations

## Resources
- Book: *The Night Before Christmas* by Clement C. Moore (Walker Books)
- Song: 'When Santa Got Stuck Up the Chimney', from *This Little Puffin* compiled by Elizabeth Matterson (Puffin)
- Paper
- Small boxes
- Cereal card
- Thick blue, black and red paints and paintbrushes
- Cotton wool
- Plasticine
- Pipe cleaners
- Glue and spreaders
- Parcel tape
- Stapler
- Construction bricks and base

 Superfvise the use of the stapler.

## Learning objectives
- To build an imaginative story around a simple concept within a song
- To introduce an alternative storyline or narrative
- To represent ideas, thoughts and feelings using a range of media, such as found materials for modelling, art and craft materials and paint

## What to do
**Circle time**
- Read the poem *The Night Before Christmas* (first published in 1822).

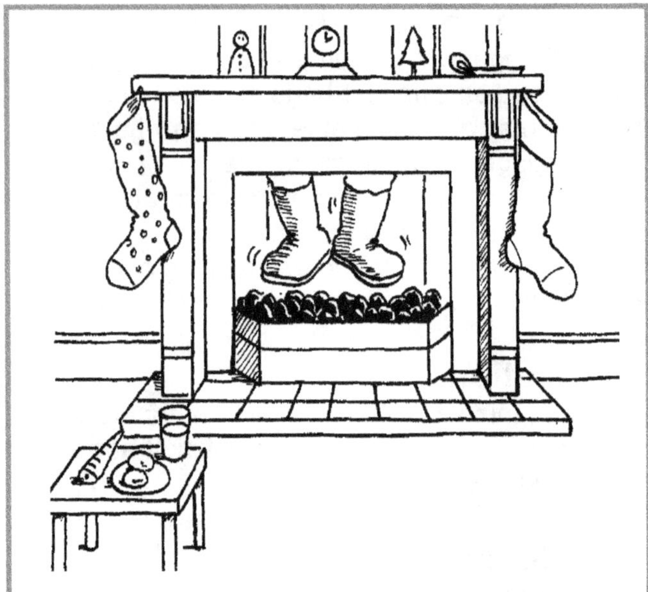

- Read the words to the song 'When Santa Got Stuck Up the Chimney'. Ask what you would see, if Santa got stuck. Suggest different view points such as seeing him through the window, stuck in the chimney next door, or inside the bedroom, if there is still a fireplace there.
- Ask what might have happened next. The children might suggest soot everywhere, Santa not fitting through the gas fire, etc. Be encouraging to all suggestions.

**Art activity**
- Suggest making a model of what they would see.
- Support the children while they are working on their models. Encourage them to keep their ideas simple and model any techniques that might help to achieve particular effects.

**Music activity**
- Learn the song 'When Santa Got Stuck Up the Chimney'.

## Extension/variation
- Paint a picture illustrating the song.

## Related activities
- Bricks (see page 93)
- Rockin' Robin (see page 150)
- Decorate a tree (see page 179)

# Soup for sale!



## Learning objectives

- To play cooperatively as part of a group
- To develop and act out a narrative as an advertisement for soup

## What to do

**Role-play activity**

- Ask the group whether they like soup.
- Ask how the people who make the soup let everyone know about their product (advertising). Ask how and where they can advertise their product. (Posters, adverts in magazines, on the television.) Show the examples that you have.
- Suggest that the group makes a DVD advert for the soup. Support the children's ideas. (If they say they don't like soup, they could make a DVD saying how horrible the soup is.)
- Support language development; suggest and encourage adjectives to describe the soup.
- Show the children how to use the camcorder. Let them take turns.
- Discuss the children's plans with them before they start to record the advertisement. Ask how they will set the scene, what props they will need, etc.

**Art activity**

- Show painting *Soup Can* and talk about how it has been created (printing).
- Ask children to make an advertising poster for their soup. Suggest that they use the computer for their writing.

## Topic

Food and shopping

## Resources

- DVD: television advertisement for soup
- Advertisement for soup from a magazine
- Small video camcorder with tape on a tripod
- Television with DVD player to play the resulting recording
- Adapter for tape if required
- Soup tins from different manufacturers with their labels
- Soup dishes
- Spoons
- Tablecloth
- Painting: *Soup Can* by Andy Warhol
- Paper, paints and paintbrushes
- Computer with different fonts available or CD-ROM: '2publish', from *Infant Video Toolkit* (2Simple Software)
- Printer and paper

## Extensions/variations

**Computer activity**

- Show the different labels on the soups. Ask the children to make a label for their own brand of soup.
- Use the computer to do the lettering. You could type in the words, and then support the children in altering the fonts and choosing which ones they would like to use.

## Links to home

- Invite parents to watch the DVD.
- Ask parents to encourage their child to look at food labels.

# The Pied Piper

## Topic
Animals

## Resources
- Story: *The Pied Piper of Hamelin* (several versions available)
- Fur, felt and other fabrics, wool, pom poms and other craft pieces
- Pipe cleaners
- Elastic
- Card
- Scissors
- PVA glue and spreaders
- Sticky tape
- Internet search: Pied Piper of Hamelin
- Music: James Galway, A Portrait
- CD Player

## Learning objectives
- To use media and materials in original ways, thinking about uses and purposes
- To represent ideas, thoughts and feelings through art and design, music, dance, imaginative role-play and stories
- To play cooperatively as part of a group to develop, act out and perform a storyline

## Preparation
- Read and discuss the story of *The Pied Piper of Hamelin* with the children.
- Check suitability and prepare music. For ease of organization, the recommended CD has all the required tracks.

## What to do
**Role-play**
- Pretend to be rats eating everything, then pretend to be the townspeople looking very frightened.
- Be the Piper arriving and asking for money and the Mayor promising him money to get rid of the rats.
- Act out the rats following the Piper and jumping into the river to drown. (There could be several small groups acting this simultaneously.)
- Pretend to be the townspeople looking very happy, then the Mayor refusing to pay the Piper and the Piper being angry.
- Act out the children following the Piper to a cave and disappearing, then one boy, who could not keep up, going back to the town and the people being sad.

**Dance activity**
- Play the music CD and encourage the children to dance and display the appropriate emotions to represent the different characters. Support them by calling out reminders of the order of the events in the story.

- **Scene 1:** Entry of the councillors and Mayor, rats running around, and entry of the Pied Piper – *Concerto No. 2, K314, in D: III–Allegro* by Mozart. The children could play percussion instruments to represent the knock at the door.
- **Scene 2:** Rats following Pied Piper and drowning – *Flight of the Bumble Bee* by Rimsky-Korsakov.
- **Scene 3:** Townspeople dancing with joy – *Belfast Hornpipe,* traditional.
- Argument between Mayor and Pied Piper – *Concerto, Wq 169, in G: III – Presto* by C. P. E. Bach.
- **Scene 4:** Children skipping and following Pied Piper – *Sonata, Op. 1 No. 11 in F, IV–Allegro* by Handel.
- Lame boy left behind – *Sonata, Op. 1 No. 11 in F, III–Siciliana* by Handel. Children could play percussion instruments to represent the landslide.
- **Scene 5:** Townspeople grieving – *Adagio of Spartacus and Phrygia* by Khatchaturian.

**Craft activities**

- Invite the children to make rat masks. Support them in cutting out shapes for the face and ears from card and fabric. Make cones for noses and attach with tabs. Complete the masks with pipe cleaner whiskers and pom pom noses. Tie elastic to fit children's heads.
- Make hats for the Mayor, the Piper and the townspeople.
- Paint a picture or make a collage to illustrate the story.
- Make a plan of Hamelin and the countryside around the town.

## Extensions/variations

- Involve the whole group in a production of the story.
- Ask which activity they liked best.

## Links to home

- Ask parents and carers to help with making costumes.
- Invite parents, carers and families to watch the performance.

Being imaginative

# Over the rainbow

## Topic

Colours

## Resources

- Paintings: *The Blind Girl* by Sir John Everett Millais (shows a double rainbow and thunderclouds; *The Rainbow* by Georges Seurat; *Pine in St Tropez* by Paul Signac
- DVD: *The Wizard of Oz*
- CD-ROM: *OZ-Intreactive Storybook* (Dorling Kindersley)
- Music: *Clair de Lune* by Claude Debussy
- Song: 'Somewhere Over The Rainbow' sung by Judy Garland, from *The Wizard of Oz*
- Clear plastic tank with water
- Mirror to fit into tank
- Coloured scarves or streamers
- Coloured papers, card, magazines, cellophane, fabrics, wool and craft pieces
- Cardboard tubes and boxes
- Aluminium foil
- Nylon stockings
- Material for stuffing
- Garden canes
- String
- Ready mixed paints
- Paintbrushes and kitchen sponges
- Shallow trays
- Potatoes
- Scissors
- PVA glue and spreaders
- Sticky tape
- Computer with CD and DVD player

 Supervise the use of garden canes and scissors.

## Learning objectives

- To choose particular colours to use for a purpose
- To capture experiences with a range of media
- To create movements in response to music
- To represent ideas, thoughts and feelings through art and design, music, dance, imaginative role-play and stories

## Preparation

- Set up the mirror in the plastic tank with water, as shown in the diagram. You will need a sunny day for this activity.
- Load the CD-ROM.
- Find some examples of paintings by Georges Seurat or Paul Signac. They painted in a style called pointillism, with lots of little dots of colour instead of brush strokes.

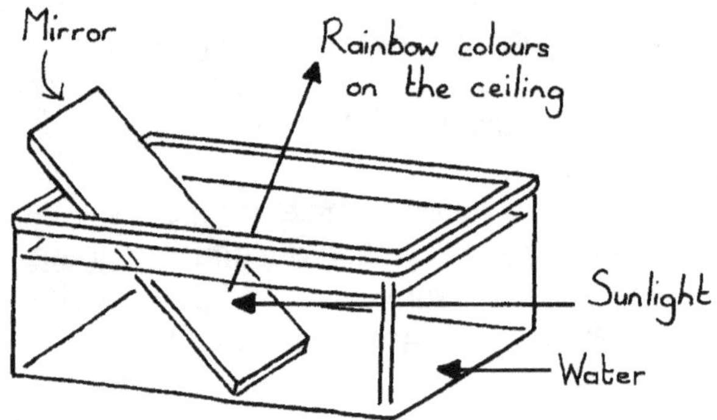


## What to do

### Make a rainbow

- Let the sun shine through the water in the box.
- Tilt the mirror inside the box so the sun hits the mirror and reflects on to the ceiling.
- Ask the children what they notice about the rainbow and if they can name its colours.

### Circle time

- Show the paintings and discuss the composition and use of colour.
- Show an excerpt from the DVD of *The Wizard of Oz.*
- Find the place where Dorothy meets the scarecrow and the song *If only I had a Brain.*
- Suggest that the scarecrow would be happier if he had a friend.

**Craft activities**

- Suggest that the children make a rainbow.
- Ask about its shape and the order of its colours and offer the children a variety of materials to choose from.
- Ask what colours and in what order.
- Ask what materials they are going to use. Supply a variety of materials, but let the children choose.
- Make a scarecrow body from stuffed stockings.
- Fasten a cane along the back so it can be stuck into the ground.
- Dress the scarecrow in colourful fabric.
- Talk to the children about the texture of the fabrics and their colours.
- Suggest to the children that there is a magical place over the rainbow where the colours are different.
- Show painting *Pine in St Tropez* by Signac. (He favoured pink, blue, orange, purple, red and green spots.)
- Suggest that the children use small pieces of potato to print similar effects. Use kitchen sponges in shallow trays covered in ready-mixed paint on top to make printing pads. Use one tray for each colour.

**Dance activities**

- Invite the children to listen to the piano music and to imagine themselves dancing to the music, to think of the steps they would take and how they would move around the room.
- Offer scarves and encourage them to dance and wave the scarves to the music.

## Extensions/variations

- The children can make a tin man and/or lion puppet.
- The scarecrow can be a gift and put in a window box.
- Play the CD-ROM *OZ-Interactive Storybook.*
- Encourage children to create pictures and patterns using coloured spots of pain from a finger or paintbrush.

## Notes for practitioner

- A rainbow is part of a circle but we only see half of it. The red is always at the top of the curve and blue is under the curve.
- To see a rainbow the sun has to be low in the sky (early morning or evening). The sunlight is bent by the raindrops and is split into the separate colours.

# Goldilocks and the Three Bears

## Topic
Homes

## Resources
- Picture storybook: *Goldilocks and the Three Bears* (Ladybird or any other edition)
- Music: The Three Bears Phantasy by Eric Coates
- Different chairs from the setting
- Catalogues with pictures of different chairs
- Small-toy or small-world figure with jointed legs (capable of sitting in a chair)
- CD player
- Percussion instruments
- Cameras
- Construction kits, bricks and blocks
- Craft and junk material
- Card and paper
- Pencils and crayons
- Paints and brushes
- PVA glue and spreaders
- Playdough
- Scissors

Supervise the use of scissors.

## Learning objectives
- To construct with a purpose in mind, using media and materials in original ways
- To represent ideas, thoughts and feelings through design and technology, art, music, dance, role-play and stories

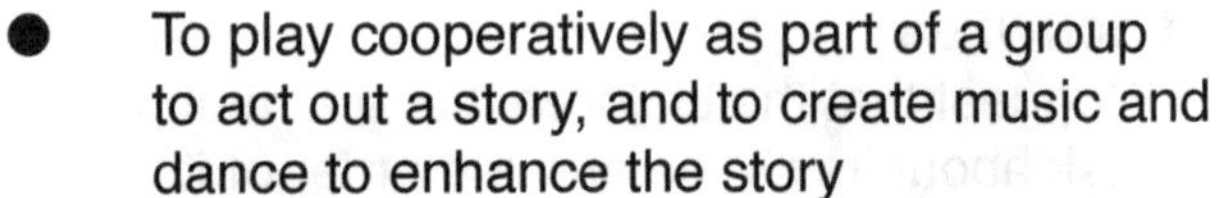

- To play cooperatively as part of a group to act out a story, and to create music and dance to enhance the story
- To describe and express opinions of the project effectively, connecting ideas and events to develop narratives and explanations

## What to do
### Circle time
- Read *Goldilocks and the Three Bears.*
- Ask children to sit in different chairs and say whether they are comfortable or not, describing them as too hard, too soft, or bouncy etc
- Talk about the functions of different chairs and the different materials they are made from, such as leather adjustable office chairs and plastic stacking school chairs. Show the children pictures of different types of chairs in a catalogue.
- Ask why Goldilocks broke Baby Bear's chair (she was too heavy for it), why she slept in his bed (she was tired) and how she got into the house uninvited the bears had not locked the door).

### Art activity
- Encourage the children to design and make a small chair to fit a toy or a small world figure. Offer them a variety of materials and methods to choose from and model techniques for shaping and joining pieces.

### Music activity
- Ask the children to choose an instrument sound to represent each of the four characters in the story. Read the story and encourage them to play the appropriate instrument each time the character is mentioned.

### Dance activity
- Play the music and ask the children to try to match the parts of the music to the story.
- There is a repeated 'Who's been sitting in my chair?' motif. Ask children to put up their hands when they hear this motif.

- Other parts of the music to listen for include:
  - knocking on the door (1.12 minutes)
  - the bears' arrival (2.42 minutes)
  - their anger (deep trombones and drums) (3.3 minutes)
  - the end of the piece, which sounds as though they try to make friends but ends with a chase.
- Ask the children to mime the story as Goldilocks, then as the bears, first without the music, then with the music.
- Support by giving instructions to the part of the story they are to mime.

**Role-play activities**

- Ask children to describe the bears' feelings and to mime their expressions of anger, sadness, surprise, etc.
- Suggest that the children work together, in groups of four, to act out the story.
- Take lots of photographs of the group work.

## Extension/variation

- Make a bed for Teddy.

## Links to home

- Practise acting out the story with children in different roles and prepare a performance.
- Invite parents/guardians and family members to watch the children in performance.

**Being imaginative**

# Who is knocking?

## Topics
Homes/People who help us

## Resources
- Books: *ABC: I Can Be* by Verna Allette Wilkins (Tamarind Books); *Alfie Gets In First* by Shirley Hughes (Walker Books); *What Am I?* by Debbie MacKinnon and Anthea Sieveking (Frances Lincoln); *Tidy Up Titch* by Pat Hutchins (Red Fox)
- Pictures and photographs of people wearing clothes that identify their jobs
- Songs: 'Patrick Was A Postman' and 'I Went To School One Morning' from *This Little Puffin* compiled by Elizabeth Matterson (Puffin)
- Playdough or self-hardening clay
- Rolling pins and other tools
- Finger puppets of people who help us
- Percussion instruments
- Items that are particularly associated with people's jobs
- Dressing-up outfits for people who help us
- Items of litter (clean packaging and wrappers, etc)
- Sugar paper or thin card
- PVA glue and spreaders
- Scissors
- Paints and brushes
- Computer and word processing program
- Printer and paper
- Percussion instruments

## Learning objectives
- To engage in imaginative role-play based on first-hand experiences
- To capture experiences by making up simple songs
- To create simple representations of events, people and objects
- To play cooperatively as part of a small group to act out a narrative
- To represent own ideas, thoughts and feelings through discussion and role-play
- To show interest in exploring and describing textures
- To show interest in different occupations and ways of life

## Preparation
- Access the word processing program in the computer

## What to do
### Circle time
- Show picture book *ABC I Can Be* and show the pictures and photographs.
- Read *Alfie Gets in First*. Ask who came to help Alfie's mum to get back into their house.
- Ask children to think of people who might come to the door and how they might be recognized by their uniforms and badges. Talk about safety and not opening the door without an adult.
- Read and show *What Am I?* and talk about the jobs illustrated.
- Share the items with children and ask who would use them and for what purpose. Ask children to talk about jobs they would like or not like to do when they are older and why. Make it very clear that both men and women may choose any job and that people of all nationalities and abilities (including those with disabilities) can work together.
- Read *Tidy up Titch.* Ask where Titch should put stuff he did not want any more.
- Talk about getting rid of rubbish.

**Art activity**

- Suggest to the children that they make identity badges of their initials or words of their choice using playdough or self-hardening clay.
- Sort different materials by type and texture and talk about them, using descriptive words such as: *smooth, rough, shiny, transparent, plastic, metal, paper, fabric, wood, stone, natural* and *man-made*. Use the materials and 'litter', such as packaging and wrappers, to make a collage for a poster. (Make sure they are clean.)

**Music activity**

- Use finger puppets of different people who help us.
- Sing '(Patrick) Was a Postman', substituting the name of a child in the group, preferably one whose name starts with 'P'. Give the child the puppet. Ask what the postman is wearing.
- Sing the song with the children, using the instruments to keep the beat.
- Choose another puppet and ask what it is wearing. Ask if that person would knock on the child's door at home and what he/she does.
- With the children make up a suitable line with the same beat, eg 'Martin was a milkman… , He delivered all the milk… ,'

**Role-play**

- Encourage the children to pretend to be people carrying out different jobs. Ask them to mime what the person would do. Offer dressing up outfits for 'people who help us' and invite them to dress in character.

**Technology activity**

- Support printing the text for the poster using a word processing package on a computer. Let the children choose the font.

## Extensions/variations

- Sing songs ('I Am The Music Man'; 'I Went To School One Morning') and make up new verses to include people who work in the community.
- Arrange a visit to a fire station or invite a police officer to come into the setting to talk to the children.
- Take the children out for a walk to see the refuse collectors collecting the dustbins.

## Links to home

- Ask parents if they could talk to their children about their jobs, uniforms and badges and whether they would like to come in and talk to the group.
- Ask for volunteers to accompany children and practitioners on a walk or visit.
- Suggest that parents talk about official visitors and recycling at home.

Ensure the correct child:adult ratio. Check regulations for taking children out of setting.

Ensure there are no sharp edges on any of the objects.

Being imaginative

# The Sorcerer's Apprentice

## Topic
Water

## Resources
- Books: *Doing the Washing* by Sarah Garland (Bodley Head Children's Books)
- For instruments to make: *The I Can't Sing Book* by Jackie Silberg (Brilliant Publications)
- DVD: *The Sorcerer's Apprentice* by Paul Dukas in *Fantasia* (Walt Disney)
- Poems: 'Clothes on the Washing Line' by Frank Flynn, from *The Oxford Treasury of Children's Poems* (OUP)
- 'Water' from *Out And About Through The Year* by Shirley Hughes (Walker Books)
- Songs: 'This is the Way We Wash Our Clothes', from *This Little Puffin* compiled by Elizabeth Matterson (Puffin); 'There's a Hole in my Bucket' – several versions available on the Internet
- CD Player
- DVD player and television or computer
- Purchased and homemade instruments
- Paint and paintbrushes
- Paper and cardboard
- Clothes pegs and string
- Scissors
- Water tray or paddling pool
- Lots of small yoghurt pots
- A few larger buckets
- Dry sand in tray or sandpit

## Learning objectives
- To choose particular colours and shapes to use for a purpose
- To capture experiences with a range of media
- To create simple representations of events, people and objects
- To safely use and explore a variety of materials, tools and techniques, experimenting with colour, design, texture and form
- To make up sounds and simple rhythms associated with a theme
- To represent ideas, thoughts and feelings through engaging in imaginative role-play
- To play cooperatively as part of a group to develop and act out a narrative or storyline

## Preparation
- Find the appropriate section on the *Fantasia* DVD.

## What to do
### Circle time
- Read the story *Doing the Washing* and the poem 'Clothes on the Washing Line'. Talk with the children about using water to wash clothes and different ways of drying them.
- Read the poem 'Water' and talk about the sounds that are being made in the swimming baths and by the little girl playing with the water.
- Invite children to think of words associated with water and introduce new vocabulary to stimulate their language development. For example: *pour, freeze, trickle, splash, bubble, drip* and *flow*.
- Watch *The Sorcerer's Apprentice* with the children. Talk with them about what went wrong for the apprentice (played by Mickey), especially when he chopped the broom.
- Ask them to imagine what the Sorcerer said when he came home and what Mickey said or did to show that he was sorry. Encourage them to think how they would have felt and what they would have done.

**Art and craft activity**

- Encourage children to draw and colour shapes to design their own clothes. Offer support if needed as the children cut out the clothes and colour both sides.
- Tie a string washing line across one end of the room and peg up the clothes.
- Paint watery pictures, using blue, white and green paints, or a scene from the story in wax resist, using wax crayons and a watery wash of blue paint.
- Design and make a sorcerer's hat from a cone of card and cut out or sticker stars.
- Design and make buckets or brooms from junk and craft materials.

**Music activity**

- Sing 'This is the Way We Wash Our Clothes' and learn the actions.
- Read the poem 'Water' and remind the children of the words.
- With the children working in pairs, encourage them to choose one of the words and make up sounds (using water if appropriate) with homemade and purchased instruments to represent it.

**Role-play activities**

- Provide buckets and small yoghurt pots in a water tray or paddling pool. Ask children to find out how many small pots of water are needed to fill the large containers and what happens if they go on pouring once the containers are full.

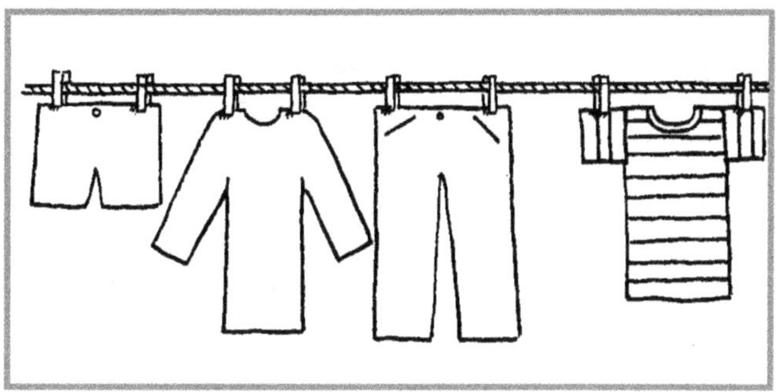

⚠ Supervise the use of scissors.
Hang the line high enough not to be reached by the children.

- Ask them to carry the buckets and to show that they are worried and afraid of what the sorcerer will do and desperately trying to stop the brooms.
- Try the same activity with dry sand.
- Sing the song 'There's a Hole in my Bucket'

## Links to home

- Ask parents to involve their children in washing and drying clothes and pegging them up to dry.
- Suggest that they take their children swimming, if possible.

# How will Teddy get there?

## Topics
Toys/Transport and travel

## Resources
- Large teddy bear
- Song: 'The Bear Went Over the Mountain', from *This Little Puffin* compiled by Elizabeth Matterson (Puffin)
- Sand tray
- Plastic bears

## Learning objectives
- To introduce a storyline or narrative into their play
- To create movement in response to music
- To initiate new combinations of movement and gesture to express feelings, ideas and experiences

## What to do
**Circle time**
- Learn the words and tune of 'The Bear Went Over the Mountain'.
- Ask the children to suggest alternative ways for the large bear to travel over the mountain, eg *hopped*, *skipped*.
- The song says that the bear saw the other side of the mountain. Ask the children to describe what they think the bear really saw.

**Outside or hall activity**
- Gather the children to sit in a circle and sing the song.
- Ask the children to remember the alternative words they thought up during circle time. Let the child who suggests a word, eg *hop*, hop with the large teddy bear round the circle, while everyone sings the song.

## Extension/variation
**Sand tray activity**
- Pile up a mound of sand in the sand tray. Provide the children with small plastic bears. Encourage the children to sing the song to themselves as they play.

## Related activities
- A bear hunt (see page 34)
- Goldilocks and the Three Bears (see pages 168–169)

# Weather dance

## Learning objectives

- To create movement in response to music
- To use movement to express feelings
- To engage in imaginative role-play based on first hand experiences
- To play alongside other children who are engaged in the same theme

## Topic

Weather

## Resources

- Large space
- Music for different types of weather, eg Debussy's *Snowflakes Are Dancing* for snow, Beethoven's *6th Symphony* for rainstorms, or piano
- Cardboard cut into 'puddle' shapes
- Paint
- Paintbrushes
- Glue
- Large sheets of paper, eg length of wallpaper
- Print of any Lowry painting

8–10

## What to do

### Circle time

- Invite the children to pretend to go outside in different types of weather, including snow, sunshine, rain and wind.

### Movement activity

#### Snowy weather

- Be a snowflake. If possible use soft flowing music for snow. Debussy's *Snowflakes Are Dancing* makes very good 'snowy' music.
- Discuss newly fallen snow. Ask the children if they think it is crunchy. Encourage them to walk as though they are crunching through deep snow, but very softly as snow blanks out sound.
- Pretend to make a snowman, then to be a snowman, standing very still.
- Pretend to dress up warmly.

#### Hot weather

- Now pretend that the weather is warm. Sit in the sun and feel the heat. Remind the children to pretend to put on suncream and sunhats. Ask them to think about what they would eat or drink in the sunshine, such as cold drinks, ice cream or candyfloss at the seaside, and to show you how they would hold an ice cream and eat it.

#### Rainy weather

- Now pretend it has begun to rain. Flutter fingers like raindrops. If you can, provide appropriate music, such as crashing music for storms and running music for rain.
- Ask the children if they can imagine rain falling and how it feels and sounds, then to imagine what they would wear in the rain and to pretend to pull on boots, put on a rain coat, or jacket and hat and put up a bright umbrella.
- Invite children to join in with a rain dance. Use cardboard shapes to resemble puddles. Ask them to jump in or over the puddles.

#### Windy weather

- Pretend that it's windy and it's hard to stand up straight. Ask the children to pretend the wind is blowing them sideways. Ask them to push hard against the wind and walk around.

## Extensions/variations

- Paint a weather wall frieze showing slanting rain, bright umbrellas and people walking slanting in the wind. A Lowry painting would show this scene.
- Make a rainbow picture on a large piece of paper; the back of a length of wallpaper would be ideal. Let the children take turns to draw an arch in each colour. Affix to the wall frieze.

## Related activity

Over the rainbow (see pages 166–167)

Being imaginative

# The farmer grows our food

## Topic
People who help us

## Resources
- Large floor space
- Bread wrappers
- Flour
- Yeast
- Variety of types of bread loaves and rolls
- Different types of music: *Carnival of the Animals* by Saint-Saens
  Windmill - *Feathers and Fins*
  Sprinkling seeds - *Birds*
  Growing - *Swan*
  Cutting, swiping - *Mules*
  Grinding - *Fossils*
  Punching dough - *Finale*
  *Harvest* by Wendy Bird from Harlequin (A & C Black)
- CD player or cassette recorder
- Climbing equipment
- Wheeled vehicles
- Collage materials
- Straws
- Glue

## Learning objectives
- To create movement in response to music
- To represent ideas, thoughts and feelings through music, dance and role-play
- To show good control and coordination in large movements

## Preparation
- Find a large safe floor space for the movement session.
- Arrange on a display table the ingredients of bread (such as flour and yeast). Add different shaped loaves and rolls.
- Find suitable music for the movement activity.

## What to do
**Circle time**
- Talk to the children about farmers. Ask them if they have ever seen a tractor at work in the fields carrying wheat, grass, hay, vegetables or apples. Encourage them to think of other things that the tractor might carry. Suggest it might carry churns of milk after the farmer has milked the cows or food for the cattle and pigs. The tractor can also pull the plough to prepare the fields.
- Tell them how the farmers help us. They grow at least half the food we need by sowing seeds and growing wheat. Tell them how it is ground into flour, made into dough and baked in the oven.

**Movement activity**
- If you have a hall or a big space, invite the children to move to music. Suggest that they wave their arms like the sails of a windmill. They could begin slowly as the wind starts to blow the sails and then wave more quickly as the wind increases.
- Play some lively music and encourage the children to scatter and sprinkle seeds with their fingers.
- Next play some growing or ascending music. Ask the children to sit on the floor. They could pretend to be seeds in the ground, getting up slowly and pretending to grow into wheat swaying in the field.
- Play some music to act out harvesting. Show the children swiping movements like cutting corn.
- Play suitable 'grinding' music. Ask them to run round in small circles, but take care that they don't become too giddy.
- Play jerky or powerful music and ask the children to pretend to knead and punch the dough before it is baked.

## Extensions/variations
- Set up some climbing equipment to resemble a tractor. Ask the children to climb up into the farmer's driving seat and pretend to drive it away.
- Provide some wheeled vehicles and push or pull them around the farmer's fields.
- Make a collage of a farm. You could use drinking straws for hay.

# Outer space



## Learning objectives

- To capture experiences and responses through music and sound effects
- To use music and sounds in original ways for particular uses and purposes
- To represent ideas, thoughts and feelings through music and sounds
- To explore the different sounds of instruments on an electronic keyboard
- To learn how sounds can be changed electronically
- To select and use technology for particular purposes

## Topic

Transport and travel

## Resources

- Poems: 'Many Ways to Travel' by Tony Mitten and 'Two, One, Zero' by Barbara Ireson, from *Transport Poems* compiled by John Foster (OUP)
- Song: 'Five Little Spacemen', from *This Little Puffin* compiled by Elizabeth Matterson (Puffin)
- Posters, photographs and non-fiction books of space exploration
- Tape recorder
- Blank cassette tape
- Percussion instruments
- Music: 'The Overture', from *The Essential Jean Michel Jarre* by Jean Michel Jarre
- CD player
- Electronic keyboard with different voices
- Music: *The Planets Suite* by Gustav Holst
- Internet: search Gustav Holst, select Planets Suite

## What to do

### Circle time

- Read the poems and encourage the children to join in.

### Music activity

- Sing the song 'Five Little Spacemen' with the children and then record individuals or groups as they sing it alone.
- Play back the recording and ask whether the children can recognize who is singing.
- When we hear our own voices we are hearing the sound through the air (which is the same as the sound recorded) and through the head (which is not recorded).
- Ask the children to put their fingers in their ears to hear the sound only through their heads.
- Record two or three different percussion instruments and replay, adjusting the balance and volume. Discuss how different this can make the sounds. Point out that sounds can be changed (electronically).
- Play music by Jean Michel Jarre, who was one of the first musicians to create and play an electronic orchestra.

## Notes for practitioner

- MIDI = musical instrument digital interface
- Synthesizer = produces an electronic sound signal sent to the amplifier and loudspeaker.

## Extensions/variations

- Explore 'preset' sounds on the electronic keyboard.
- Encourage pairs and small groups of children to further explore sounds on an electronic keyboard, by creating a soundscape describing a spaceship travelling through deep space.
- Play *The Planets Suite* to illustrate how music can be inspired by outer space.

## Links to home

- Enquire if any parents can compose with electronic keyboard and effects board. Ask if they would come and demonstrate to the children.

## Related activity

- Tick, tock, hum, click (see page 116)

# Fantastic animals

## Topic
Animals

## Resources
- DVD: 'The Pastoral Symphony (No. 6)' by Beethoven, in *Fantasia* (Buena Vista–Walt Disney)
- DVD player and television
- CD player
- Music: *The Pastoral Symphony (No. 6)* by Ludwig van Beethoven
- Paper, brushes and paints
- Playdough or clay
- Sugar paper or card
- Fabrics, scrap papers, found materials for collage
- Scissors
- PVA glue and spreaders
- Book: *Remarkable Animals* by Tony Meeuwissen (Frances Lincoln)

## Learning objectives
- To use imagination to represent their own ideas and thoughts through art and design and dance
- To initiate new combinations of movement and gesture in order to express and respond to feelings and ideas
- To use what has been learnt about media and materials in original ways

## Preparation
- Find section on DVD and CD.

## What to do
### Circle time
- Explain that the children are going to see on the DVD a cartoon of gods and fantastic mythical creatures that the Greeks believed existed many years ago.
  - Pan plays pipes.
  - Cupids bring lovers together.
  - Pegasus is the flying horse.
  - Centaurs are half human and half horse.
  - Unicorns are horses with a single horn.
  - Bacchus is the god of wine and festivals.
  - Zeus is the King of all the gods.
  - Hephaestus, his son, makes the thunderbolts.

  (Note: The rainbow has been painted upside-down! The blue colour should be under the curve.)

### Story activity
- Ask the children to describe the story. (Pegasus with foals playing, centaurs falling in love and having a party which ends with a thunderstorm. After the storm a rainbow is formed. The sun sets and the moon and stars come out.)

### Dance activity
- Play Beethovan's *Pastoral Symphony*. Ask the children to dance, showing how they feel – when the pan pipes are playing (happy), and when the storm comes (frightened).

## Extensions/variations
- Ask the children to make a painting, model or collage of a mythological animal of their own.
- Explain that many of the creatures are half animal and half human. Look at the book *Remarkable Animals* and discuss some ideas.

# Decorate a tree

## Learning objectives
- To use media and materials in original ways
- To represent ideas imaginatively through art and design

## What to do
**Art activity**
- Suggest to the children that they decorate the twig they have collected or brought from home (see **Links to home**).
- Ask the children to describe the shape of their twigs and to say what they remind them of.
- Encourage the children to add other materials (natural and made) to the twig. Suggest using newspaper, cotton wool, fabrics and threads to add textures.
- Add a base to make the decorated twig balance.

## Extensions/variations
- Ask the children to describe what they are making and how they are using the materials in their work.
- You could varnish the finished products (away from the children) to make them last longer.
- Decorate a tree in the garden.
- Decorate a tree for Christmas.

## Links to home
- Ask parents to help their child obtain an interesting looking twig no more than 50cm long.

## Related activities
- Autumn leaves (see page 113)
- Stuck up the chimney (see page 162)
- Trees (see page 128)

## Topics
Celebrations/Gardening

## Resources
- Newspaper
- Wallpaper paste (no fungicide)
- Tray for papier-mâché
- Brushes
- PVA glue and spreaders
- Stapler
- String
- Medium sized twigs
- Fabrics and wool
- Material for base (eg Plasticine)
- Varnish (for use by practitioner)
- Christmas tree decorations

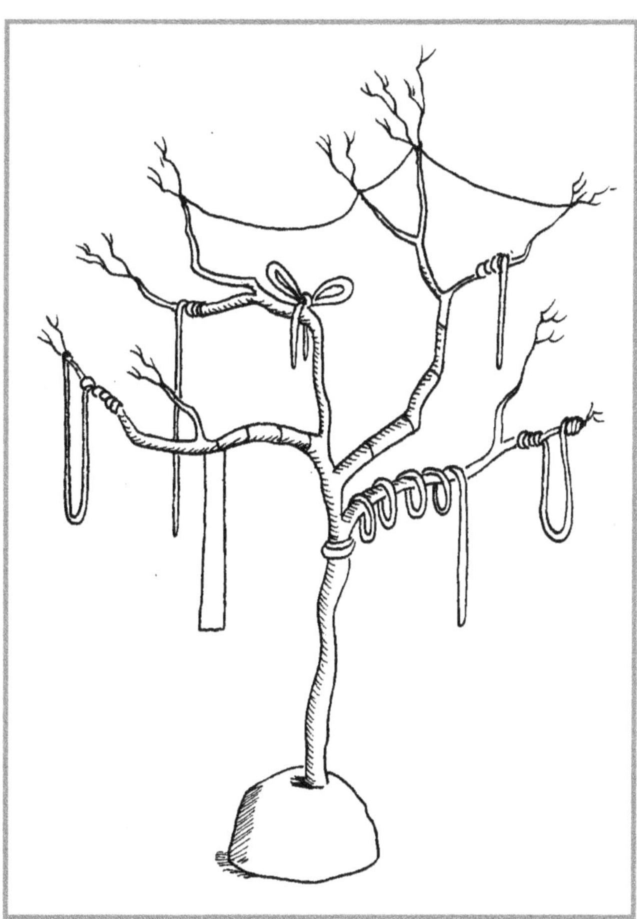

# My imaginary life

## Topic
Myself

## Resources
- Book: *Cinderella*
- Photographs of (separately) child, their family, and three others, eg their home, pet, garden, car
- Three A4 sheets of paper folded to A5, and stapled to make a book
- White paper
- Computer and printer
- Coloured magazines with pictures of people, homes, gardens, toys, playground equipment, etc, as required
- Scissors
- Crayons
- Glue and spreaders
- Guillotine (for use by practitioner)
- CD-ROM '2publish' from *Infant Video Toolkit* (2Simple Software)

Supervise the use of scissors.

## Learning objectives
- To represent own ideas, thoughts and feelings through design and technology, art and stories
- To use phonic knowledge and memory skills to recognize and read or write some common words and familiar names
- To use technology, with support, for a particular purpose

## Preparation
- Collect magazines and pictures for activity.
- Prepare booklets.
- Access word processing program on computer, eg '2publish', and select suitable layout for books.

## What to do
**Circle time**
- Read *Cinderella* up to the point where the fairy godmother changes Cinderella for the ball.
- Invite children to describe how they would like to be and how they would wish their homes and gardens to be, if a fairy godmother could change them.
- Suggest that they make a book to show their ideas.

**Computer activity**
- Support printing text for the booklet.
  - **Page 1 (title)**
    My life, … by
  - **Pages 2–3**
    This is me … but I would like to be like this.
  - **Pages 4–5**
    This is my home … but I would like to live here, etc.
  - **Page 6**
    This is my family … but I love them as they are!
- Add their own drawings to the text.

**Art activity**
- Stick the collage and photographs on white paper first, then into the booklet when the children are satisfied with their efforts.
- Left-sided page will show their photographs and the right side will be made of a collage from magazines to show their imaginary ideas.
- For example, opposite the photograph of their dog could be a cut-out picture of a dinosaur; opposite their flat could be a picture of a fairy castle, and their garden could be a jungle or pictures of playground equipment on a drawn grass background.

## Extensions/variations
- The children could make drawings of themselves and their homes and other pictures, instead of using photographs.
- Give the booklet as a Mother's or Father's Day gift.

## Links to home
- Ask parents for photographs that can be used.

## Related activity
- Over the rainbow (see page 166–167)

# Clowns



## Learning objectives

- To create movement and dance in response to music
- To create simple representations of particular people
- To represent ideas, thoughts and feelings through art and dance

## Preparation

- Find Act II, Scene 2, on the *Pagliacci* DVD.

## What to do

**Group storytime activity**

- Tell the children that you are going to show them a DVD of a play about clowns. Act II, Scene 2, contains a slapstick routine.
- Explain that the style of singing is called opera and that the language is Italian because the composer was Italian. Talk about the training that opera singers must have.
- Support children in learning new words and understanding that the *soprano* (Nedda) sings very high; the *tenor* (Canio) sings fairly high and the *baritone* (Tonio) sings low.

**Art activity**

- Ask the children to paint a face of a clown on a paper plate.
- A practitioner (or parent) could offer to copy the designs onto children's faces if they would like their faces painted.
- Take photographs of the children.

**Dance activity**

- Play 'Tears of a Clown'. Encourage the children to dance to the music as though they are clowns.

## Extensions/variations

- Draw the children's attention to the appearance of the harlequin clown in *The Nutcracker Ballet.* Ask the children how his appearance differs from other clowns that they might have seen.
- Make the plate into a mask. Cut out eyeholes and attach elastic.

## Notes for practitioner

- *Pagliacci* is a story about a clown, Canio, whose beautiful young wife, Nedda, loves a young man, Silvio. Canio sings at the end of Act I 'Vesti la giubba', heartbroken at his wife's infidelity. The drama concludes tragically during the clowns' performance, when jealous Canio stabs his wife and her lover. This part is unsuitable for young children.
- However, this production does show traditional clowns in costume (Harlequin, Columbine and Pagliaccio) with an amusing slapstick routine in Act II, Scene 2.

## Topic

Toys

## Resources

- DVD: *Pagliacci* by Ruggero Leoncavallo (Philips 1982 version with Plácido Domingo, filmed by Franco Zeffirelli)
- Face paints
- Cotton wool
- Towels
- White paper plates and crayons
- Fabrics and wool
- Glue and spreaders
- Camera
- Elastic
- Song: 'Tears of a Clown' by Smokey Robinson
- CD or tape player
- DVD recorder and television

## Link to home

- Before offering face paints, find out from parents if any children have allergies or any families have objections to them.

## Related activity

- The Nutcracker (see pages 118–119)

# Are we there yet?

## Topic
Transport and travel

## Resources
- Poems: 'Are We Nearly There Yet?' and 'I Feel Sick', from *Wish You Were Here (And I Wasn't)* by Colin McNaughton (Walker Books)
- Wheeled toys
- Toy cars
- Play mat of road in the country
- Song: 'Going by Car', from *Start with a Song* by Mavis de Mierre (Brilliant Publications)
- Book: *Are We There Yet?* by Verna Allette Wilkins (Tamarind Books)

## Learning objectives
- To engage in imaginative role-play based on own first-hand experiences
- To explore and discuss similarities and differences between people and families and to understand the importance of equal opportunities
- To recount an event within a small group, connecting and expressing ideas and events effectively, using past, present and future forms accurately and showing awareness of listeners' needs

## What to do
**Circle time**
- Read the poems, and ask the children if that is how they felt about going on a trip.
- Encourage the children to talk about their own day out.

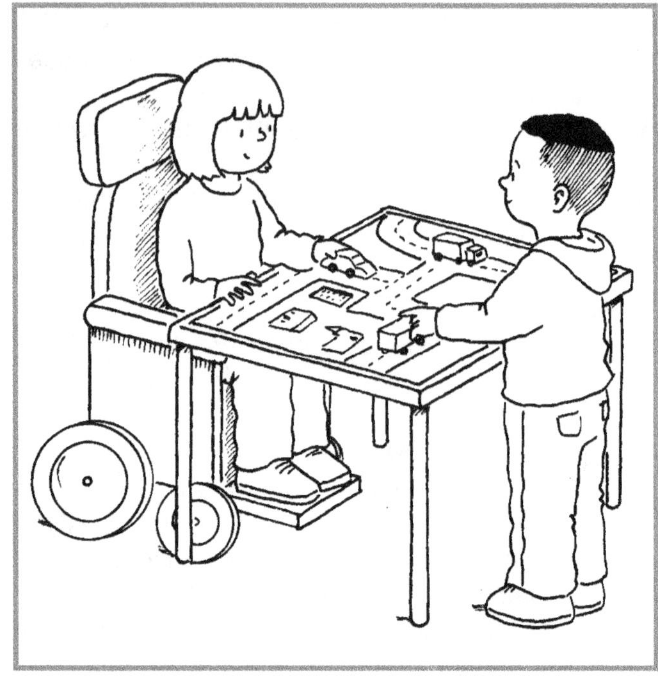

**Imaginative play activity**
- While playing on the mat, encourage the children to pretend that they are going in a car to a theme park or seaside.
- Ask them what they can see on their journey.
- Ask how they feel about going on the trip, and what they might do when they get there.

**Music activity**
- Learn the song 'Going by Car'.

## Extensions/variations
- Read the story *Are We There Yet?*
- The father in this story is in a wheelchair. There could be discussion about equal opportunities and access when disabled people go out. Some of the children may be disabled; others may have disabled parents.

## Links to home
- Tell parents about the activity, and ask them to talk to their child about a day out that they have experienced recently.

## Related activity
- Seaside (see pages 102–103)

# Windy weather

Being imaginative

## Learning objectives

- To capture experiences with music, sounds and words
- To work cooperatively as part of a group to develop a song
- To explore different sounds and use voices and instruments in original ways
- To sing songs and make music and experiment with ways of changing them

## Topic

Weather

## Resources

- CD: *BBC Sound Effects* (BBC Worldwide)
- CD player
- Poem: 'The Wind Came Running' by Ivy O. Eastwick, from *Days Like This* compiled by Simon James (Walker Books)
- Song: 'The Wind Finds', from *Start with a Song* by Mavis de Mierre (Brilliant Publications)
- Percussion instruments
- Book: *Chimp and Zee and the Big Storm* by Catherine and Laurence Anholt (Frances Lincoln)

## What to do

### Music activity

- Read 'The Wind Came Running'.
- Play the sound effects CD, and ask the children to first think inside their head how to make sounds like the wind with their voices.
- Invite each child in turn to make a sound like the wind with their voice.
- Ask all the children to make their wind sounds very quietly. Put a finger to your mouth to encourage a quiet sound.
- Ask children to make the sound louder, medium volume, then louder still. Signal this by bringing hands away from each other as the sound becomes louder. (Do not raise and lower your hand to signal quiet and loud, as that signal is used to indicate changes in pitch.)
- Support the children's language development by introducing and explaining words such as: *loud*, *quiet*, *crescendo*, *volume* and *in unison.*
- When the children have learned 'The Wind Finds', divide the group into two.
- Invite one group to make the sound effects while the other sings, then swap roles and repeat.
- End with playing the percussion instruments with a bang.

## Extensions/variations

- Accompany the poem 'The Wind Came Running' with the children's sound effects, varying the volume.
- Read *Chimp and Zee and the Big Storm.*

# Peter and the Wolf

## Topic
Animals

## Resources
- *Peter and the Wolf* storybook – any version with simple words and clear pictures
- CD of the music *Peter and the Wolf*
- Large floor space
- Coloured chalk or hoops to mark zones
- Long sheet of paper to make frieze
- Paints and paintbrushes
- Tissue paper
- Scissors
- Glue
- Pictures of the story characters and their musical instruments

 Ensure that floor space is free from splinters.

## Learning objectives
- To create and use spontaneous movement and dance in response to particular musical sounds
- To imaginatively express and represent feelings experienced while listening to the music and the story
- To show an interest in the way musical instruments sound
- To experiment with different ways of moving
- To move in a range of ways, safely negotiating space
- To respond to feelings experienced when listening to the music and the story

## Preparation
- In a safe place mark the various zones with coloured hoops or chalk:
  - meadow green zone
  - tree brown zone
  - pond blue zone
  - grass black zone
  - house red zone
  - forest yellow zone
- Have the music ready to play.
- Make picture cards showing each of the characters.

## What to do
### Circle time
- Read the book *Peter and the Wolf*. Make sure that children are familiar with all the characters. Discuss why different instruments are used to represent the characters, the different sound qualities and how they can reflect personalities. Show pictures of the instruments and the characters. Invite the children to choose which parts they would like to play.

### Movement activity
- Ask the children to remember which part they are playing, to listen carefully, and to role-play the relevant part when the correct music begins.
- Explain that there is a special instrument for each character:

| | | | |
|---|---|---|---|
| bird | flute | duck | oboe |
| Peter | strings | cat | clarinet |
| rifle shots | drums | wolf | horn |
| grandfather | bassoon | | |

- Play the music and act out the story. You may have to assist the younger children in remembering which colour is their zone. Hold up the relevant character pictures to remind children when they are unsure.

## Extension/variation
- Make a long wall frieze showing the procession through the village street, for example grandfather, Peter, bird, cart, and the wolf. Stick a picture of the duck onto the wolf's stomach. To add further texture, make tissue paper collages of the cat and the bird.

## Links to home
- Ask if family members play any of the instruments and if they would be willing to come into the setting to demonstrate and play for the children.
- Plan and prepare a musical performance involving all of the children and invite families to watch.

## Related activities
- What's the time, Mr Wolf? (see page 28)
- Noah's animals (see page 109)

# Carnival of Animals

**Being imaginative**

## Learning objectives

- To create new movements and gestures to respond to music and express ideas and feelings imaginatively
- To play cooperatively as part of a group to act out a narrative
- To concentrate and experiment with different ways of moving
- To move confidently in a range of ways, safely negotiating space

## Topic

Animals

## Resources

- CD of *Carnival of Animals* by Saint-Saens
- CD player
- Large safe area
- Large cardboard boxes
- Paints
- Scissors

Ensure children respect each other's space.
Pay special attention to the use of scissors.

## What to do

### Movement activity

- Invite children to create their own original movements to represent the animals on the CD. Explain that they will be taking part in a 'Carnival of Animals'.
- Ask the children to sit on the floor and to listen and concentrate very carefully. As each animal is mentioned, encourage them to create appropriate actions and role-plays. For example:
  - lion – slink and roar
  - rooster – flap and crow
  - jackass – laugh
  - turtle/tortoise – crawl slowly
  - fish – float and wriggle
  - mules – trot slowly
  - cuckoo and other birds – flap wings
  - fossils and bones in museum – shake limbs
  - swan – sway gracefully

## Extension/variation

- Offer children the opportunity to discover what it would be like to be a tortoise or a turtle. Cut out an archway shape each side of a large cardboard box big enough to fit over the child's shoulders. Cut another archway for the child's head. Ask the children to paint a turtle shell pattern over the box. The children will like taking turns to crawl slowly like a turtle.

## Related activity

- Can you squirm like a worm? (see page 35)

# Kumbh mela

## Topic
Celebrations

## Resources
- Small pieces of climbing apparatus
- Long piece of wallpaper
- Orange or grapefruit halves
- Thread or string
- Night lights
- Boxes/containers suitable for making baskets
- Paper
- Paint and paintbrushes
- Coloured tissue paper
- Scissors
- Glue

Do not light the candles in the setting.

## Learning objectives
- To initiate new combinations of movement and gesture to express feelings, ideas and experiences
- To play cooperatively as part of a group to develop and act out a narrative
- To move with confidence and imagination, safely negotiating space
- To show an interest in different traditions and ways of life

## Preparation
- Find a safe large floor space. Place small pieces of climbing apparatus around the room.

## What to do
**Movement activities**
- Tell the children about the festival of Kumbh mela that takes place every twelve years in Haridwar in India. Advise them that there are lots of small shops, and plenty of bathing in the river. Station some apparatus around the room with a child to each to depict the stalls and shops. Lay a piece of rolled out wallpaper in one corner for the river.
- Have some of the children asleep on the floor (in their tents). Suggest they awake excitedly and run across the red bridge (a piece of apparatus).
- Some children can pretend to sweep the streets, making large sweeping movements with their arms and moving sideways as they progress. Others can be policemen patrolling the town, walking along importantly, heads held high in the air.
  Some of the children can weave in and out as they walk through the narrow streets. As they pass the stalls ask the shop children to hold out their hand as if displaying trinkets and call out 'Buy some treasures.'
- Next, pretend that it is time for bathing. Ask the children to run to the river Ganges and pretend to take off their clothes and step into the river to find out whether the water is warm. Suggest that they jump up and down and then crouch down low in the water.
- Now pretend it is evening and the river is brightly lit with candles. Shake out coins as offerings; flutter fingers to drop petals into the river.

## Extensions/variations
- Make lights for along the river. Use empty orange or grapefruit halves. Thread some thread or string through the sides. Take the children outside or into a large space and ask them to stand or sit still and keep well back while an adult lights the candles for them to watch.
- Make baskets of flowers to send down the river. Use empty strawberry punnets, margarine tubs or other small containers. Cover with paper and paint them yellow.
- Cut out petal shapes and paste them with glue. Stick on coloured crumpled tissue paper and lay the flowers in the baskets.

## Links to home
- Display a notice in advance asking parents to save orange or grapefruit halves after eating them at home and to bring them into the setting.

# Who has eaten the lettuce?

**Being imaginative**

## Learning objectives

- To create a simple representation of an object, creature or person
- To use media and materials in original ways
- To represent own ideas and thoughts through art and design

## What to do

**Circle time**

- Show the painting *L'Escargot (The Snail)* represented by a spiral collage of coloured paper rectangles.
- Ask the children what they think it is. Give them the clue that it will eat the lettuce in their garden.
- Tell them the title. Point out how the rectangles of paper make a spiral shape.
- Suggest that they make a picture from shaped paper.

**Art activity**

- The children can use cut out or torn coloured paper, handmade paper, or cut out of gummed paper shapes or stickers.
- Ask the children what they are making, and discuss their choice of presentation and use of colours.

## Extensions/variations

- Paint paper using mixed colours or print a pattern on the paper first.
- Cut or tear the paper and then use to make the collage.

## Related activity

- Creepy-crawly mini-beasts (see pages 98–99)

## Topics

Animals/Colours

## Resources

- Painting: *L'Escargot* by Henri Matisse
- Paper
- Paintbrushes
- Paints
- Scissors
- Glue and spreaders
- Gummed shapes or stickers
- Smooth coloured paper

 Supervise the use of scissors.

# Tree template

# Skeleton template

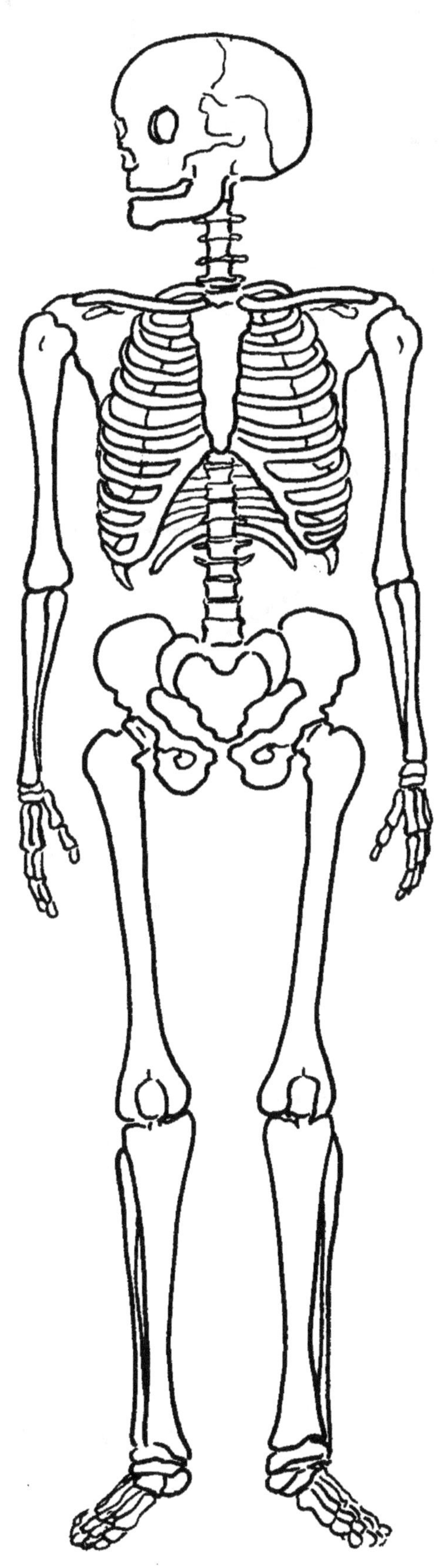

# Flags template

**The Union Jack**
**United Kingdom flag**
Red, white and blue

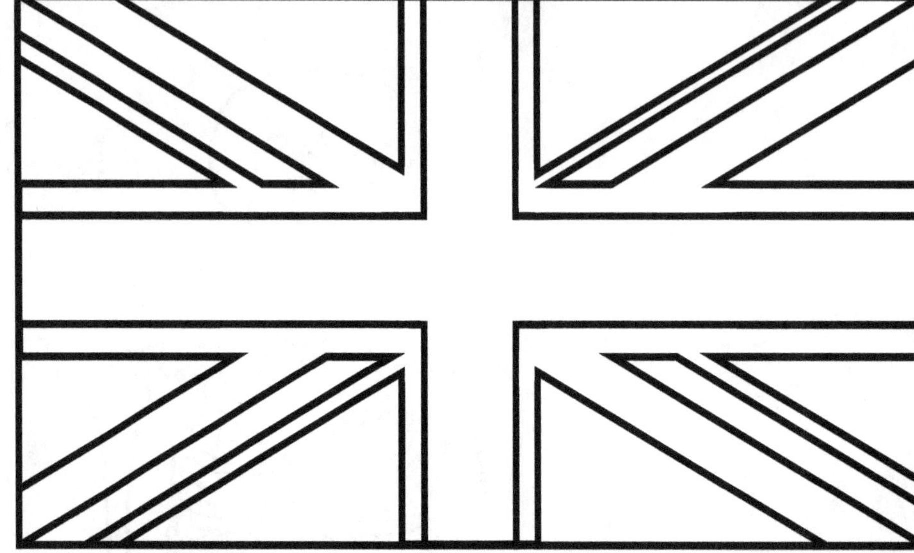

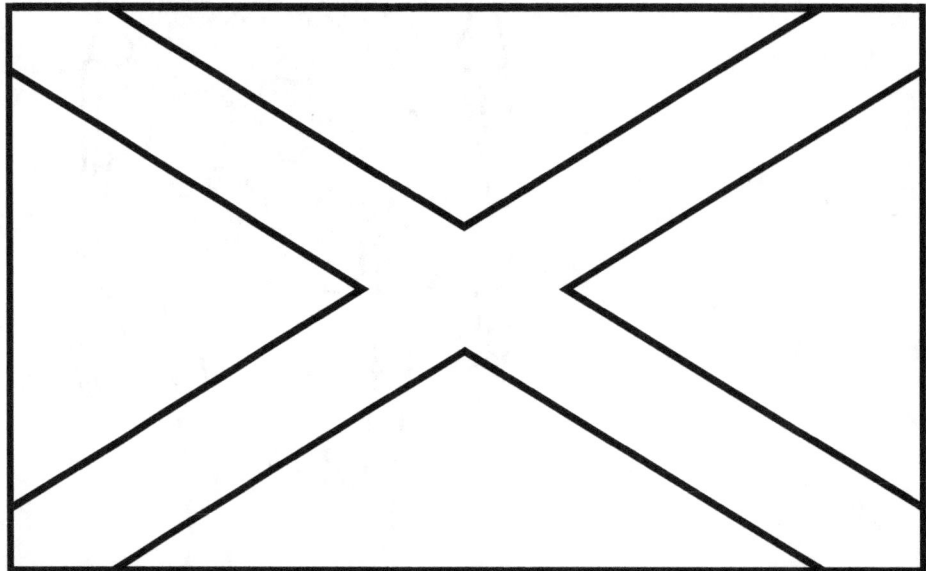

**St. Andrew**
**Sottish flag**
White and blue

**St. Patrick**
**Irish flag**
White and red

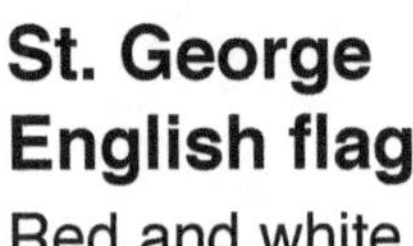

**St. George**
**English flag**
Red and white

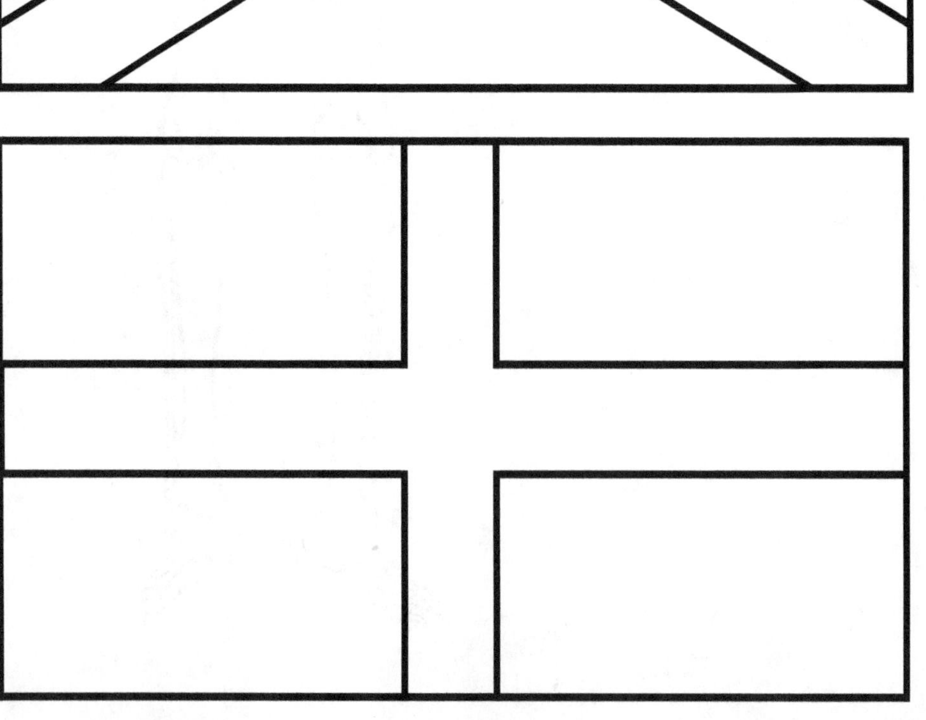

# Dolls template

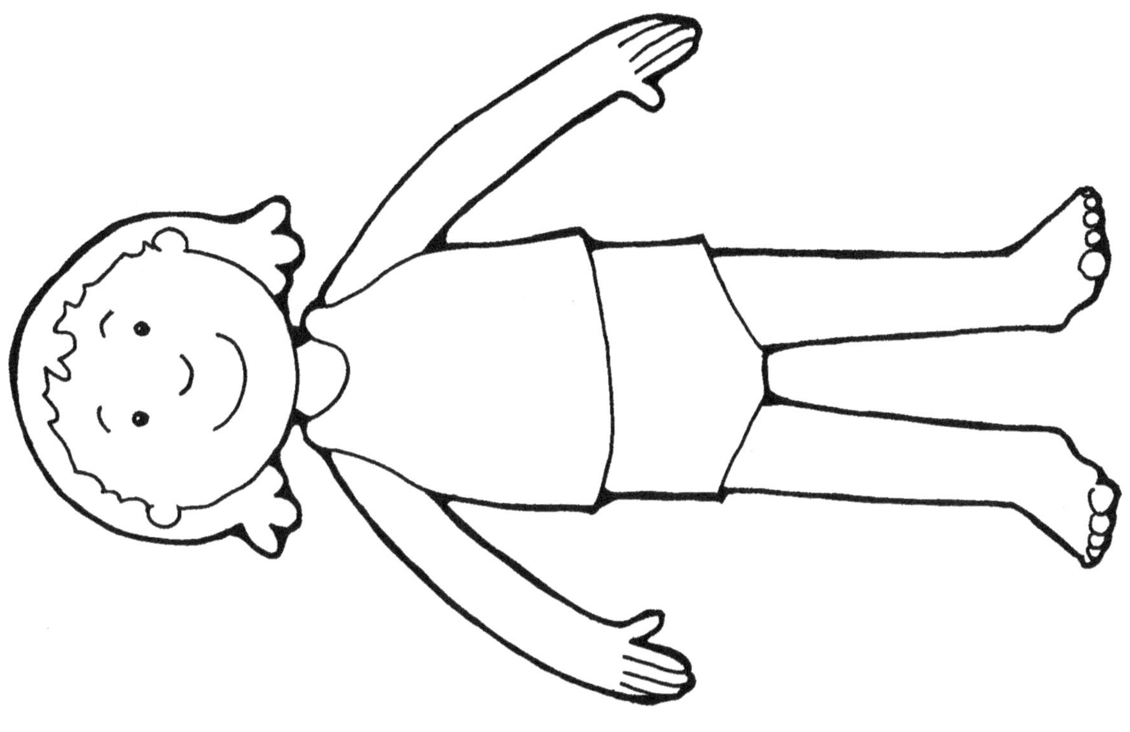

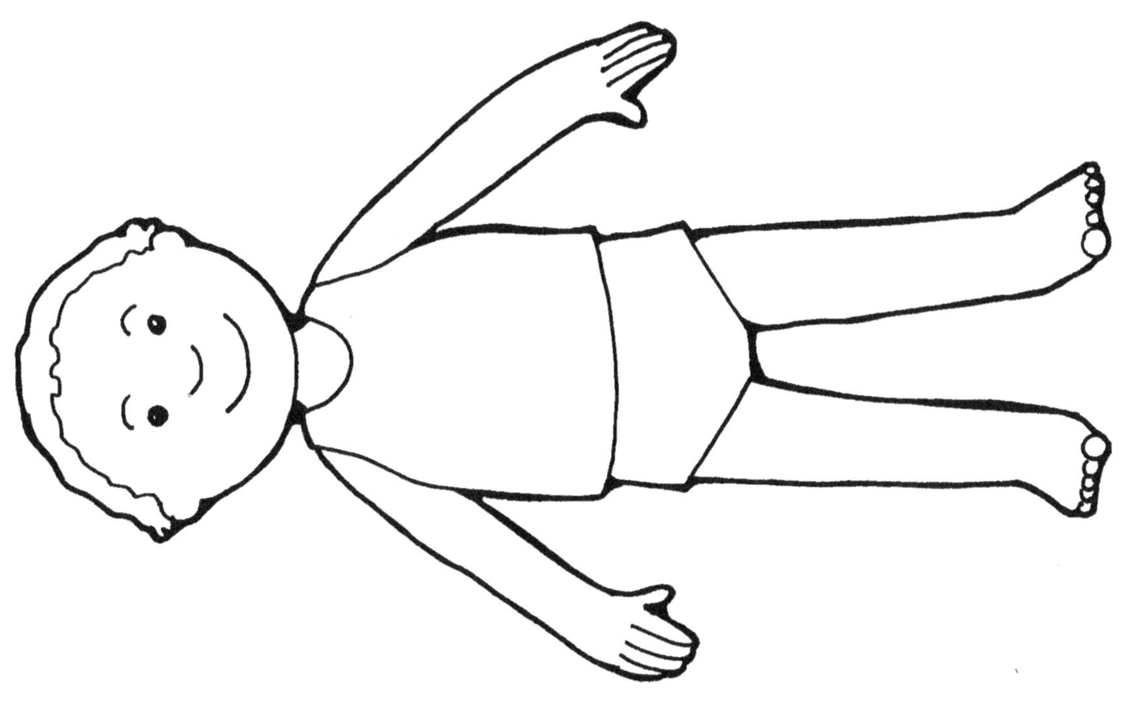

# Heart template

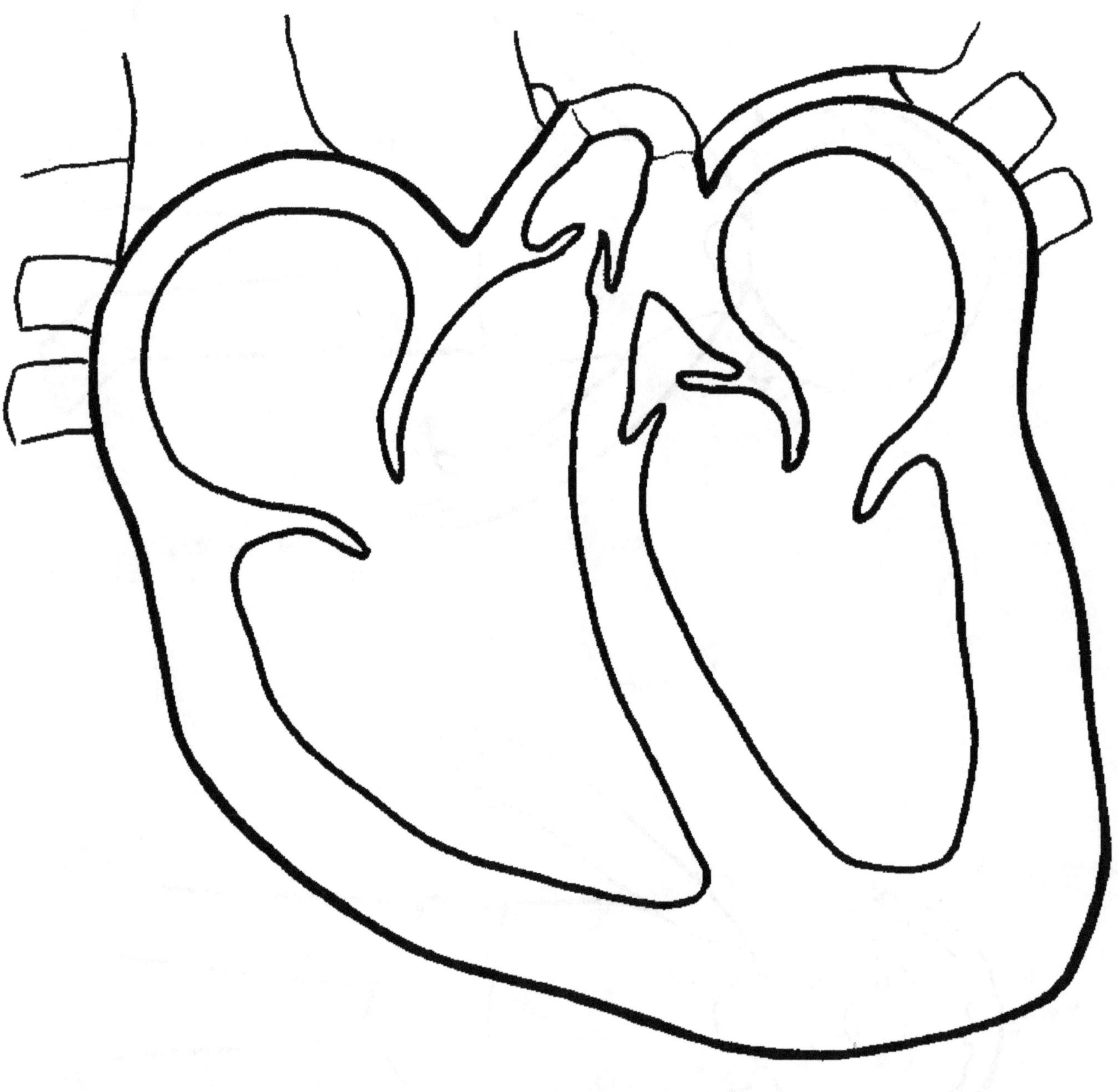

# Glossary

**abstract**
A picture reduced to its essential visual elements (eg lines, shapes, colours)

**acoustic**
Non-electronic means of sound production (as in acoustic instruments)

**aesthetic**
Relates to what is considered to be beautiful or artistic

**armature**
A frame supporting a 3D sculpture

**beat**
The regular pulse of music

**body percussion**
A percussive sound created using the body (eg stomp, pat, clap, snap)

**choreography**
Planning and arranging dance movements into a finished dance work

**closed sounds**
Sound is dull and short, eg a triangle held by the hand to stop it vibrating

**collage**
2D image created by gluing materials such as paper and fabric scraps to a flat surface

**context**
Circumstances influencing the creation of the work, such as intention, time and place, eg skipping songs

**cool down**
After activity, to help children's heart rates return to normal and to help them become still

**dance drama**
Individual or group drama based on movements that tell a story, with music as either stimulus or accompaniment

**duration**
Long or short rhythmic patterns

**dynamics**
In music, the degree of loudness or softness, ie volume; in dance, one of the five elements of movement; refers to how the body is moving

**found instruments**
Everyday objects used as classroom instruments to create music (eg PVC piping, pots and pans, kitchen utensils)

**found objects**
Everyday objects recycled or incorporated into an artwork

**found sounds**
Body sounds, found instruments, traditional instruments, voices, natural sounds, synthetic sounds to create a music composition (see soundscape)

**graphics**
2D images produced by processes such as printmaking, photography, and computer graphic applications

**harmony**
The combination of pitched notes in a way that is musically significant

**installation**
A 3D arrangement often constructed of found objects and involving mixed media

**logo**
A symbolic design to identify an organization

**maquette**
A small sculpture made as a trial or sketch for a larger piece

**melody**
The arrangement and sequence of pitches

**MIDI**
Musical Instrument Digital Interface – standard specifications that enable electronic instruments such as synthesizers, samplers, sequencers, or drum machines to communicate with one another and with computers

**monoprint**
Printing by transferring a painted design on to paper by laying the paper over the painted surface; only one print can be made of each design

**narrative**
Follows a story line

**open sounds**
When the sound is bright and resonates by using a metal beater and allowing the instrument to vibrate

**Orff instruments**
A set of barred instruments (glockenspiels, metallophones, and xylophones) for teaching music

**ostinato (plural ostinati)**
A rhythmic or melodic pattern that is repeated persistently throughout a composition

**pattern**
Repetition of one or more of the elements in a planned way, eg a sequence of three different movements, shapes and colours, or verse followed by chorus

**percussion instrument**
Any instrument that is played by striking, shaking or scraping

**performance**
A production of dance, drama or music for an audience

**personal space**
The 'space bubble' that a dancer occupies, including all levels, planes, and directions both near to and far from the body's centre

**pitch**
High and low notes (result of many or few vibrations)

**poster**
A sign used to advertise a simple message

**programme music**
Music inspired by a story or visual image, eg *Peer Gynt suite*, *Carnival of the Animals*, *Peter and the Wolf* (also known as illustrative music)

**repertoire**
Music and dance learned, performed or listened to

**rhythm**
In music, the arrangement of notes and silences of varying duration; the beat may be slow, but each note having a short duration results in a running rhythm

**round**
The same melody sung by two or more parts, beginning one after another; all parts sing at the same pitch

**solfa**
Notation that uses syllabic names (do, re, mi, fa, so, la, ti, do) to represent the notes of the scale relative to the tonic

**soundscape**
A free-form composition using any arrangement or ordering of sounds and any combination of traditional instruments, non-traditional instruments, voices, body percussion, natural sounds, found sounds, synthetic sounds, technology, and so on

**style**
A distinctive quality given to a creation by its creator or performer, eg ballet and the lambada are styles of dance

**tempo**
Slower and faster beats; a brisk march has a faster tempo than a slow waltz

**timbre**
The characteristic or quality of the sound that distinguishes one instrument, voice or sound source from another, eg a clarinet can be distinguished from a horn

**vocables**
The voice is used as an instrument as opposed to singing words

**warm up**
Before physical activity, a series of movements and exercises to prepare the body

# Characteristics of Effective Learning

Throughout all activities, practitioners need to be aware of the four themes of the Early Years Foundation Stage. Every child must be considered a *unique child* and given opportunities to form *positive relationships* within an enabling environment in order to make progress in *learning and development* in each of the prime and specific areas.

In addition to the *Learning Objectives and Early Learning Goals* listed for each activity, practitioners will seek always to encourage and observe the following *Characteristics of Effective Learning*.

## Playing and Exploring

Children will find out and explore by showing curiosity and developing particular interests, using their senses and engaging in activities. They will play with what they know, acting out their own experiences through pretending and imaginative role play. They should be willing to 'have a go' by seeking new and challenging activities and being confident to try things out.

Practitioners should join in with children's play without taking over, helping, supporting and modelling ideas, challenges and risk taking and setting an example that effort and practice improves and mistakes can be learned from.

Children need flexible and stimulating resources provided within calm and ordered indoor and outdoor spaces and uninterrupted periods of time to play and explore.

## Active Learning

Children will learn to become involved and concentrate on their chosen activities, displaying high levels of fascination and attention to details, maintaining focus and ignoring minor distractions. They need to develop perserverence, effort and persistence to 'keep on trying' through challenges and believe that a solution to a problem may be found or accept that an idea may not work out exactly as planned. They should enjoy meeting their own goals and challenges and be proud of their own accomplishments and achievements, without relying heavily on external praise or rewards.

Practitioners should support children in choosing their own activities, methods, plans and goals and talk with them about progress, challenges and successes. They may be encouraged to work together and learn from each other when appropriate. Specific praise for particular efforts, persistence, problem solving, good ideas and new skills acquired will help children to develop their own motivations.

Children should be provided with new and unusual activities that are linked to their current interests and given enough time and freedom for all to contribute and to become deeply involved.

## Creating and Thinking Critcially

Children will have their own ideas, think of new ways to do things and find ways of solving problems for themselves. As they make connections and notice patterns and sequences within their experiences, they will learn to make predictions, test and develop their ideas and understand cause and effect. They will then be able to make informed decisions and plans, check and change their strategies as they work and play and eventually review their approaches and activities.

Practitioners should model thinking aloud, describing problems, remembering previous experiences, making connections, finding out and trying different ideas and approaches. If children's interests and conversations are supported, and sustained shared thinking is offered when appropriate, they will learn to use the 'plan-do-review' process effectively.

Children should always engage in activities in order to find their own ways to represent and develop their own ideas, using techniques and processes that they may learn from others. Routines should be recognizable and understandable to both children and adults, but also flexible enough to ensure that both security and independent development are available within the learning community.

# Table of learning opportunities

| Activity | Page no. | Communication and Language | | | Physical Development | | Personal, Social and Emotional Development | | | Literacy | | Maths | | Understanding the World | | | Expressive Arts and Design | |
|---|---|---|---|---|---|---|---|---|---|---|---|---|---|---|---|---|---|---|
| | | Listening and attention | Understanding | Speaking | Moving and handling | Health and self-care | Self-confidence and self-awareness | Managing feelings and behaviour | Making relationships | Reading | Writing | Numbers | Shape, space and measures | People and communities | The world | Technology | Exploring and using media and materials | Being imaginative |
| Five Currant Buns | 18 | ✔ | | | ✔ | | | | | | | | | | | | | |
| Can you grow like a bean? | 19 | | | | ✔ | | | | | | | | | | | | | ✔ |
| Holiday homes | 20 | | | | ✔ | | | | | | | | | | | | ✔ | |
| The Queen's palace | 21 | | | | ✔ | | | | | | | | | | | | | |
| Catch the robber | 22 | | | | ✔ | ✔ | | | | | | | | | | | | |
| Let's play trains | 23 | | | | ✔ | | | | | | | | | | | | | |
| Sing a limb | 24 | | | | ✔ | | | | | | | | | | | | | ✔ |
| Use your senses | 25 | | | | ✔ | | | | | | | | | | ✔ | | ✔ | |
| Horsey, Horsey, Don't You Stop | 26 | | | | ✔ | | | | | | | | | | | | ✔ | |
| Spring plants and animals | 27 | | | | ✔ | | | | | | | | | | ✔ | | | |
| What's the time Mr Wolf? | 28 | | | | ✔ | | | ✔ | | | | | | | | | | |
| Acting out colours | 29 | | | | ✔ | | | | | | | | | | | | | ✔ |
| Shape necklaces | 30 | | | | ✔ | | | | | | | | | | | | ✔ | |
| Fishes in the sea | 31 | | | | ✔ | | | | | | | | | | | | | ✔ |

| Activity | Page no. | Communication and Language | | | Physical Develop-ment | | Personal, Social and Emotional Development | | | Literacy | | Maths | | Understanding the World | | | Expressive Arts and Design | |
|---|---|---|---|---|---|---|---|---|---|---|---|---|---|---|---|---|---|---|
| | | Listening and attention | Understanding | Speaking | Moving and handling | Health and self-care | Self-confidence and self-awareness | Managing feelings and behaviour | Making relationships | Reading | Writing | Numbers | Shape, space and measures | People and communities | The world | Technology | Exploring and using media and materials | Being imaginative |
| Build a house | 32 | | | | ✔ | | | | | | | | | | | | | |
| Reflections | 33 | | | | ✔ | | | | | | | | | | | | ✔ | |
| A bear hunt | 34 | | | | ✔ | | | | | | | | | | | | | ✔ |
| Can you squirm like a worm? | 35 | | | | ✔ | | | | | | | | | | | | | ✔ |
| British bulldog | 36 | | ✔ | | ✔ | | | | ✔ | | | | | | | | | |
| Battle ball | 37 | | | | ✔ | | | | ✔ | | | | | ✔ | | | ✔ | |
| Packing groceries | 38 | ✔ | | | ✔ | | | | | | | ✔ | | | | | | |
| Body shapes | 39 | | | | ✔ | | | | | | | | | | | | | |
| Treasure trail | 40 | | | ✔ | ✔ | | | | | | | | ✔ | | | | | |
| Journey to the stars | 41 | | | | ✔ | | | | | | | | | | | | | ✔ |
| Look what I can do | 42 | | | | | | | | | | | | | | | | | |
| Find the smugglers' cave | 43 | | | | ✔ | | | | | | | | | | | | | ✔ |
| Cross the sea | 44 | | ✔ | | ✔ | | | | | | | | | | ✔ | | ✔ | |
| Cross the forest canopy | 45 | | | | ✔ | | | | | | | | | | | | | ✔ |
| Archway touch | 46 | | | | ✔ | | | | ✔ | | | | | | | | | |
| I can balance | 47 | | | | ✔ | | | | | | | | | | | | | |
| Let's ride the train | 48 | | | | ✔ | | | | | | | | | | | | ✔ | |
| Bony business | 49 | | | | ✔ | | | | | | | | | | | | ✔ | |

| Activity | Page no. | Communication and Language | | | Physical Development | | Personal, Social and Emotional Development | | | Literacy | | Mathematics | | Understanding the World | | | Expressive Arts and Design | |
|---|---|---|---|---|---|---|---|---|---|---|---|---|---|---|---|---|---|---|
| | | Listening and attention | Understanding | Speaking | Moving and handling | Health and self-care | Self-confidence and self-awareness | Managing feelings and behaviour | Making relationships | Reading | Writing | Numbers | Shape, space and measures | People and communities | The world | Technology | Exploring and using media and materials | Being imaginative |
| Winter | 50 | | | | ✔ | | | | | | | | | | | | ✔ | |
| Shipwreck | 51 | | ✔ | | ✔ | | | | | | | | | | | | | |
| Family coach | 52 | ✔ | | | ✔ | | | ✔ | | | | | | | | | | |
| Toy ball | 53 | | | | ✔ | | ✔ | | | | | | | | | | | |
| Careful not to bump! | 54 | | | | ✔ | | | ✔ | | | | | | | | | | |
| I prefer this hand | 55 | | | | ✔ | | | | | | | | | | | | | |
| Obstacle course | 56 | | | | ✔ | | | | | | | | | | | | ✔ | |
| Scare the crows | 57 | | | | ✔ | | | | ✔ | | | | | | | | ✔ | |
| Water wheel | 58 | | | | ✔ | | | | | | | | | | ✔ | | | |
| Pets help to keep us healthy | 60 | | | | | ✔ | ✔ | | | | | | | | | | | |
| Healthy eating | 61 | | | | | ✔ | | | | | | | | ✔ | | | | |
| Vegetable and fruit faces | 62 | | | | | ✔ | | | | | | | | | | | | ✔ |
| We need to eat and sleep | 63 | | | | | ✔ | ✔ | | | | | | | ✔ | | | | |
| Hygiene in role-play | 64 | | | | | ✔ | ✔ | | | | | | | | | | | |
| Effects of activities on the body | 65 | | | | ✔ | ✔ | | | | | | | | | | | | |
| Teddy bears celebrate! | 66 | | | | ✔ | ✔ | | | ✔ | | | | | | | ✔ | | ✔ |

| Activity | Page no. | Communication and Language | | | Physical Develop-ment | | Personal, Social and Emotional Development | | | Literacy | | Math-ematics | | Understanding the World | | | Expressive Arts and Design | |
|---|---|---|---|---|---|---|---|---|---|---|---|---|---|---|---|---|---|---|
| | | Listening and attention | Understanding | Speaking | Moving and handling | Health and self-care | Self-confidence and self-awareness | Managing feelings and behaviour | Making relationships | Reading | Writing | Numbers | Shape, space and measures | People and communities | The world | Technology | Exploring and using media and materials | Being imaginative |
| Healthy foods for celebrations | 67 | | | | ✔ | ✔ | | | | | | | | ✔ | | | ✔ | |
| Water is great to drink! | 68 | | | | | ✔ | | | | | | | | ✔ | | | | ✔ |
| I help at home | 69 | | | | | ✔ | | ✔ | | | | | | | | | | ✔ |
| Pastry babies | 70 | | | | ✔ | ✔ | | | | | | | | | ✔ | | | |
| Dressing for the weather | 71 | | | | | ✔ | ✔ | | | | | | | | | | | |
| Help me put on my sari! | 72 | | | | | ✔ | | | | | | | | ✔ | | | ✔ | |
| The land of health | 73 | | | | ✔ | ✔ | | | | | ✔ | ✔ | | | | | | ✔ |
| Garden by the sea | 74 | | | | | ✔ | | | | | | | | | | | | ✔ |
| Can you be a doctor? | 75 | | | | | ✔ | | | ✔ | | | ✔ | | | | | | |
| Fire! Fire! | 78 | | | | ✔ | ✔ | | | | | | | | | | | ✔ | |
| Summer means holidays | 79 | | | | ✔ | | | | | | | | | | | | ✔ | ✔ |
| The Grand Old Duke of York | 80 | | | | ✔ | | | | | | | | | | | | ✔ | |
| Time to go home | 81 | | | | | | | | | | | | | | | | ✔ | ✔ |
| Fruitful | 82 | | | | | | | | | | | | | | | | ✔ | ✔ |

| Activity | Page no. | Communication and Language | | | Physical Develop-ment | | Personal, Social and Emotional Development | | | Literacy | | Math-ematics | | Understanding the World | | | Expressive Arts and Design | |
|---|---|---|---|---|---|---|---|---|---|---|---|---|---|---|---|---|---|---|
| | | Listening and attention | Understanding | Speaking | Moving and handling | Health and self-care | Self-confidence and self-awareness | Managing feelings and behaviour | Making relationships | Reading | Writing | Numbers | Shape, space and measures | People and communities | The world | Technology | Exploring and using media and materials | Being imaginative |
| Quiet as a mouse | 83 | | | | | | | | | | | | | | | | ✓ | |
| Statues | 84 | | | | ✓ | | | | | | | | | | | | ✓ | ✓ |
| Paint the town red | 85 | | | | | | | | | | | | | | | | ✓ | |
| Making biscuits | 86 | | | | ✓ | ✓ | | | | | | | | | ✓ | | ✓ | |
| Make Christmas decorations | 87 | | | | | | | | | | | | | | | | ✓ | |
| Sponge prints | 88 | | | | | | | | | | | | | | | | ✓ | ✓ |
| Marble painting | 89 | | | | | | | | | | | | | | | | ✓ | ✓ |
| Mehendi hand | 90 | | | | | | | | | | | | | ✓ | | | ✓ | ✓ |
| Porridge | 91 | | | | | | | | | | | | | | | | ✓ | |
| Banananana | 92 | | | | | | | | | | | | | | | | ✓ | ✓ |
| Bricks | 93 | | | | | | | | | | | | | | | | ✓ | |
| Changing pitch | 94 | | | | | | | | | | | | | | | | ✓ | |
| Dicing with colour | 95 | | ✓ | | ✓ | | | | | | | | | | | | ✓ | |
| Pebble pet | 96 | | | | | | | | | | | | | | | | ✓ | ✓ |
| Under my umbrella | 97 | | | | | | | | | | | | | ✓ | | | ✓ | ✓ |
| Creepy-crawly mini-beasts | 98–99 | | | | | | | | | | | | | | | | ✓ | ✓ |
| Growing up | 100–101 | | | | | | | | | | | | | | | | ✓ | |

| Activity | Page no. | Communication and Language | | | Physical Development | | Personal, Social and Emotional Development | | | Literacy | | Mathematics | | Understanding the World | | | Expressive Arts and Design | |
|---|---|---|---|---|---|---|---|---|---|---|---|---|---|---|---|---|---|---|
| | | Listening and attention | Understanding | Speaking | Moving and handling | Health and self-care | Self-confidence and self-awareness | Managing feelings and behaviour | Making relationships | Reading | Writing | Numbers | Shape, space and measures | People and communities | The world | Technology | Exploring and using media and materials | Being imaginative |
| Seaside | 102–103 | | | | | | | | | | | | | | | | ✔ | |
| The Farmer's In His Den | 104 | | | | | | | | | | | | | | | | ✔ | |
| Spring is here | 105 | | | | | | | | | | | | | | | | ✔ | ✔ |
| From tadpole to frog | 106 | | | | ✔ | | | | | | | | | | | | ✔ | |
| Jewels in the crown | 107 | | | | | | | | | | | | | | | | ✔ | |
| Texture collages | 108 | | | | | | | | | | | | | | | | ✔ | |
| Noah's animals | 109 | | | | | | | | | | | | | | | | ✔ | ✔ |
| Hats | 110-111 | | | | | | | | | | | | | | | | ✔ | |
| Spring flowers | 112 | | | | | | | | | | | | | | | | ✔ | ✔ |
| Autumn leaves | 113 | | | | | | | | | | | | | | ✔ | | ✔ | |
| Tiles | 114 | | | | ✔ | | | | | | | | ✔ | | | | ✔ | |
| Add water | 115 | | | | | | | | | | | | | | | | ✔ | |
| Tick, tock, hum, click | 116 | | | | ✔ | | | | | | | | | | | | ✔ | |
| Running water | 117 | | | | ✔ | | | | | | | | | | | | ✔ | ✔ |
| The Nutcracker | 118–119 | | | | | | | | | | | | | | | | ✔ | |
| The Hokey Cokey | 120 | | | | ✔ | | | | | | | | | | | | ✔ | |

| Activity | Page no. | Communication and Language | | | Physical Development | | Personal, Social and Emotional Development | | | Literacy | | Mathematics | | Understanding the World | | | Expressive Arts and Design | |
|---|---|---|---|---|---|---|---|---|---|---|---|---|---|---|---|---|---|---|
| | | Listening and attention | Understanding | Speaking | Moving and handling | Health and self-care | Self-confidence and self-awareness | Managing feelings and behaviour | Making relationships | Reading | Writing | Numbers | Shape, space and measures | People and communities | The world | Technology | Exploring and using media and materials | Being imaginative |
| Let's travel by plane | 121 | | | | ✔ | | | | | | | | | ✔ | | | ✔ | |
| Cheese straws | 122 | | | | ✔ | ✔ | | | | | | | | | | | ✔ | |
| Hip hip hooray | 123 | | | ✔ | | | | | | | | | | | | | ✔ | |
| Kwanzaa | 124–125 | | | | | | | | | | | | | ✔ | | | | ✔ |
| Wedding | 126–127 | | | | | | | | | | | | | | | | ✔ | ✔ |
| Trees | 128 | | | | | | | | | | | | | | | | ✔ | ✔ |
| Morris dancing | 129 | | | | ✔ | | | | | | | | | | | | ✔ | |
| Today's weather | 130 | | | | | | | | | | | | | | | | ✔ | |
| The Alley Alley O | 131 | | | | ✔ | | | | | | | | | | | | ✔ | |
| The Selfish Giant | 132–133 | | | | | | | | | | | | | | | | ✔ | |
| Freezing cold | 134–135 | | | | ✔ | ✔ | | | | | | | | | | | ✔ | ✔ |
| Lines | 136 | | | | | | | | | | | | ✔ | | | | ✔ | |
| Marzipan play | 137 | | | | ✔ | ✔ | | | | | | | | | | | ✔ | |
| Miss Polly had a Dolly | 139 | | | | | | | | | | | | | | | | | ✔ |
| Hairdressing salon | 140 | | | | ✔ | ✔ | | | ✔ | | | | | | | | ✔ | ✔ |
| Can you be a tree? | 141 | | | | ✔ | | | | | | | | | | | | ✔ | ✔ |

| Activity | Page no. | Communication and Language | | | Physical Development | | Personal, Social and Emotional Development | | | Literacy | | Mathematics | | Understanding the World | | | Expressive Arts and Design | |
|---|---|---|---|---|---|---|---|---|---|---|---|---|---|---|---|---|---|---|
| | | Listening and attention | Understanding | Speaking | Moving and handling | Health and self-care | Self-confidence and self-awareness | Managing feelings and behaviour | Making relationships | Reading | Writing | Numbers | Shape, space and measures | People and communities | The world | Technology | Exploring and using media and materials | Being imaginative |
| Thank you for the music | 142 | | | | | | | | | | | | | | | | ✔ | ✔ |
| A foggy day | 143 | | | | ✔ | | | | | | | | | | | | | ✔ |
| Storm | 144 | | | | ✔ | | | | | | | | | | | | ✔ | ✔ |
| Family fingers | 145 | | | | | | | | | | | | | | | | | ✔ |
| Hello Grandma | 146 | | | | | | | | | | | | | | | ✔ | | ✔ |
| Crossing the road | 147 | | ✔ | | | | | | | | | | | | ✔ | | | ✔ |
| A nice cup of tea | 148 | | | | | | | | | | | | | | | | | ✔ |
| Noah's music | 149 | | | | | | | | | | | | | | | | | ✔ |
| Rockin' Robin | 150 | | | | | | | | | | | | | | | | ✔ | |
| Sing to your pet | 151 | | | | | | | | | | | | | | | | ✔ | ✔ |
| Sing a song of soap | 152 | ✔ | | | | | | | | | | | | | | | | ✔ |
| Rattle those pans | 153 | | | | | | | | | | | | | | | | ✔ | ✔ |
| Tra-la | 154 | | | ✔ | | | | | | | | | | | | | | ✔ |
| Moving house | 155 | | | ✔ | | | | | | | | | | | | | | ✔ |
| The King's breakfast | 156–157 | | | | | | | | | | | | | | | | ✔ | ✔ |
| Messing about in boats | 158 | | | | | | ✔ | | ✔ | | | | | | ✔ | | | ✔ |
| Lollipop person | 159 | | | | | | ✔ | | | | | | | ✔ | | | | ✔ |

| Activity | Page no. | Communication and Language | | | Physical Develop-ment | | Personal, Social and Emotional Development | | | Literacy | | Math-ematics | | Understanding the World | | | Expressive Arts and Design | |
|---|---|---|---|---|---|---|---|---|---|---|---|---|---|---|---|---|---|---|
| | | Listening and attention | Understanding | Speaking | Moving and handling | Health and self-care | Self-confidence and self-awareness | Managing feelings and behaviour | Making relationships | Reading | Writing | Numbers | Shape, space and measures | People and communities | The world | Technology | Exploring and using media and materials | Being imaginative |
| The park in the dark | 160 | ✔ | | | | | | | | | | | | | | | | ✔ |
| Down on the farm | 161 | | | | | | | | | | | | | | | | | ✔ |
| Stuck up the chimney | 162 | | | | | | | | | | | | | | | | | ✔ |
| Soup for sale! | 163 | | | | | | | | | | | | | | | ✔ | | ✔ |
| The Pied Piper | 164-165 | ✔ | ✔ | | | | | ✔ | ✔ | | | | | | | | ✔ | ✔ |
| Over the rainbow | 166-167 | | | | | | | | | | | | | | ✔ | | ✔ | ✔ |
| Goldilocks and the Three Bears | 168-169 | | | ✔ | | | | ✔ | | | | | | | | | ✔ | ✔ |
| Who is knocking? | 170-172 | | | | | | | | | | | | | ✔ | | | | ✔ |
| The Sorcerer's Apprentice | 172-173 | | | | | | | | | | | | | | | | | ✔ |
| How will Teddy get there? | 174 | | | | | | | | | | | | | | | | | ✔ |
| Weather dance | 175 | | | | | | | | | | | | | | | | | ✔ |
| The farmer grows our food | 176 | | | | ✔ | | | | | | | | | | | | | ✔ |
| Outer space | 177 | | | | | | | | | | | | | | | ✔ | ✔ | ✔ |

| Activity | Page no. | Communication and Language | | | Physical Develop-ment | | Personal, Social and Emotional Development | | | Literacy | | Math-ematics | | Understanding the World | | | Expressive Arts and Design | |
|---|---|---|---|---|---|---|---|---|---|---|---|---|---|---|---|---|---|---|
| | | Listening and attention | Understanding | Speaking | Moving and handling | Health and self-care | Self-confidence and self-awareness | Managing feelings and behaviour | Making relationships | Reading | Writing | Numbers | Shape, space and measures | People and communities | The world | Technology | Exploring and using media and materials | Being imaginative |
| Fantastic animals | 178 | | | | | | | | | | | | | | | | | ✔ |
| Decorate a tree | 179 | | | | | | | | | | | | | | ✔ | | | ✔ |
| My imaginary life | 180 | | | | | | | | | ✔ | ✔ | | | | | ✔ | | ✔ |
| Clowns | 181 | | | | | | | | | | | | | | | | | ✔ |
| Are we there yet? | 182 | | | ✔ | | | | | | | | | | ✔ | | | | ✔ |
| Windy weather | 183 | | | | | | | | | | | | | | | | ✔ | ✔ |
| Peter and the Wolf | 184 | | | | ✔ | | | | | | | | | | | | | ✔ |
| Carnival of animals | 185 | | | | ✔ | | | | | | | | | | | | | ✔ |
| Kumbh mela | 186 | | | | ✔ | | | | | | | | | ✔ | | | | ✔ |
| Who has eaten the lettuce? | 187 | | | | | | | | | | | | | | | | | ✔ |

# Index of topics

www.ingramcontent.com/pod-product-compliance
Lightning Source LLC
Chambersburg PA
CBHW080843270326
41928CB00014B/2880
* 9 7 8 0 8 5 7 4 7 6 7 4 6 *